VOODOO
CONTRA

Novels by Robert Gover

ONE HUNDRED DOLLAR MISUNDERSTANDING
HERE GOES KITTEN
J. C. SAVES
THE MANIAC RESPONSIBLE
POORBOY AT THE PARTY
GOING FOR MR. BIG
TO MORROW NOW OCCURS AGAIN
GETTING PRETTY ON THE TABLE
THE J. C. KITTEN TRILOGY
BRING ME THE HEAD OF RONA BARRETT

VOODOO CONTRA

Robert Gover

SAMUEL WEISER, INC.
York Beach, Maine

First published in 1985 by
Samuel Weiser, Inc.
Box 612
York Beach, ME 03910

ISBN 0-87728-619-1

Library of Congress Catalog Card Number: 84-52293

Typeset in 10 point Souvenir by
Positive Type, Millerton, NY
Printed in the United States by
McNaughton & Gunn, Inc., Ann Arbor, MI

Contents

Acknowledgments

Hundreds of people helped me with this book—most of them encountered by chance in remote parts of the world. Special thanks go to the following:

Ishmael Reed of Oakland, California, for the news of books and information about Voodoo we exchanged over the years.

Lennox Raphael of Trinidad and New York, for helping me embark upon the odyssey of experiences from which this book is culled.

Dan Greene of Washington, D. C., who revived me from culture shock and introduced me to—

King Efuntola of Oyotunji Village, South Carolina, whose clarity and eloquence sharpened my focus on the theology of Voodoo.

Hari Das Baba, originally of India and late of Santa Cruz, California, for his uncanny insights and encouragement.

and finally, to Charles and Julia Campbell of Phoenix, Arizona, for demonstrating the balance of determination and humor needed to push such an offbeat work as this through to completion.

Preface

The power of the word *Voodoo* is such that once, when I mentioned it to a university professor, he jumped like he'd been stuck with a hat pin. I merely asked if his university offered a course that would introduce young students to the history, beliefs and traditions of Voodoo. But at the sound of those two syllables, he was immediately on his guard, as though even *hearing* that word threatened him with the spooks and haunts and black magic that most people erroneously associate with this ancient religion.

I encountered many such reactions during the years I spent studying this subject, for there are millions of North Americans and Europeans who back away in horror when they hear the word *Voodoo*. The word itself carries so much power that I almost decided to drop it from this work.

But what other word can one use? For there are many other millions in the New World who practice what goes by the generic term *Voodoo*. The point is, their religion is a far cry from what most North Americans and Europeans suppose Voodoo is.

That is why I find myself in a catch-22 when people ask if I *practice* Voodoo, and if I have *faith* in it. The concept of Voodoo that has been conditioned into their minds has nothing at all to do with the Voodoo that I spent so many years in search of—the search that this book is about.

The ancient, literal, enduring meaning of the word *Voodoo* is "Creator of the Universe." Are they asking me, then, if I have faith in the Creator of the Universe? That's like asking if some sub-atomic particle involved in the composition of my left little toe has faith in *me*, the *being* that it is a part of. I doubt that the sub-atomic particle has any real concept of who or what I am. And I, likewise, doubt that we humans—being comparably situated in regard to the *Being* that is the Universe—have any clear idea of Who or What He or She or It is.

It is certain that the Voodooist's concept of the Creator is not the same as the Judeo-Christian concept. Biblical characters spoke to their God, prayed to Him and even heard directly from Him. Voodooists consider the Great Creator far too remote for such intimacy. Rather, they relate to the "firstborn" of God—the gods and goddesses who fashion our tiny solar system, our planet, and us.

No, I do not "practice" Voodoo in social ceremonies. My experience has taken the shape of "conversations" with the gods and goddesses—much the way one might talk to one's inner self.

As for "faith," I trust in the transcultural, transdenominational theology of Voodoo. It is universal enough to include the deities of all mankind's religions, and it invites its practitioners to creative and eclectic improvisation. Voodoo is often practiced by individuals alone in meditative trance—what present-day psychologists call creative visualization. Voodoo is but one path toward awareness of the inner self.

But the Voodoo path involves one large, other dimension: gods and goddesses and spirits. Whether mankind invented gods or gods created us is a question I, for one, do not expect to answer in this lifetime. One thing I have observed repeatedly, though, is that the Voodoo way of creative visualization can be reliable, effective, even amazingly powerful. It is this and other Voodoo "secrets" I wish to share with the reader.

Robert Gover
Santa Barbara, CA 1985

1 A Voodoo Primer

How did a West African word meaning God get translated as meaning evil black magic? That's the question we must begin with, for the original, literal meaning of the word *Voodoo* is Creator of the Universe.

Why, then, are people in Europe and North America taught to equate this powerful word's midnight consonants and rolling thunder vowels with evil and depravity? Why does it suggest satanic powers rising from steamy tropical mists, killer zombies, human sacrifices, unnamed terrors, and any number of other mythical and mysterious horrors?

Strictly speaking, the word *Voodoo* applies only to African-derived religious rites practiced in Haiti and parts of the United States. But the word has been confused and misused for so long a time to characterize the pantheistic beliefs of all black and brown people that its present, common meaning is vastly enlarged. It is this larger, contemporary meaning I intend to explore: the pantheistic beliefs, and thus the culture, that came from Africa and now unites a loose confederation of millions in the Americas.

Even as its original meaning expanded over the centuries to imply a whole complex of cultural influences derived from Africa and amalgamated in the New World, its contradictory, derogatory meaning likewise spread. Modern American politicians have used it to accuse each other of "voodoo economics" and "voodoo arms control." It's been used to discredit scientific hypotheses and to denigrate the religions of Native Americans, Hawaiians, and Orientals, as well as to scoff at the experiments of parapsychologists.

It is not my intention to win converts for Voodoo. What motivates me is Western ignorance. My desire is to undermine that ignorance by revealing how people from Voodoo cultures view the world. They know how Westerners view the world, but most Europeans and Americans are either in the dark or utterly misled concerning the mind-set of millions of people with whom we share this planet.

From the Voodoo perspective, the Creator of the Universe is the source of all, good and evil, yet not directly involved in what humans find good or evil. Yes, black magic is Voodoo, and so is white magic. Everything in the cosmos is Voodoo (God), but it is Voodoo's firstborn, the gods and goddesses, who are directly involved in earthly affairs. It is this belief in gods and spirits as the eldest children of the Great Creator that Voodooists in the Americas share with all other pantheistic occultists and religionists.

The names of the cults are many, and they descend from two primary historic streams. From the Yoruba Kingdom come Santeria, Lucumi, Candomble, Macumba, and others. From the old Kingdom of Dahomey come Dahome, Rada, Nago, Petra, Obeah, and Dogan. And it is the word *Voodoo*, used in its broadest sense as an all-inclusive generic term, that describes this mix of Afro-oriented cults. And it is this same word that is so misunderstood by Europeans and Americans, white and black.

• • •

My interest in this subject began at a tender age. I had a grandmother who used herbs and what she called her helpful spirits to heal people. Her detractors called her "the Voodoo lady." One preacher accused her of "trafficking with the devil," but when he became sick and was not helped by licensed physicians, he turned to her and was healed.

As the years went by, it gradually dawned on me that the word *Voodoo* implies far more than its westernized meaning suggests. Eventually I discovered that it implies a way of perceiving reality that is virtually contradictory to the Western way. Thus, the title of this book, *Voodoo Contra:* the contradictory Voodoo vision of the world.

For more than twenty years I have made it my business to investigate this other meaning of Voodoo, to come to grips with it as a belief system, a cultural mind-set derived from Africa but transformed when transplanted in the Western Hemisphere. This book attempts to make those beliefs understandable to Western people, and to provide a sense of what I have come to think of as the Voodoo reality.

The aim of this introductory chapter, then, is to clarify the basic beliefs of the Voodoo culture, to trace their African origins and their transformations in the Americas and West Indies.

Following this introduction to Voodoo, the book shifts to a narrative of three parts: preparations for a Voodoo ceremony by fasting, a haunted stopover before the ceremony, and the ceremony itself. The aim of this narrative is to provide the reader with a vicarious experience of the Voodoo culture. Because this book addresses westernized people, the ceremony I have chosen is for possession of the Christ spirit, known in most Voodoo cults as Obatala or Oshala.

• • •

The word itself has been spelled in a number of variations: Vodu, Vudo, Vaudoux, Voudoun, Voudou, Voh-dong, and so forth. Most students of the subject agree it comes from Dahomey in West Africa. A London report from 1789 tells us that ten to twelve thousand slaves were exported yearly from Dahomey to the French Antilles, primarily to Dominique, as Haiti was then called.[1]

As for the original meaning of the word, we have the writings of Moreau de Saint-Mery, scholar, lawyer, politician, and relative of the Empress Josephine. He tells us Voodoo, according to the Negroes from Dahomey, is the god who knows the past, present, and future.[2] In Yoruba this god is called Orunmila, Ifa. In English this supreme being is called, simply, God. Why did this one particular Dohomean word grow in common usage and expand into contradictory meanings in the New World? No one knows for sure, but speculation is rife. Alfred Metraux, the French anthropologist, in his book *Voodoo in Haiti* says this: "Some people, in their anxiety to whitewash the Voodoo cults, saw it [the word] as a corruption of 'Vaudois' (the name of a sect founded in the twelfth century by Father Valdesius),

---

[1] Janheinz Jahn, *Muntu*, trans. Marjorie Grene (London: Faber & Faber, 1961), 29.
[2] Jahn, *Muntu*, 30.

but which had finally become a term applied vaguely to heretics and sorcerers."[3]

Early colonialists, fresh from that bloodbath known as the Inquisition, may have shuddered with revulsion when they heard those dark, rumbling vowels they associated with evil black magic and witchcraft.

Yet I've also been told by one knowledgeable source that the African word was confused with an old French word, *Voudous,* which appears in the *Talmud* and refers to the "descent of the holy spirit." All Voodoo cults practice mediumship and spirit possession, so perhaps the modern word *Voodoo* descended from a combination of African and French and thus spread through Europe and the Americas.

In any case, the Inquisition and its aftereffects certainly colored how Europeans came to regard Voodoo. Early colonialists saw clearly that the Africans worshipped gods, goddesses, and ancestral spirits, and the Inquisition had cursed such pantheistic beliefs as heathen and heretical. Holders of such beliefs had been banished, tortured, or put to death by fire. The colonialists were survivors of that epidemic of missionary zeal, and in the spirit of the Crusades they were militant about spreading the notion that all religions except Christianity were heathen and heretical. Africans and Native Americans who refused to call the Creator of the Universe dog spelled backward were to be dealt with as the Inquisition had dealt with their pantheistic counterparts in Europe.

This martian (ogoonian) sort of missionary decree was not obeyed uniformly, however. Spanish and Portuguese slave traders, in accordance with Roman Catholic slave laws, dutifully baptized their human cargoes on shipboard. Yet in their Catholic colonies, it was illegal to break up families; whereas in Protestant colonies, families were systematically parted as a precaution against rebellion. Spanish Louisiana was the only place in North America where African families remained together on their arrival, according to some sources, but Maryland also contained many Catholic colonialists, who may have kept their slave families together as well.

In any case, the cultural impact must have been mind-shattering. An alien religion that demanded your obedience or your life, a strange new language to learn, a new culture that placed you on a social level with domestic animals, and back-breaking labor from dawn till dusk.

[3]Alfred Metraux, *Voodoo in Haiti* (New York: Schocken Books, 1972), 27.

For a hint of how this "civilizing" process began, let's turn to *Agotime: Her Legend* by Judith Gleason.[4] Agotime tells us:

> ...on the fifth day out, the ship's priest, Father Martinho, decided to break the monotony by baptizing all of us. ...Whereupon [he] arose from the companionway in a cloud of black cloth.
>
> The priest was a curious combination of the ecstatic and the ridiculous....Now for all the world like a masquerader, he sprang into our midst, climbed the ladder to the poop and thence up to the captain's place behind the binnacle. Raising the captain's speaking trumpet he bellowed forth his intentions in a language that I alone of all the slaves could understand. He would baptize us, he roared, in order that "those whose lusty bodies had been lately clothed in baft might not sink to damnation with shamelessly naked souls." Then he prayed aloud in what I took at once to be the secret language of his cult. Latin?

Father Martinho gave each slave a Christian name and had each repeat the name back to him. Then:

> He proceeded to mark us with a quick crisscross upon forehead and breast. Then followed something even more suspicious. With his own fingers he pried open our lips and placed a pinch of salt on every tongue. Did this salt contain a few grains of medicine that was strong enough to give the whiteman perpetual power over one? I know better now but then I was so terrified that I broke out into a sweat, tried not to swallow and fought against that unknown force with every resource I commanded. I could tell from their eyes, when their turn came around, that everyone felt as I did. But none of us dared cry out, dared refuse or reject the salt, until Father Martinho came to the strongest of the men in the bow, the slave we all called Gbaguideguide.

[4]Judith Gleason, *Agotime: Her Legend* (New York: Viking Compass Books, 1970). © Judith Gleason. Used by permission of the author.

Agotime tells us she had guessed this man was "a thunder worshipper," an initiate of Shango:

> But I did not know for sure until they branded him on the beach. Unlike the rest of us, he felt no pain, no shame. He did not clench his fists or bite his lip till the blood came. I watched him closely then, for I thought if anyone would choose that moment to revolt, to strike out at his oppressors, it would be he. But no, as the hot brand touched his flesh, Gbaguide-guide's face lit up with a fierce joy. His bloodshot eyes gleamed with the incandescence of a supernatural manliness. At that moment he could have walked through the bonfire, heaped coals upon his head, run a steel knife through his swollen tongue. I turned my eyes away, and when I looked again he had come back to himself.

This man, when his turn came at the baptism, spat the salt into the priest's face. He was quickly grabbed by sailors and bound to the capstan, and the priest continued the baptism "as if nothing had happened."

After portioning out Christian names and salt communion, Father Martinho jumped up on the bowsprit and through the captain's speaking trumpet performed "the final exorcism."

> "I conjure you," he said, "every unclean spirit, in the name of the Father, Son and Holy Ghost, depart from these creatures all and most especially from this violent savage whom our lord has called to his holy ark. Begone, I say, depart." Upon which he stepped down, picked up a waterbucket the cook had set out upon the bow for him, and wove back the way he had come, ladling out a scant amount onto the head of each new Christian.

Following that ceremony, the priest brought onto deck a large statue of St. Anthony and placed it in the center of the ship. Agotime says:

> Anthony was the first Portuguese *vodu* they [the slaves] had seen and naturally they began to clap. The tension broken thus, they then began to dance, drumming upon the deck with their feet. "Silence," cried Father Martinho.... "You see before you a powerful provocator of winds, patron saint of this and all Christian ships that venture forth upon the fickle

surface of the sea. Stay, Anthony, and provide us release from our chains, whip us up a breeze sufficient to the amplitude of our undertaking. Now, my little brothers, you may continue your dance." With this the priest retired to his cabin—all wrung out from the look of him.[5]

This "civilizing" process was more successful among the Protestants of North America, whose beliefs did not encompass anything as close to African customs as the worship of saints. In South America and the West Indies, where the landscape was not so different from Africa's, slaves escaped by the thousands, or committed suicide, or were allowed to perpetuate African ways by overseers interested only in agricultural production. Today in Surinam and Brazil there are upriver villages founded by runaway slaves, each with its own oral tradition.

Thus did the mind-set that is uniquely African find its way to the European-dominated New World. Given the nature of that domination, it's a wonder any of the African ways survived. Yet as Harold Courlander says in *A Treasury of Afro-American Folklore:*

> Looking at the Western Hemisphere as a whole, it is abundantly evident that many tangible elements of African ways, customs, attitudes, values and views of life survived the Atlantic crossing. In differing degrees, according to the complex of social forces at work, numerous Negro communities in the Americas continue to draw from the African wellspring. In the upper river jungle country of Surinam, for example, descendants of African slaves live in a style reminiscent of the West African bush village. Haiti, though overlaid with a heavy veneer of French custom, manifests . many characteristics of African life. Black communities in Cuba, the English-speaking West Indies, Brazil, Venezuela, Guiana, the French Caribbean and the United States—all preserve something of the African past, and sufficiently so that it is possible to perceive the shared African inheritance."[6]

It is this "outer edge of the African cultural complex," as Courlander calls it, that is what I here call the Voodoo culture. Just as

[5] Judith Gleason, *Agotime: Her Legend* (New York: Viking Compass Books, 1970), 5.
[6] Harold Courlander, *Treasury of Afro-American Folklore* (New York: Crown, 1976), 2.

the descendants of early European immigrants developed their own distinct brand of Western civilization on these shores (I'm tempted to call it the cowboy culture), so the descendants of African slaves developed a view of life distinctly different from the European. As Courlander says:

> A devotee of the Macumba cult in Brazil may be, and probably is, a Catholic; if he speaks some ritual words in Yoruba, his native language is Brazilian Portuguese; if he holds a number of superstitions a good many of them probably came from Europe; if he responds to African-style music he also responds to music more in the Caboclo and Iberian traditions. Although he is a devotee of Macumba, so are countless whites. And as has been pointed out by various studies of this cult, Macumba today is compounded of African, European, Catholic, Indian, spiritist and even more diverse and exotic elements.[7]

• • •

How did a West African word meaning God become in Western culture a handy tool to denigrate, insult, or vilify? Or to imply primitive black magic, witchcraft, ignorant superstition?

Early Europeans who recorded their observations of Africans were often shocked and baffled by the customs they encountered on the "dark continent." They were especially nonplussed by what they regarded at first as "snake worship," which was closely associated with a word they first spelled as *Voh-dong*.

Among the more sympathetic accounts is one written in 1608 by a Catholic priest, Pere Labat, who describes what his friend, Pere Braguez, witnessed in Whydah, West Africa:

> The people on their knees and in silence are withdrawn some distance apart; the King alone with the priest of the country entered the enclosure, where after prolonged prostrations, prayers and ceremonies, the priest drew near a hole where supposedly he had a serpent. He spoke to him on behalf of the King and questioned him as regards the number of vessels that would arrive the following year, war, harvest and other

---

[7]Harold Courlander, *Treasury of Afro-American Folklore* (New York: Crown, 1976), 5.

topics. According as the serpent replied to a question, the priest carried the answer to the King who was kneeling a short distance away in an attitude of supplication. This by-play having been repeated a number of times, it was finally announced that the following year would be prosperous, that it would have much trade, and that they would take many slaves. The multitude expressed their joy by loud shouts, dancing and feasting.[8]

Pere Braguez then tells Pere Labat that he interviewed the officiating priest and was told:

> That the cult rendered to the serpent was only a cult in its relation to the Supreme Being, of whom they were all creatures. That the choice was not left to themselves, but that they had adopted it through obedience to the common Master's orders, which were always founded on sound principles. The Creator knew perfectly the dispositions of the creatures who had come from His hands, and appreciated only too well man's pride and vanity, not to take every means suitable to humble him; for which purpose nothing seemed more effective than to oblige him to bow down before a serpent, which is the most despicable and vilest of all animals.[9]

What seems to have been lost in translation is that only one kind of snake, the python, was the object of such ceremony. Modern science tells us the python has two sense organs on either side of its head, and that these organs are "heat sensitive." Science calls them "labial pits" but doesn't know what information the python picks up through these organs.

Those worshippers of the creator god, Voh-dong, who communed with the python, crossed the Atlantic among the thousands of slaves from Africa. Their European owners then outlawed their traditional religions and, to one degree or another, made an attempt to Christianize them. Combined with the European

---

[8]Quoted in Joseph J. Williams, *Voodoos and Obeahs: Phases of West Indian Witchcraft* (New York: Dial Press, 1932), 22.
[9]Williams, *Voodoos and Obeahs: Phases of West Indian Witchcraft*, 22.

response to those two awesome syllables, *Voh-dong*, this attempt succeeded in hopelessly confusing traditional African religion with witchcraft. The distinction between priest and magician blurred, and the word *Voodoo* took on added dimension.

From an anonymous Frenchman we have this: "The slaves are strictly forbidden to practice the dance which in Surinam is called 'Water Mama' and in our colonies 'Mae d'Agua.' They therefore make a great secret of it, and all we know is that it highly inflames their imaginations. They make immense efforts to do evil things. The leader of the plot falls into such transports that he loses consciousness."[10]

The pre-Christianized European pantheists, the ancestors of those early colonialists, would have seen such scenes differently, no doubt, for pantheism/polytheism/paganism is the same, essentially, for all humanity. But the rise of the Roman Church and the Inquisition probably eradicated from the European mind any awareness of their own ancestral water deities. And it outlawed such frolicsome methods of worship as dance.

African pantheism was most ruthlessly suppressed in the North American colonies that became the United States. It was just as misunderstood elsewhere, however. In his book, *Voodoos and Obeahs*, Joseph J. Williams describes how attempts to outlaw the African religion resulted in a confusion of priests and wizards:

> It is probable that many of the African priests became simple Obeah men after coming to Jamaica, for the simple reason that they could not openly practice their legitimate profession. But when known as Obeah men, however much they might be treated with respect, they still were hated and feared. Every evil was attributed to them. The very name of them spread dread.[11]

In Ashanti, where the majority of Jamaican slaves came from, the Okomfo (priest) was in constant and open combat with the Obayifo (wizard or evil magician). But in the New World, where the white master saw no distinction between priest and wizard, the former

---

[10]Quoted in Joseph J. Williams, *Voodoos and Obeahs: Phases of West Indian Witchcraft* (New York: Dial Press, 1932), 145.

[11]Quoted in Joseph J. Williams, *Voodoos and Obeahs: Phases of West Indian Witchcraft* (New York: Dial Press, 1932), 145. Williams is quoting from *Twentieth Century Jamaica*, by Herbert G. de Lisser, published in 1913 in Kingston, Jamaica.

were forced into the sort of hiding and secrecy which had characterized the latter. Thus the distinction between them became blurred, even to their countrymen.

Like Voodoo in Haiti, Obeah in Jamaica was also used by rebellious slaves against their masters, focusing European attention on African magic and subtle methods of herbal poisoning. And the word *Voodoo* was steadily growing as the most commonly used one to designate such activities. Voodoo priests were beaten, jailed, or killed in the United States. The idea that Voodoo also pertained to religion became unthinkable—especially to Europeans, who found nothing sacred about such Voodoo scenes as the following, reported in the *New Orleans Times*, June 26, 1872:

> ...the sudden entrance of a hoydenish flaxen-haired white girl, who whirled around the room in the arms of a Negro blacker than the ace of spades.... There could be no mistake about it. Set adrift on the rapids of depravity in real earnest, she had reached the center of the vortex. The pallid wanton face actually beamed with exuberant levity, and La Dame aux Camelias, in her wildest hours, could not have displayed an abandon more complete. Even the negresses gazed at her with a look of wonder. While the maddening whirl continued our reporter watched the wretched creature, as one after another the ebony suiters sought her hand; he saw her shrink out into the darkness, and more wanton than ever rush back to the revel, and mute with amazement he also turned away.[12]

To the above account one can add countless others describing human sacrifices, massive orgies, boiling pots filled with blood, snakes, toads, owl's heads, rabbit's feet, etc. Where the fancies of such observers diverge from the facts we shall probably never know.

It must be remembered, however, that in the forced migration from Africa, priests and sorcerers, royalty and criminals were all thrown together, and to the eyes of Europeans all were savages. From that perspective came the mangled notion of Voodoo that has found its way into novels and movies. It became a notion so pervasive in Christendom that it created its own wall of racial bigotry and religious intolerance.

---

[12]Robert Tallant, *Voodoo in New Orleans* (New York: The Macmillan Co., 1946), 36, 37.

A small hole was made in that wall in 1929 when *The Magic Island* by W.B. Seabrook appeared. Seabrook undermined the notion of Voodoo as savage superstition and hailed it as religion:

> I believe in such ceremonies. I hope that they will never die out or be abolished. I believe that in some form or another they answer a deep need of the universal human soul. I, who in a sense believe in no religion, believe yet in them all, asking only that they be alive—as religions. Codes of rational ethics and human brotherly love are useful, but they do not touch this thing underneath. Let religion have its bloody sacrifices, yes, even human sacrifices, if thus our souls may be kept alive. Better a black *papaloi* (Voodoo priest) in Haiti with blood-stained hands who believes in his living gods than a frock-coated minister on Fifth Avenue reducing Christ to a solar myth and rationalizing the Immaculate Conception.[13]

In 1947, Maya Deren went to Haiti to make a film in which Haitian dance was to be portrayed as "purely a dance of form." Four years and three trips later she published *Divine Horsemen: The Voodoo Gods of Haiti*. It was written, she tells us in her preface, "not because I had so intended but in spite of my intentions...I end by recording, as humbly and accurately as I can, the logics of a reality which had forced me to recognize its integrity."[14]

Maya Deren's *Divine Horsemen* is eloquent and profoundly philosophical, and it takes one deep into Haitian Voodoo. Other descriptions of Afro-American cults have since appeared, but to my mind none with the powerful insight of Deren's.

For instance, the American novelist A.J. Langguth makes a valiant effort to come to grips with Brazilian Voodoo in his chronicle titled *Macumba*.[15] He spent three months in the rural village of Camaru, in the state of Bahia, nicknamed "the Voodoo Vatican." The result is a swift read and a compact encyclopedia of gods and goddesses, symbols and paraphernalia.

Unlike Deren in Haiti, however, Langguth's vigorous attempt to comprehend the subject falls short. He decides it's crucial he get out of Bahia or else "I'd start to rant and flail." He concludes:

---

[13]W.B. Seabrook, *Magic Island* (New York: Harcourt, Brace, 1929), 61-62.
[14]Maya Deren, *Divine Horsemen: The Voodoo Gods of Haiti* (London: Thames and Hudson, 1953), 5-6.
[15]A.J. Langguth, *Macumba* (New York: Harper and Row, 1975).

I'm not sorry I spent these three months searching after spirits. Where I went wrong was in not recognizing that the mystery lay closer to hand than a forest in Bahia. Writing fiction is my communion with spirits; it is all one mystery. And since I have known better than to analyze my own impulse too closely, I should simply accept and enjoy the Brazilian effort to recast and gladden an unsatisfactory world, at least until science overtakes us all.[16]

So for all his careful gathering of data, Langguth only adds weight to the notion of Voodoo as superstition and/or a "lost mystery," which is definitely not for North Americans or even urbanized *brazileiros.*

But if that were really the case, why is it that so much of the Western Hemisphere is so firmly grounded in the complex of shared beliefs that constitute the Voodoo culture?

• • •

Even in North America, where African traditions were most ruthlessly suppressed, there are obvious differences between white and black folkways and outlooks on life. And the farther south toward Brazil one goes, the stronger and more influential transplanted African culture becomes. In the United States blacks speak of soul brothers, soul food, soulful gospel. In Brazil, Yoruba and Bantu words are often combined with Brazilian Portuguese to say what cannot quite be said in the European languages.

Throughout the Americas, African rhythms and dance movements are evident influences. What is not so obvious are the values and beliefs supporting such influences. What constitutes the Voodoo culture, then, are these commonly held values and beliefs, whether held consciously or otherwise.

For centuries Europeans considered the African way of thinking "primitive," or as Levy Bruhl called it, "pre-logical."[17] Not many attempts were made to make this outlook understandable in Western terms until after World War II. By then it had become

[16]A.J. Langguth, *Macumba* (New York: Harper and Row, 1975), 264.
[17]See Janheinz Jahn, *Muntu,* trans. Marjorie Grene (London: Faber & Faber, 1961), 97, for more on French anthropologist Levy Bruhl.

obvious that African culture can absorb what it pleases from Western culture without losing its essential integrity.

One of the best studies of African thinking is Janheinz Jahn's *Muntu,* a Bantu word meaning "human being." Jahn quotes Alexis Kagame, a Bantu who wrote in French, explaining that his native language is structured around four categories: *Muntu* (human being), *Kintu* (thing), *Hantu* (place and time), and *Kuntu* (modality). Everything belongs in one of these four categories—not only as substance but primarily as force.[18]

"Man is a force, all things are forces, place and time are forces, and the 'modalities' are forces." Beauty and laughter are modalities, and as forces they are related to each other. And all forces are related to *ntu,* the stem of the Bantu word for the four categories.[19]

"NTU is the universal force as such, which, however, never occurs apart from its manifestations: Muntu, Kintu, Hantu and Kuntu. NTU is that force in which Being and beings coalesce."[20]

As the Yoruba writer Abebayo Adesanya puts it, "This is not simply a coherence of fact and faith, nor of reason and traditional beliefs, nor of reason and contingent facts, but a coherence and compatibility among all disciplines."[21]

To the African mind, there is no such thing in reality as contradiction, no mutually exclusive propositions, as there are in European thinking. Says Adesanya: "God might be banished from Greek thought without any harm being done to the logical architecture of it, but this is impossible in the case of Yoruba thought, since faith and reason are mutually dependent. . . .In modern times, God has no place in scientific thinking."[22] But this is impossible in African thinking, for the source of everything permeates everything.

When sacrifices are made in Voodoo ceremonies, it is not to an idol or an image of a god or ancestor that the food or animal is offered but to the *force,* the *spirit* of the god or ancestor. And that force is not something separate or distant; it is part of the universal force and related to all forces everywhere.

---

[18] Janheinz Jahn, *Muntu,* trans. Marjorie Grene (London: Faber & Faber, 1961), 100.
[19] Jahn, *Muntu,* 100.
[20] Jahn, *Muntu,* 101.
[21] Jahn, *Muntu,* 96.
[22] Jahn, *Muntu,* 97.

Jahn quotes the Yoruba novelist Amos Tutuola to explain the African concept of modality:

> We knew "Laugh" personally on that night, because as every one of them stopped laughing at us, "Laugh" did not stop for two hours. As "Laugh" was laughing at us that night, my wife and myself forgot our pains and laughed with him, because he was laughing with curious voices that we never heard before in our life. We did not know the time that we fell into this laugh, but when we were only laughing at "Laugh's" laugh and nobody who heard him when laughing would not laugh, so if somebody continue to laugh with "Laugh" himself, he or she would die or faint at once for long laughing, because laugh was his profession and he was feeding on it.[23]

In African thinking, the physical individual and his personal soul are one during life, and when parted at death, the soul needs the living it has left behind as descendants. As a spiritual force, the soul remains in communication with its descendants, and only when it cannot do this is it considered "entirely dead." In Afro-American Voodoo cults, the attention of the living to the souls of ancestors keeps those souls alive. If such prayerful attentions are done properly and regularly, the souls of ancestors are strengthened.

Things, plants, animals, and minerals, are forces without intelligence. It is the human being who imbues things with intelligence and meaning. Man does this with words. Words *are* the forces of life. Naming creates magic. In the Voodoo culture, it is the spiritual forces of plant medicines that effect healings, not chemical compounds.

When someone falls ill in a Voodoo community, his priest divines to name the source of his illness—its spiritual force. Usually another priest then conjures a counter word, a stronger spiritual force, which will bring about the healing.

Note the difference between this African belief in the power of words and the Christian "In the beginning was the Word, and the Word was with God, and the Word was God" (John 1:1).[24] In the Christian mind, the word remains with God. In the African view, the word was with the Great Creator in the beginning and is still with Him,

---

[23]Janheinz Jahn, *Muntu,* trans. Marjorie Grene (London: Faber & Faber, 1961), 103. Jahn is quoting from *Palm Wine Drinkard,* by Amos Tutuola.
[24]All Bible references from the King James Version.

but it is also with man and continues to be with man. Man's word continues to create and procreate. Words give force to gods and goddesses and strengthen the souls of ancestors. Words bring intelligence to plants, animals, and minerals, giving the spiritual forces of such things meaning and usefulness.

All human reality is based on words, sounds made meaningful. And all words are part of the Great Creator's original Word, just as rivers and oceans, lakes, and springs are all of water.

It is this belief in spirits and words that crossed the Atlantic and now forms the foundation of the Voodoo culture. All Voodoo cults, no matter how wildly different they may seem to Western observers, hold this belief in words as spiritual forces. Conversely, in Western culture it is *things* that have power. The things of disease are treated with the things of medicinal remedies. Often one chemical remedy will come onto the market in the guise of a dozen or more names, put out by various companies and in various compounds with other, inactive chemicals. But it's not these many names that are thought to have power; it's the one chemical remedy.

The Western belief in things has been undermined lately by what is called the "placebo effect," a name for the fact that patients often respond as well when they *think* they've been given the proper pill as they do when they actually have been given the proper pill. It is said that the cure rate is especially high in experiments in which the doctor thinks he is dispensing the prescribed chemical but is actually giving his patients a placebo. Such experiments support the African contention that it's the word, not the thing, that has power.

In Western culture, the words *mind* and *brain* are often used synonymously, as if they mean the same thing. In the African tradition from which Voodoo arises, those two words have distinctly different meanings. The brain is the *organ* of the mind. The mind, on the other hand, is a nonphysical entity composed of thoughts, which when worded acquire forces.

In the Voodoo culture close attention is paid to the effects of thoughts (spiritual forces) on the physical human being. Whereas Western medicine considers the autonomic nervous system to function independently of conscious thought, Voodooists consider the autonomic nervous system quite vulnerable to the spiritual forces of worded thought.

Western doctors see the proverbial "witch doctor" as employing hypnotic suggestion to affect their patients or victims. But

Voodoo practitioners have a far more sophisticated concept of mind, both conscious and unconscious. For example, an American scientist arrives in a Voodoo community to do an anthropological study. He attributes the local priest's powers to the community's shared beliefs. If you believe he can heal or hex you, he can; if you don't believe it, he can't. The scientist crosses the priest, who puts a hex on him. The scientist falls ill and is taken to the nearest hospital. Doctors there diagnose his illness in their terms and treat him accordingly. Whether he recovers or dies, neither he nor his doctors will see any connection between his illness and the Voodoo priest's anger. Thus, both Western scientists and Voodoo practitioners find verifying evidence for their different beliefs.

Whereas Western culture has produced astounding ways to manipulate the physical environment, the genius of Voodoo culture is to manipulate the spiritual environment—which Westerners do not believe exists. But if you theorize the existence of Voodoo's spiritual world and its means of manipulation, there is ample evidence to support the theory.

If the writings of Sigmund Freud had been correctly translated, Americans might not find it so difficult to grasp the Voodoo concept of "the invisibles." Freud used the word *psyche* to mean what it has always meant since its Greek origins: soul. I suppose "soul-analysis" was not considered "scientific" in America, thus the mistranslation, and American culture took another giant step away from occult awareness. Now many Americans find it difficult even to imagine the realms of souls and spiritual forces that compose the ordinary reality of Voodooists.

Another reason Westerners have difficulty confronting the evidence of Voodoo reality is this: in Christendom there is said to be but one God, and yet there are almost as many notions of who or what that one God is as there are believers. I've heard Christians say it's not God who brings such natural catastrophes as earthquakes and hurricanes but rather God who helps people survive such tragedies. On the other hand, the Christian god is said to be everywhere, in everything, and eternal.

One does not encounter such mutually excluding beliefs among Voodooists, who regard the uproars of nature to be the doing of those children of God—the gods and spiritual forces. From the Voodoo perspective, the Creator of the Universe has far larger concerns and does not bother with the joys and sorrows of one species on one tiny planet in His vast cosmos. Whereas Christendom has many concepts of its one God, Voodoo has many gods and goddesses, souls and spiritual forces.

To help bring the Voodoo belief system into clearer focus, we will next talk with a Voodoo priest. I have interviewed more than a hundred priests of various cults that fit the expanded meaning of the word *Voodoo*. The one I have chosen to present here is a very articulate American dedicated to preserving the Yoruba Voodoo tradition.

● ● ●

I brought notebook and tape recorder to interview the king of Oyotunji Village near the tiny town of Sheldon, South Carolina. This king was born in Detroit in 1928 and christened, aptly enough, Walter Serge King. He studied commercial art in high school, then joined the Katherine Dunham African dance troup and toured Europe. He was initiated as a Voodoo priest first in Cuba and later in Nigeria. Now his name is Oseijeman Adejunmi. In Yoruba, those names mean "savior of the people" and "the crown has been given to him."

His priestly name is Efuntola. *Efun* is a white powder symbolizing the creativity and purity of the sun god, Obatala, the Voodoo Christ. Efuntola means a person who is a medium for the power of Obatala.

Efuntola obviously has considerable white blood in his mixed lineage, for he's light-skinned and fine-featured enough to be mistakenly classified as white. The last time I spoke with him he had five wives and presided over a village of close to one hundred people. They are all classified as blacks in this country. Most are from big cities, and many are well educated. They live without piped-in water, gas, or electricity. They dress as their pre-slave African ancestors did, speak the Yoruba language among themselves, and are devout worshippers of the Voodoo gods and ancestral spirits.

Their king, according to African tradition, has absolute power over his people and village, and he retains that power as long as all goes well. In the case of calamity or extended misfortune, the king must sacrifice his life.

To reach Oyotunji Village, you leave the paved road near Sheldon, park your car near a farmhouse, and walk back along a dirt road. Soon you pass a sign saying you are now leaving the United

States and entering a Yoruba kingdom where the Voodoo gods of African ancestry are worshipped. When you arrive in the center of the village, the feeling is that you have definitely left Western culture and are now in precolonial Africa. About the only thing you find here that speaks of modern America is plywood, used in the construction of houses that are essentially African in style.

Many people travel great distances to seek Efuntola's healings or advice, so you must wait your turn before being ushered into the king's compound. For our interview, Efuntola sat on a platform in an overstuffed chair of vivid purple, wearing a white robe and smoking Norwegian tobacco in a briar pipe.

• • •

Gover: Obatala, I take it, is Oshala, the Sun god.

Efuntola: In Brazil they call this god Oshala, but that's a corruption of *Orisha-nla. Orisha* is the Yoruba term for a god, and *nla* means great. So this god is the great god, and he's the patron of this village. And of all creative people, as a matter of fact—artists, musicians, writers, scientists, philosophers. He is the father of all the gods, and according to the Yoruba tradition, he created the solid earth and the first human beings.

Gover: And how does Obatala relate, in your pantheon, to Eshu?

Efuntola: Eshu is the messenger of all the gods. He's the youngest, and Obatala is much older.

Gover: Does your Eshu correspond to Lucifer, the bringer of light? [Such a correspondence is made in Brazil.]

Efuntola: Well, not necessarily. Light was already brought by Obatala. For us, Eshu simply becomes the messenger. Whatever the gods have to communicate to man, Eshu is expected to communicate. However, Eshu is very unpredictable because of his youthfulness. For that reason, a god may be sending a person luck, but the person is liable to be having bad luck. So everyone worships Eshu, hoping to avoid his mischievousness in changing the directions of the god who ordered him. Eshu, then, is the unpredictable element in life.

Gover: I've been impressed by the idea that the theory of relativity is an expression of one god, Damballah—or the one you call

Orunmila—and that the quantum theory is an expression of Eshu. Do you see it that way?

Efuntola: Not necessarily. All the gods together is what relativity represents, the relationship of all forces to one another.

Gover: And quantum?

Efuntola: Eshu works very closely with Orunmila; they work like a hand in a glove—predestiny and the unpredictable. Orunmila is the fact that all is order and all is organized. Eshu often confuses this. But if the individual worships Eshu, he can then receive the ordered gifts and advantages of the universe. You see, Eshu is at the opposite end of the spectrum from Orunmila—or, as we sometimes call him, Ifa. Ifa is everything that has already happened or is going to happen or is happening now. He is the fact that every life being lived now has already been lived many times before. Through our system of divination, one can correspond with the god who knows what has gone on before and who will tell you what to do in order to solve every single problem. On the other hand, this orderly, predictable element is constantly being interrupted and confused by Eshu.

Gover: Is it possible to deduce that the theory of relativity is an expression of Obatala, since he brings enlightenment?

Efuntola: Well, you see, Ifa—Orunmila—is an even higher concept than Obatala. Obatala corresponds to the planets Sun and Jupiter, but for Orunmila—Ira—there is no planet. He is the knowledge of all the planets, all the gods and all their destinies. And of all rules and laws. He is known elsewhere as Ilam Aballah, or the whole zodiac.

Gover: All right, so relativity comes from Orunmila, Ifa.

Efuntola: Yes, I would say so.

Gover: How do your other gods express through the planets of our solar system? Which, for instance, is your Venus?

Efuntola: In our pantheon, Venus is Oshun. The Moon is Yemanja. Mercury corresponds to Eshu, Mars to Ogun, and Earth to Obaluaye. But this seems confusing because Saturn is also Obaluaye, the Great Teacher. In our system Earth is considered more like man, in the sense that in the trinity concept the Sun is father, the Moon is mother, and the Earth is everyman, or Jesus Christ who suffers in material form. This is the basic concept behind the original trinity. Well then, Shango corresponds to Uranus, Neptune to Olokun. *Okun* means oceans, so Olokun is ruler of the oceans. And this is the god, incidentally, who rules over the African race. So whenever the planet Neptune moves into another constellation, we know that this is going to be the expression of blacks for the next fourteen years, since it takes about that long for Neptune to transit each constellation. *Gover:* It's in Sagittarius now. [*Now* being Summer, 1976].

Efuntola: Yes, and when it was in Libra, the emphasis on "black is beautiful" came out, and the cry for justice. The cultural movement began then, and we produced the dashiki. Blacks became conscious of their own attractiveness and began to wear their hair in the "natural." And when Neptune went into Scorpio, you had the rise of the Black Panthers, Malcolm X, and so forth, a more aggressive influence. This more intense, more dynamic force took over the blacks. Then, as soon as Neptune went into Sagittarius—which is the sign of organization, institutionalization—the Panthers completely changed, and we of the cultural movement went south and began to establish and institutionalize our work here. The blacks who were into integration decided to organize by going into black caucuses and into government, formulating new methods to solidify control. Blacks in the middle of the road, between integration and nationalism, decided to organize schools of thought, so a number of black schools were set up around the country.

Gover: And what will be the effect on blacks when Neptune goes into Capricorn?

Efuntola: The industrial era will be undermined and come to a conclusion. People will have to return to the earth, to the soil. The luxury in which many have lived during the industrial era will completely constrict and contract. There's going to be land reform in the world generally, particularly in America and other industrialized nations. Blacks, for the most part, are going to have very hard times in the cities. That's one of the reasons we moved south—to prepare an alternative way of life for blacks when they are compelled to leave the cities.

Gover: Well, that analysis seems to make sense. Now we have one more planet, Pluto.

Efuntola: Pluto, the ruler of Scorpio, is the goddess we call Oya. She is one of the wives of Shango. She is a warrior queen, very intense and, if she is negatively aspected, subversive. On the other hand, she's the crusader who changes whole eras. She gets out the crusading type of people who begin to reorganize, to reorder the social system.

Gover: Then Pluto transiting through Libra, where she is now, brings the force of Oya to love and the arts, to legality and justice, dredging up government corruption. Is that so?

Efuntola: Yes, and when negatively aspected, it brings up all kinds of sexual perversions and aberrations, degeneracy, a love of ease and luxury.

Gover: In recent times, East and West seem to be having that meeting that "never the twain" would have, according to an earlier assumption. Yet it seems to me that one of the world's three primary races, the African, is still grossly misunderstood by both East and West. Do you agree?

Efuntola: Well, not entirely. The East and the African worlds are quite similar. They have a basic understanding. Actually, the East and West will never understand each other. They'll meet only superficially.

Gover: What I'm suggesting is that Voodoo—using that word as a generic term for the African-oriented cultural perspective—is the link for a true understanding between East and West.

Efuntola: Well, it would seem so, but because of the very nature, the very genius of the West, that genius is not able to live and express itself harmoniously with either the Eastern or African geniuses.

Gover: You see Ogun, then, as the genius of the West? Mars, god of war?

Efuntola: Exactly. We say of the Caucasian people that they are Arien, or Martian. Africans are a Piscean race—Olokun, Neptune. Obviously, then, there's going to be a terrific cultural difference. The East is ruled by Eshu, Mercury. The West is Ogun, and as it has been developed here in the United States, it's also Shango, Uranus.

Gover: Shango and Ogun combine to dominate the internal combustion engine and the assembly line, things of that nature.

Efuntola: Exactly. And both are terrifically powerful *auxiliary* energies. But they are not necessarily intellectually profound energies.

Gover: Would you say *dense* is the word?

Efuntola: Yes, that fits them very well, because Ogun is the consciousness of minerals, which are of a dense molecular structure. But when properly directed, Ogun is the force of the seed battling out of its pod to grow toward the finer energies, like the sun. But when left to his own devices, he's like the nuclear bomb. Both Ogun and Shango need strong direction by the older, wiser gods. Otherwise, they can become the most destructive forces imaginable.

Gover: Yes, well...I'd like to move on now to the relationship of the gods to individuals. What I'm trying to do is find a way to explain, in Western terms, the old gods as composing the life force of each individual. Or in other words, as the archetypes of the energy science tells us is all at various rates of vibration.

Efuntola: All right, I think our Voodoo doctrine of multiple souls will be helpful here. We believe the human individual is not motivated by one soul but by nine souls. The ancient Egyptians had this concept too. Each soul is a force in some aspect of life on this planet. And each also has an area of worship, relationships, and factors that give it expression, which the individual, in one way or another, at one time or another, ritualizes.

Now the first of these is the *universal* soul. This unites man with the universe and everything in it. Being a part of the universe, whatever happens in the universe affects man, sooner or later. If there's an earthquake on Krakatoa, people in America will in time be affected somehow. A sunspot, whether we even know of its existence or not, in one way or another will affect energies on this planet. This universal soul, then, can be taken for granted. Man doesn't have to worship it formally. This is the universal God, which we call Olodumare or Olorun, the supreme universal force permeating everything.

Now after that, man has a *human* soul. This narrows man down from being just an amorphous element in the universe and gives him a particular form. This gives him his relationships with other forms and other human beings. Whatever he does, he thinks of in human terms. Wherever he goes, this human soul enables him to relate to other human beings on a basic level. There may be other ways in which humans are unable to relate, but one human can correspond with other humans on this basic level, whereas he may or may not be able to relate to a turtle or a tree. So this human soul is another factor that guides, controls, and limits the behavior of the individual. And this soul corresponds to Obatala, the begetter of earthly forms.

Now after that, men are born into different races, and each has a *racial* soul. Each racial soul has its own genius, its own character. This is expressed by each particular race in the same way individuals or groups have certain talents and behaviors and geniuses. Each race also has this. The individual's acts and reactions to stimuli are going to basically be those of an Oriental, an African, or a European. We say Europeans are ruled by Ogun, Orientals by Eshu, and Africans by Olokun, and we consider the American Indian primarily Eshu.

Then after that is the *sexual* soul. Each race is divided into males and females. In every civilization there's a masculine ideal and a feminine ideal. The behavior of all human beings is motivated and controlled and limited by this spiritual force that was created in their ancient past, long before they were born. Its laws, rules, and expressiveness were created long ago in each culture. Men in Arabia often walk around holding hands. That's not done in the Western world. The American ideal of masculinity is based on the cowboy, for the most part, which goes back to Valhalla and the ideal of fighting and dying and living in Valhalla and still fighting, still competing.

After the sexual soul, then, each person has an *astral* soul. Each male and female has some particular talent, or *odu,* as we call it. His *orisha* gives him a particular talent, and he's able to be a plumber or a writer, a killer or a decorator, a mystic or whatever, based on this astral force, this spiritual force we call a soul. And this one too limits, controls, and motivates the individual. This is the individual's archetypal god. And as we know, each god has his own rituals and symbols and elements and how a man should relate to it.

Now then, after the astral soul comes the *national* soul. People are born into various nations, and each nation has its own character, its own spirit. The American spirit is one thing, the Japanese spirit another. The Yoruba spirit is one thing, the Bushman spirit another. Whatever nation a person is born into, he carries this spiritual quality called the character of that nation. He acts like a Frenchman, or a Russian, or a Chinaman. He's mystical like a Hindu, and so forth. People develop popular notions about how each nationality is supposed to act. An Indian is supposed to be stern and silent. Orientals are supposed to be insidious and unpredictable. The Yoruba is supposed to be vigorously happy, strong, and sensual. So this national soul is a very real and influential thing, if you're willing to admit it and trace it out behind popular prejudices. And a person has to worship it if he is to integrate totally his complete identity, composed of all these souls, each expressing the characteristics of one god or another.

After this national soul, the person has an *ancestral* soul. This is his own personal family within the nation. And each family's pattern of behavior—if they're criminals, warriors, businessmen, factory workers, farmers, or whatever—has come down through the family to affect the individual. In the African system, of course, human beings are considered to reincarnate within the same family, so this particular soul is worshipped very intensely. There's a very elaborate system of worship attached to it.

After the ancestral soul, each person has a *historic* soul—what Shakespeare called the age and body of the time—the *spirit* of the time one is born into. Those born in the time of slavery are going to have quite a different historical soul, speaking of blacks. And there are revolutionary times, innovative generations. This is a generation that is highly spiritual, much as we had two thousand years ago when religions in the Middle East were developing. People are born into wartime with a warrior historical soul, and into times of plenty, times of deprivation, artistic and scientific advancements, and so forth.

Then, finally, each individual has his own *personal* soul—in other words, his ego. This is his personal destiny, what he personally is going to do, or what he's expected to do, would like to do, or has the ability to do during one lifetime, which may last eighty years, more or less. In the Yoruba Voodoo culture, we each have a little vessel we worship, which represents our own personal destiny. It's called your *odu*, the reading you came from heaven with. And this soul also controls your life, motivates it, and limits it by prescribing what you are capable of doing, the type of people you are best to associate with and the type you can't even get along with. Also the type of things you should eat and what you should avoid eating—your *odu* writes out completely your individual life. [End of interview]

• • •

Unlike the Western theological tradition, within the Voodoo culture one is never asked to accept any belief on faith. As the Yoruba writer Adesanya points out, the ideal that God has no place in scientific thinking is an impossible proposition in African thinking. Olodumare, the source of all, permeates all, including scientific thinking. From the Voodoo perspective, every thought—scientific or otherwise—is from the realm of one god or another. Every undertaking—personal, family, social, political, or international—shows the old gods participating in human affairs, for those able to read the evidence.

In order to read the evidence, one must first consider the possibility that the African world of spiritual forces is valid. But within the modern, rational, scientific community, it is practically taboo even to suppose there are gods and spirits, and that words conjure forces that can be directed and used. The energy science proposes is all at various rates of vibration—that energy is not alive and conscious, nor can it be divided into those archetypal realms called gods and goddesses.

From the Voodoo perspective, that scientific taboo, or faith, is itself from the realm of Ogun, for that deity's most notorious faults are narrow-minded self-righteousness. When Ogun gets such a self-limiting, dead-end notion in his head, there is no point in trying to argue with him. So there is no point in my attempting to prove the logical integrity of Voodoo in a way that would be acceptable to the scientific community.

But for Westerners who are willing to discard the scientific taboo and consider the basic beliefs of Voodoo as possibilities, there is more than enough validating evidence. What so often confuses this process for Westerners, however, is the lack of any standard pantheon of deities throughout the Voodoo culture. Voodooists are polytheists, and each priest is a pope in his own cult. In some cults, the American Indian theology is the strongest; in others, Dahomean, Bantu or Congolese names and customs prevail.

To avoid that impasse, that confusion of different names and customs, I will stick with Efuntola's Yoruba pantheon. For one thing, the Yoruba people have been elucidating their theology for thousands of years and have become quite adept at making it clear and comprehensible. Transplanted to the New World, it has been this clearly defined Yoruba version of African pantheism that has become dominant. And Efuntola is among those who seek to preserve the Yoruba tradition as purely as possible.

The interview I presented above was edited from five hours of taped sessions. I also spent time with Efuntola informally and had the opportunity of watching him work, using the spiritual forces of various animals and things to heal some people and end the misfortunes of others, and to divine—to commune with Ifa, the knowledge of past, present, and future.

In one instance, a good friend, who was then a feature writer for a major newspaper, asked Efuntola to divine the destiny of that newspaper. Efuntola threw the traditional Yoruba *opele* and the reading came that if the paper were a person it could be said to be suffering a blood disease, like leukemia, a subtle kind of bleeding. Since money is the lifeblood of such an entity as a newspaper, its financial system would have to be thoroughly cleansed or else it would go belly-up financially. It did, within the year.

I asked Efuntola to divine the destiny of this book, which I was then working on. His reading said the book would take much longer than I had anticipated (it has) but that when I finally brought it under control, it would be welcomed on three continents—which remains to be seen.

One reason the book has taken so long to complete is that for about five years I grappled with the confusing external differences found in the various Voodoo cults. It wasn't until I decided to shed as much exotic detail as possible and seek the common denominators uniting all of these seemingly different cults that the task became manageable.

Then too, it became clear over the years that Voodoo cannot be grasped as theory only, the way one can learn math from a textbook. To validate the theories of the Voodoo belief system, it is necessary to enter the Voodoo culture and experience it. I have made various attempts over the years to burrow deeply enough into the Voodoo reality to capture its essentials as personal experiences, to understand it from the inside out.

But such attempts did not succeed until I realized that like so many others conditioned by Western culture I had some very powerful built-in psychological blocks. As long as these blocks remained unidentified, unnamed, they acted as a stone wall.

For example, I never consciously held the belief that the souls of my ancestors were parked in heaven, hell, or purgatory, far from the living. Nor had I bought the belief of the rational—that death is oblivion and that there is no such entity as a soul or spirit. I could entertain the notion of reincarnation but neither believed nor disbelieved it. I had been conditioned by my culture to suspend belief, which was good. What was not good was that I blocked on looking for evidence, pro or con.

I didn't identify that block until evidence of reincarnation found me. A Santa Barbara hypnotist, Karl Larsson, guided me into a deep trance and got me to come up with my name and date of birth for a series of past lives, and we recorded the session. One of the persons I described myself as having been was a Captain John Worthington, whose main occupation during the mid-1600s had been transporting slaves from Africa to the Americas. Captain John had four wives—in London, Brazil, New Orleans, and Annapolis. About a week after that session, I chanced on an American genealogy book and looked up my surname. I found, to my utter amazement, that it recorded my first European ancestor to these shores as one Robert Gover, whose son,

Andrew, married Pricilla Worthington, daughter of Captain John and Hannah Worthington of Pendemy on the Severn, Annapolis! Since it's virually impossible that I could have tucked that bit of information away in my subconscious, I had to admit it as evidence of reincarnation. It is also evidence of the Voodoo belief that souls reincarnate within family lines—that an interwoven mix of bloodline and soul exists and evolves through time.

I realize that such evidence cannot be put forward as strictly scientific, since it did not emerge from a controlled experiment. But I can't deny it or dismiss it as coincidence on strictly scientific grounds, for I know how it came to me and how it revealed a psychological block: an inability to accept the information-gathering capabilities of my own mind. I had been conditioned to look "out there" rather than "in here."

Another block I eventually discovered was that I unconsciously bought into that old American saw, "If he's so smart, why ain't he rich?" I found I was paying more respectful attention to wealthy, educated, urbanized Voodoo priests than to their dirt-poor rural counterparts. I became aware of this hangup when I encountered a Voodoo priest who was watching an American news telecast in the jungles of French Guiana. After that, I didn't hesitate to find a translator and go sloshing into muddy villages of banana-leaf huts to seek out the ancient wisdom.

Without mentioning all the cultural baggage I had to toss overboard, I should include the one block I think of as my final breakthrough. That block I call the idea that mental telepathy is sporadic at best and usually unreliable. Since I was so often dealing through translators with Voodoo priests, I took the advice of one and paid close attention to the thoughts that came to me in his presence and later in dreams, imaginings, and visions. I found that not only did the priest's message jump the language barrier into my mind telepathically but that this brought home in no uncertain way the power of thought/spirit. After that, my interviews became translingual and transcultural, and Voodoo pantheism became stunningly real. Indeed it is a transtheological belief system, harmoniously integrated and logically verifiable.

Having found my own personal verifications, I was still left with the problem of how to convey the subject to my fellow countrymen. I made more attempts than I care to remember before going back to square one: theory precedes discovery of evidence; you won't find what you're not looking for nor what you don't suppose can possibly exist.

A jungle tribesman may look up and see a jet fly by and consider it a supernatural phenomenon, having no knowledge of the theories on which the jet is built and flies. So an urban Westerner with no knowledge of the theories (gods and spirits) of Voodoo will consider ceremonial possession either a supernatural event or a fraud.

Thus, this first chapter is intended as a quick primer, an outline of Voodoo beliefs posed as theoretical possibilities. In contradiction to the Western belief that Voodoo is ancient and barbaric superstition, my aim is to show it as quite modern, highly developed, and the natural perspective from which millions of people view life.

No longer are these people remote and far away from us. We are now all part of the same "global village" and increasingly interdependent. Thousands are acquiring Western educations and finding they are able to integrate their native beliefs with Western beliefs. They know the Western perspective on life, but Westerners generally don't know theirs. That ignorance hinders the evolution of humanity. And Voodoo, with its contradictory meanings, is the cornerstone of that hindering ignorance.

This primer about the Voodoo belief system, then, is followed by a condensed narrative of my own search for evidence of the theories. It's as though I shot ten hours of film and edited it to one hour in an effort to capture the essence of the subject. My focus is on the internal effects of the Voodoo culture, for it is in mind, thought, spirit, and inner dialogue that the stuff of any culture resides. Even such spectacular manifestations of Western culture as the nuclear bomb derive from beliefs, theories that have found evidence of themselves.

I thought of the journey I will describe as a modern update of the Native American vision quest. To guide the first steps of this vision quest, I called on my old friend, Lennox, who had grown up in a Shango Voodoo culture in Trinidad. He had experienced Brazilian and Haitian Voodoo as well, and had the best collection of books on the subject I've ever run across.

My friend was living with his wife in a rented house that perched on a steep incline along Fort George Road, near Port of Spain. I stayed in their guest room downstairs in the back, overlooking the village in the valley below. All day I heard the chorus of voices and the clamor of work; each evening brought the sound of steel drum bands practicing and each night the noisy travels of dog packs roaming the neighborhood. In the predawn stillness it was not unusual to see the tiny distant lights of Voodoo candles dotting the landscape. Lennox proved to be an excellent guide into the Voodoo culture. But I soon found that trying to deal with my experience in straightforward prose was like trying to wrestle an octopus. My culture demanded I intellectualize, whereas what was needed to obtain the Voodoo perspective was a leap of intuition.

Too often I found myself involved in inner conflicts between those two *I*s, intellect and intuition. Until, that is, I realized my intellect is an expression of my personal soul and my intuition an expression of my astral soul. Eventually, I settled for these two personas of my *odu*—Gover, my personal soul and intellect, and O. Govi, the name I gave my astral soul and intuition. I turned these two entities loose in the dialogue that follows.

2 Entering the Voodoo Reality

O. Govi: He sleeps under mosquito netting in his friend's guest room. I, as his dreaming self, venture forth and spy ferocious guardians at the gates of Voodoo. If I conveyed such images to his sleeping mind, he'd pop awake from a nightmare. I withhold them. Perhaps later I'll share them. Yet I shiver and quake at the treacherous tangle of contradictions he has set out to explore—White Voodoo as black magic and Black Voodoo as white magic.

• • •

Gover: Today I begin fasting. Fasting is common in the Voodoo culture as a means of purification. I've been preparing for the past two weeks by eating nothing but raw fruits and vegetables. From now on, until I feel thoroughly cleansed, I will take in nothing but orange juice and the sun-purified milk of green coconuts.

I'm up at five a.m. to go with Lennox to a Shango Voodoo shrine in the countryside. He's described it as centering around a beautiful waterfall way back in the hills. Lennox has been up since four A.M., he tells me, doing Hatha Yoga and jogging up the very steep Fort George Road. This is his fifteenth day of fasting.

An hour of driving brings us to the foot of another very steep hill, deep in a rain forest full of magnificent fruit trees. I'm amazed by the heavy-hanging abundance growing on both sides of the road. Has it been left to grow in untamed wildness?

No, for further up the road we pass a government work crew pruning trees. I want to stop so I can pick one of these luxuriant gifts of Mother Nature. I promise only to sniff and fondle it, but Lennox won't stop because he says the first day of a fast is the most difficult and there's no point making it more difficult than it has to be. He stashed a sack of green coconuts and a machete in the back seat. "Today we drink the sun-kissed milk of the coconut, nothing more," he says in the clipped English of his West Indian dialect.

The road climbs toward a cloud-covered peak. Near the end of the road the grade becomes so steep the car falters. We park it and continue up a hiking trail. "From here it's about a mile," says Lennox, then sets out at a fast pace up a single-lane dirt and stone thoroughfare. The angle of ascent soon becomes something for mountain goats. I'm panting and sweating; my legs give out, and I have to call for a rest.

• • •

O. Govi: His pursuit of the old gods might have taken us to a more fashionable place, like Findhorn in Scotland. But that would not have satisfied his fascination with the word *Voodoo.* Well, I'm not sure that dragging me, his much-abused autonomic nervous system, through such tortures as this will bring him any satisfaction either. His boozing and smoking have taken a heavy toll. That's why Lennox has advised that he fast—to get rid of the gunk of "civilized" living and clean up this wreck, this body, this "temple of his soul," and make it habitable for decent spirits.

• • •

Gover: I was educated to suppose that fasting is debilitating. And no doubt if you stop eating and drinking entirely, you will wither away and die. But witnessing Lennox's dynamo vigor after fifteen days of nothing but orange juice and coconut milk reminds me that energy—force—is not the stuff you chew and swallow and digest. What I need now is that type of energy named Ogun (Mars).

I struggle on, watching Lennox's "dreadlocks" swing to and fro. Occasionally the dreadlocks whirl as he turns to see if I'm still on my feet. I've known him for fifteen years and never before have I seen him so strong, so glowingly healthy and sure of himself. His new wife, Cuiqui, is due to deliver their first offspring in a week.

At the crest of our climb he stands grinning down at me as I come groaning up the last of the ascent. Before us is a brief valley surrounded on three sides by cliffs. At the far end is a waterfall that feeds a rushing stream along the valley's floor. White water spumes over the top of the cliff then cascades down, becoming every color of the rainbow as it falls. Here it tumbles down in solid streams, elsewhere in slender trickles, and everywhere it sends out mists that hover in the sparkling sunlight or go flying in the wind.

We descend into the valley and approach the waterfall. Its rocky face is thick with moss that glows: deep purples, blues, greens, yellows, and glints of silver. All around are rocks and boulders, some eight or ten feet high. On top of the boulders and around their bases are plates of food, half-emptied bottles of rum, Coca-Cola, homemade breads stuffed with herbs, and candles—lots and lots of candles. I'm amazed by the number of offerings—not moldy old leftovers but fresh foods, neatly arranged among candles set in appropriate designs.

The path into this captivating valley and the floor of the valley itself are obviously well cared for. The tropical growth is kept trimmed back from the path, the old offerings to the gods picked up. "Who keeps this place so clean?" I ask.

"Whoever the spirits move to do so."

We wander about awhile, then each fall into our separate meditations. I open my notebook and pick up my pen, but the atmosphere of the place, the steady sound of the waterfall and rushing stream compel a wordless trance.

● ● ●

O. Govi: He would like to write something appealing to the rational Western mind—a syncretism of Voodoo and science. Or if he cannot find words for that, something about the overwhelmingly awesome atmosphere of this place. But he is struck dumb by the presence of towering intelligences far too vast to be contained by rational English.

And that is as it should be, for if the old gods were so easily conveyed in rational language, there would be no need for him to be here having this nonverbal experience.

Gover: I lost track of time and don't know how long we stayed there, entranced. Walking back down the hill, Lennox pauses to point out offerings at the base of a silk-cotton tree. We pause again to gather some fallen nutmeg to bring home. And now I notice here and there along the narrow thoroughfare—wide enough for two or three people but not for a car—people have constructed little rock bridges over natural gullies. That touch, plus the trimmed-back growth of the rain forest, are the only evidence of human tampering.

I'm reminded of what the Oxford-educated Bantu witch doctor Credo Mutwa said in his book, *My People:*[25] it's a great insult to divine creation for people to invent mechanical or technological ways to revise nature. Obviously, the Shango Voodoo worshippers at this natural shrine know this. I get the feeling that this place is so well guarded by such powerful invisibles that it would withstand the most severe geophysical catastrophe.

Where the stream widens and deepens we stop for a swim. It's like bathing in holy water. Then we lie out on rocks to dry off in the sunshine.

As we get back into the car I vow to myself to never mention the name and location of this place to anyone. If it ever became a tourist attraction, it would quickly fall into ruin.

• • •

O. Govi: He smiles to himself then, for he thinks he has taken a step into the Voodoo reality and now understands why such shrines are kept secret: the Christianized would scoff at feeding the pagan gods, and the rationalized would want to turn such a charming site into a public park.

Well yes, he has taken one step into the Voodoo reality, and he's about to take the next step.

• • •

Gover: At the first crossroads, an elderly man carrying a satchel flags us down with insistent arm-waving. He's between sixty and seventy but as spry and quick-witted as a man of twenty, as I soon

---

[25]Credo Mutwa, *My People*. I ran across this book while I was in Trinidad. I have not been able to find this book in the United States. It was originally published in London.

discover. He wears a black cloth band around his right wrist and a red one around his left. In Shango Voodoo these are called "shield rings." He's going to Port of Spain, he tells us, on an urgent mission.

As we fly over the blacktop, Lennox engages him in that clipped, British-flavored Trinidadian lingo that is a language of its own. I catch enough of it to realize I have just encountered my first Shango Voodoo priest.

"Oh, but I have nothing to do with *evil* spirits," he says for my benefit. Centuries of experience has taught Voodooists to be cautious around white people.

Seeing that he carries flowers and herbs in his satchel, I ask about the mission he's on.

"I go on a mission of healing. You see, mon, some people think they can call down an evil power and put it on somebody else and that's the end of it. But no, no sir, that's *not* the end of it. Because the power one person call down and put on another always go back to the first person, and then that person is in trouble. You know what I mean, mon?"

He explains that he's going to give a bush bath—an herbal spiritual cleansing—to a girl who is suffering what Westerners would call a psychotic episode. He'll use the spirits of his flowers and herbs to end the diabolic squabbling in his distraught patient. "She call down evil on somebody and now that evil make her suffer too." He shows us the flowers and herbs he's picked, holding up each with reverence. "First I get ready the bush bath, then I read Psalm Ninety-one and Psalm Twenty-three, and when I'm done with the body, I read the Fifth of Saint James."

Such an amalgamation of Christianity and Voodoo is not unusual in this part of the world, especially among the English-speaking. But the healing of mental illness by exorcism is neither Christian nor psychiatric. So he is a kind of Christianized Voodoo psychiatrist. With this in mind, I idly ask, "And does the bush bath always work?"

An instant later I want to eat my words. Both he and Lennox gape at me with irritation and contempt. My question has undermined the purity of intention, the intense conjuring needed for a successful healing. Well no, it hasn't really undermined anything in their minds, but it's made them feel they should not have discussed any of this with me, a white man.

"I never know it to fail," the old man says emphatically, then falls silent.

A while later, Lennox mentions my interest in Shango Voodoo and tells him we have just come from visiting the outdoor shrine. That lightens the mood, and the priest tells me there is really no difference between Christianity and the ancient African religion. "Oh yes, they *seem* different," he says, "but no no, at the heart of it all they are both quite the same."

I agree enthusiastically, glad to have gotten beyond my thoughtless question, and I mention the Seven African Powers candle, which depicts the Voodoo gods as Catholic saints and is widely used throughout the Americas. He is pleased to learn I consider saints Catholic symbols of the old gods.

Our rapport is so good now that as we near his destination I am tempted to ask if I can go with him and watch him work. But he deals with my question before I ask it. He makes it clear that what he's about to do is a strictly private affair between his patient, the spirits involved, and himself. Absolutely no visitors allowed, especially not an American who, even though he understands a thing or two about the Old Religion, as he calls it, has blurted out a question that shows he doesn't understand the concentration of purpose needed to succeed.

When we let him out, he graciously thanks us both for the ride, wishes me well in my quest to comprehend the Old Religion, then turns and takes off running. He runs through a busy intersection with long, loping strides, dodging cars like a lanky football player dodging tacklers.

We drive on, and Lennox gently reminds me that the British colonialists tried everything they could think of to destroy Voodoo and Christianize the "savages." Forced to bow to the Christian pantheon, the Africans made obvious (to them) correspondences between the old gods and these new characters called saints. So although it appeared to the Christian clergy that their obedient "darkies" had been converted, the blacks were really worshipping the Voodoo gods as the informing spirits of the Christian pantheon.

Well, I already knew that from reading books. "But the essential difference," I say, "is that Christians worship Jesus as a dead hero, who has promised to return, while the Voodooists worship Obatala as the Christ spirit present always and everywhere, who takes temporary possession of those able to invoke him."

We agree that there is this very important difference: whereas Christians worship the Christ spirit, they are unaware of it acting out in people, plants, and everything else, and Voodooists are aware of it!

O. Govi: One step forward, one step backward. My esteemed collaborator tends to overlook the fact that knowledge *about* is not experience *of.*

• • •

Gover: Even though I can legitimately claim to be the author of this, O. Govi has a way of coming up with thoughts that are strictly his, not mine. Sometimes I agree and sometimes, even as I jot them down, I wonder.

• • •

O. Govi: Words are the costumes of thoughts. Styles change. The same thoughts enjoy dressing up in different costumes.

• • •

Gover: I decided to create O. Govi after several Voodoo priests advised that I develop a way to listen to my inner voice, my subconscious, my dreams. Well, writing poetry and fiction is a process of harkening to one's inner voice, or *voices.* I've been doing that since earliest recollection.

But fictitious characters come as inner voices *via* the writer's subconscious. Creating a dialogue *with* the subconscious is something else. And this is not fiction; it's a condensed version of actual experience. I give O. Govi existence, definition, even form of a kind, and yet . . . .

• • •

O. Govi: And what form does he suppose I take? A bee in his bonnet? How easy it is to lose track of the *spirit* of things, to think in literal terms about abstractions. Although it's true the old gods manifest through physical matter, to the *eye* of the *informed* observer, such spirits are as abstract as scientific theories.

It is recorded that the ancient Pythagoreans were attempting to square the circle. Well, I am a sphere contained within a cube that is Robert Gover. Anyone's so-called subconscious is a universe, the whole sphere of his mental grasp, the parameters of his awareness, his personal flying saucer through inner space. I am the vehicle he must ride to the Voodoo experience.

Gover: Second day of fasting. It's Saturday night, and Lennox and I have decided to go to the Savannah, Port of Spain's sprawling central park, for a big revival meeting to be conducted by a Pentecostal preacher from the United States.

A large crowd is already there by the time we arrive. We park, then work our way through this throng toward the brightly lit platform, where an organist is playing bouncy gospel tunes. Presently, the preacher steps forward and prepares to do his thing, with the aid of microphone and loudspeakers.

A long line of people await his blessing. In countries such as Trinidad, anyone advertised as spiritual draws a crowd. We manage to station ourselves by the platform's off-ramp, just as the line begins to move, the blessings happen, and the whole show gets under way.

It reminds me of an assembly line. Like bottles in a cola factory, each human vessel is filled with a Christian blessing. The preacher claps a palm smartly over each forehead and yells, "Heal, heal, heal! Heal in the name of Jesus!" Occasionally he cups a cheek gently, or holds a shoulder, or lays a hand on an ailing limb. Then each of the blessed in turn bounces, plods, or runs down the off-ramp, past our close inspection. Those who are especially touched by the blessing stagger down the ramp into the waiting arms of a couple of Pentecostal assistants.

Some are bored, and others go through this process just for a Saturday night kick. There are children of all ages, beautifully healthy young adults, the old and lame, maimed, blind and deaf, and all this blessing is happening to a musical accompaniment—a young lady behind the preacher enthusiastically bangs out waltzy hymns on her electric organ. When she's into an especially lively number, the crowd keeps time with hand clapping.

The preacher wears a raincoat for the first fifteen minutes or so, then he takes it off and is in a blue suit, white shirt, and subdued necktie. He is plump and jowly, and he's working away at this blessing business at a frenzied pace. It's a cool, damp night, but he's soon sweating. A thoughtful assistant hands him a cup of coffee, which he sips quickly between blessings. "Heal, heal, heal"—sip, sip—"heal in the name of Jesus!" Sip, sip.

The rhythmic efficiency of the preacher and the figures floating past me down the ramp are spellbinding. A multiracial mix of Afro, Hindu, Amerindian, Chinese, and brown-Spanish, -French, -Dutch, -English. Such a great ethnic variety, and yet after awhile they all seem to blend before my spellbound eyes into one.

Momentarily I snap out of the trance and wonder why so many are here tonight. Very few, if any, are Pentecostal. They are Anglican, Catholic, Protestants of one kind or another, Moslems, Hindus, Baptists, Baptist Shouters, Shangoists, and, no doubt, a few who secretly maintain the ancient Yoruba tradition. In the United States, this preacher could not possibly draw such a large crowd from so many other faiths. So why, I wonder, have these people come?

The answer to that is in their behavior. It's well understood here that the gods are the same by whatever name. That is a primary difference between these two cultures I call Western and Voodoo. Christianized Westerners believe their particular faith is the only true one. But these people know that everyone has discovered and/or invented essentially the same gods and goddesses.

And many of these people are experts at acquiring possession of their deities, to one degree of another. Or to put it another way, they have been trained to be spirit mediums. And occasionally I see someone who appears on the verge of becoming possessed in the preacher's hands. Hanging in the air is the strong hint that sooner or later this Pentecostal ceremony is going to be spiced by some Voodoo.

Sure enough, suddenly the preacher has his hands on a young woman who trembles at his touch, screams, flings up her arms, falls backward, then pops up and grabs him in a vibrating bear hug. He lifts his face heavenward and yells, "Jesus, Jesus, save this soul." But the spirit that has this woman has the preacher in its embrace and won't let go. The woman's body is trembling like she's about to have an orgasm. A hush comes over the crowd. The organist changes her tune. The preacher keeps yelling heavenward, and finally the woman regains her ordinary senses and lets go, reels backward and almost falls off the stage. The two assistants escort her gently down the off-ramp. The preacher pulls out a handkerchief and mops his brow. There is a huge sigh from the crowd—a kind of subdued mirth and the feeling of being spent.

The preacher accepts a second cup of coffee in a Styrofoam container and after a couple of sips gets back to work. All goes smoothly for a few minutes, then it happens again. Looks like the same prankster from the realm of Eshu, this time invading the body of a short, squarely built, middle-aged woman. Her arms lock around the preacher's midsection and her body vibrates orgastically. Again the preacher shouts skyward to his version of the Great Creator's human son, but again this female Eshu prankster won't let go till she's good and ready. And since she's riding a stronger woman this time, the preacher is being bounced up and down. For awhile it looks like the pair of them are going to go bouncing down the ramp together. The crowd loves it.

Finally the woman regains her selfhood, and/or the prankster spirit departs, and she goes reeling down the ramp into the arms of the assistants. Again the crowd sighs, the preacher takes a brief coffee break, and it's back to work...but not for long. That rakish female Eshu spirit has another in her grasp, a slender young thing about eighteen years old. This time, though, the preacher is able to peel her encircling arms off his body and hold her at arm's length a moment, before she whirls away and seemingly flies down the ramp into the clutches of the assistants, then falls on the ground, while her body throbs, undulates, and pulsates. I'm in the front row of the crowd that quickly swarms around her, and it's clear that no human being could move like that in her ordinary state.

Then down the ramp comes the preacher in a rush to the rescue, followed by another woman apparently possessed by the same mischievous entity—for she is running around with her arms extended like "Daisy Mae" chasing "Li'l Abner." The circle of people opens to admit the preacher and his pursuer, then closes for a closer look at the action. The preacher drops to his knees, claps a hand on the prone and pulsating lady, lifts his face to the night and yells for Jesus to remove this "demon." The second lady dances around the pair of them with such furiously fast footwork she resembles a hummingbird. "Jesus, Jesus, Jesus," yells the preacher, "take this devil *out!*" Then he bends down—or else the lady rises up—and they lock into an extremely sexual embrace.

I find myself standing next to one of the assistants. We exchange a glance and he says, "This happens sometimes. Evil spirit. He'll get rid of it, don't worry."

I'm amazed by his cool, controlled tone of voice. "Where will he send it?" I ask.

The assistant shrugs his shoulder, and we both return our attention to the action—the troublesome spirit has departed now and the preacher and lady are getting to their feet, both of them panting. The "hummingbird" dancing has ceased too, and the three participants in this seance are staring at each other with stunned expressions, as though wondering how they got here and what the hell is happening.

Then the preacher wraps one arm around both ladies and raises the other like a victorious boxer, lifts his face, and shouts loud thanks to Jesus. A triumphant cheer goes up from the encircling crowd and spreads throughout the park.

Pulling both ladies behind him, the preacher strides briskly up the ramp onto the stage and grabs the microphone. Then, with an intensity that is startling, he launches into a raging, snarling diatribe. This is such an unexpected turn of events that I can't understand what he's shouting at first. I think maybe he's "speaking in tongues," as the saying has it, but no. Gradually his roaring separates into words I can understand. I turn to Lennox, who is grinning broadly. He winks. I scan the faces around me. Everyone is amused, some near the point of having falling-down laughing fits. And I realize we have arrived at the highlight of this evening's religious extravaganza.

The preacher is possessed. In the name of his notion of deity he is cursing the gods of Africa and India. He is baring his teeth with rage, snarling, shaking his fist, and bellowing like the Christian Lord of Absolute Evil. His hoarse voice cracks with the effort.

"Cast out those evil Shango idols! Cast them *out,* I say. Turn your backs on those Hindu spooks and haunts, those so-called gods and goddesses! Destroy all profane objects! Burn ouija boards! Cast out *all* the instruments of the devil. There is but *one* god. Jesus is his oh-nly begotten son! Don't let anyone ever tell you *otherwise!* If they try, say, 'Devil, be *gone!'* Say, 'Devil, be gone' and call upon your *savior!* Jesus *is* your savior! Shango idolatry is the devil's device of deception. Be *not* deceived! *Remove* the blindfold of superstition and come, come, come to *Jesus!"*

After an initial torrential outburst of such invectives, he pauses, mops sweat from his brow, and continues in a less rageful tone. "These poor girls were possessed," he says, tugging them toward the front of the stage. "For *years* they've been possessed. For years the devil has had them in his evil grasp. They've tried Shango witch doctors and Hindu idols, but that didn't help them. Perhaps they even tried doctors and psychiatrists, but they didn't help. The devil stayed right there and rose up to make their lives miserable. They tried every which way to get the devil out . . . but there *is* but *one* way. Jesus is the way, the light, the life everlasting. Jesus came down tonight—you saw it, it happened right over there—Jesus came down and took the devil out. Took the devil right out of this girl, and this one."

The two young ladies, who never dreamed they'd been devil-possessed for all those years, who may or may not be Shangoists or worshippers of Hindu gods and goddesses, who look like they probably attend Anglican services each Sunday, are clearly uncomfortable and anxious to escape. They glance at each other, then out at the crowd, turn and look behind themselves, and give every indication of wanting to get out of this preacher's show.

"Now they're saved, glory be to Jesus. Isn't that a blessing?" The preacher pauses for reaction but the crowd remains stone silent. "You *bet* it is. So what about all those gods and goddesses? All that *eye*-doll-itry? All that oh-*cult* nonsense? Get rid of that sinfulness, I tell you. Cast it all out, I say. Turn your backs on superstitious savagery and come, come, come to Jesus."

The spirit that's been riding the preacher is clearly from the realm of Ogun, whose main fault is narrow-minded self-righteousness. As the old myths point out, Ogun needs the guidance of higher, older, more intelligent gods, for otherwise his thick-headed, stubborn self-righteousness can result in such behavior as this. But the possessing spirit has departed now, and the preacher has released the two young ladies, who have disappeared into the crowd. The line of people awaiting the preacher's blessing has shortened considerably, and when the preacher returns to his assembly line work, I hear the sound of car engines starting in the distance and see people leaving in droves. The show they came to see is over. Lennox nudges me and says, "Let's buy some coconuts."

We stroll away from the bright lights of the stage toward the street and join a group gathered around the pickup truck of a coconut vendor. He stands amid his coconuts and, holding out one at a time with his left hand, whacks it open with his machete, then hands it to a customer, pockets some coins, and gets busy whacking open the next coconut. His customers drink the milk of the green coconuts without straws and without spilling a drop—a trick I have not yet mastered. Lennox and I have two apiece, and by the time I'm ready for my second, my shirtfront is soaked.

From the distant loudspeakers we are still haunted by the preacher's "Heal, heal, heal," shouted out like orders issued by a Marine drill instructor. The gathering of coconut milk drinkers I'm now part of is in a jovial mood and is soon speculating about the preacher's connections to his government. Since I'm the only American present, a few call for my opinion as an expert witness. But others hoot before I can come up with an opinion. "How could an American know?" someone says. "Ask a Latino, not an American." The coconut vendor, a sparkling happy and healthy old man, settles the debate: "Ask," he says tapping his forehead with a forefinger, "dee inner mon."

O. Govi: That's me. And my answer is, yes and no. The preacher has no formal government connection, but there is no real separation between church and state. The preacher and his government are both products of the same culture.

Having brought this to his mind, I remind my esteemed collaborator of the very different roles Christianity and Voodoo have played in the histories of their very different cultures.

• • •

Gover: I think tonight's performance by the Pentecostal shows that Voodoo has not been Christianized through contact with Western culture; on the contrary, it is Christianity that has been Voodooized.

In *Muntu,* Janheinz Jahn offers the following explanation:

> The polytheists are gladly prepared to add an additional and obviously powerful divinity to their pantheon. They participate in the ceremonies required of them, allow themselves to be baptized and willingly learn the prayers and usages with which the new divinity is to be served. And from now on, they serve all their divinities, old and new, each according to custom and propriety. The monotheists cannot understand this and are horrified by it, and the polytheists cannot understand why the monotheists are so distressed. For the latter the very foundation of their monotheistic world is at stake, so much the more so as their God now no longer opposes the others but—recognized alongside others—threatens to be transformed from the one and only God to just one more divinity among many others. Thus the polytheists seem to them apostates, heretics, who sin against the most sacred of all commandments, "I am the Lord thy God, and thou shalt have no other Gods but me." Everything the polytheists do appears in the light of the most terrible crime, and the more deeply their life is permeated by religion, the more does it appear false, idolatrous, abominable. The whole wrath of Jahweh and Moses against the apostates who danced before the golden calf comes to life in the disap-

pointed missionaries; curses of banishment come to their lips and in their distress they become the images of their god and say: "I am the Lord...and thou shalt!"[26]

That preacher tonight realized he was dealing with a crowd who are basically polytheistic, for in Trinidad many gods and goddesses are tolerated, worshipped, discussed, and compared. And because religion is the backbone of culture, he was up against that hard wall of prejudice that separates Christian and Voodoo cultures. So he banged his head on the wall and screamed, and in the minds of most of his audience he made a damned fool of himself. One could even say he found his own evil mirrored in his own wall of prejudice.

Monotheists construct monolithic social orders and cannot tolerate the diversities of polytheistic social orders. As Efuntola pointed out, Voodooists understand that Western culture is dominated by Ogun (Mars) and understand too that the Great Warrior can be confused by the Great Trickster, Eshu. From the Voodoo perspective, Eshu was sent tonight to confuse the preacher's Ogun. But there was no malice intended, for the Eshu spirit was lighthearted and erotically playful. If a heavier Eshu spirit had arrived, the preacher would have found himself in deep trouble. As it turned out, he and his Jesus were welcomed, even while the old gods revealed themselves, just to keep the whole event from becoming a bore.

• • •

O. Govi: He sleeps, and as his dreaming self, I am free to roam the dream dimension. Here I encounter many other dreaming selves wandering this dimension. And after considerable travel and investigation I decide to report my findings to his sleeping consciousness. He dreams he is trapped in a cave with a lot of primitive brown people who regard him with suspicion, for they are trapped in this cave by primitive white people brandishing weapons. Those in the cave have no defense against those weapons, and they talk of throwing him out in the hope that their enemies will be satisfied to kill him and go away. He pleads that he is not one of their enemies, but the skin-color distinction prevails, and he pops awake with a fright just as he is being rudely forced out of the cave.

---

[26]Janheinz Jahn, *Muntu,* trans. Marjorie Grene (London: Faber & Faber, 1961), 59.

Gover: Third day of fasting. Lennox tells me that after the third day I won't be so tempted to break the fast, and the body will then get rid of the accumulated poisons of junk food, booze, and cigarettes. I want to believe him, but it isn't a temptation to end the fast that tortures me today; it's an awful feeling of depression punctuated by angry thoughts. Alternately I wallow in a self-pitying sense of futility—the feeling that my life has gone awry and there's no point in continuing—and visits of rage that boil up inside me. Memories of being wronged ignite my emotions and make me lust for revenge. Then I realize the lust for revenge only exacerbates the pain of the wrongs, and I fall back into depression.

When I confide this to Lennox, he smiles and says it's just part of the process of fasting. To counteract it he advises a hike up Fort George Hill. The day is hot, the hill is steep, and I'm lethargic, but I force myself to do it.

I'm soon drenched with sweat and winded, gulping in the hot, moist air and continuing the forced march only because of the flaringly angry thoughts that keep haunting me. On certain holidays hundreds of Trinidadians hike up this hill and then, around sundown, go calypso-singing and dancing their way down to the city again. Lennox's house is near the foot of the hill, so I've seen such parties pass. Near the top I realize it's exorcism as well as exercise, for my focus of attention changes to the gnat-sized cars on the roads below, the ant-sized tankers riding at anchor in the bay.

At the top a sign informs me that this fort of heavy stone was established in 1804 and in its time was "considered well nigh impregnable." "In times of rumors of war, the merchants of Port of Spain would store their records, cash and valuables here." But the fort was never involved in a battle. That's nice.

There's another building up here which was used as a signal station for ships. It was designed by one "Prince Kofi Nli, son of King Kofi Calachi of Ashantee, West Africa." Beside the squat stone structure of the fort it appears tall, wooden, and vulnerable. Yet the two buildings seem to have weathered the decades equally well.

Standing on the fort's wall overlooking a panoramic scene of land and sea, I feel as if I could spread my arms and soar through the air like a seagull. The rageful thoughts and depression seem to have gushed out of my pores with the sweat, and I'm surprised to realize that the fast has not made me hungry for food; it's made me hungry for the pure joy of life I felt as a child.

If, as the Voodoo belief has it, each element has its spiritual component, the residues of poisons I've ingested in civilized Western life are the physical components of the evil spirits I must rid myself of during this fast. Then I will be able to host good spirits, even the high ones who bring enlightenment.

That's a Voodoo idea I wasn't sure whether to believe or disbelieve a couple of weeks ago. But gradually it has grown valid in my mind, and now, up here on Fort George Hill, I suddenly see it as an absolute certainty. I try to imagine the countless millions of human beings who have fasted for the same reason down through the countless centuries. It comforts me to feel part of that seemingly endless river of souls.

Around sundown I walk back down the hill, the rage and depression gone, replaced by what I think of as the angels of healing.

• • •

O. Govi: It would tighten his intercourse with reality to realize he's the boss of his healing angels. The sooner he starts snapping orders, the sooner he'll be cleansed and ready for more arduous ordeals.

One of the old habits he's got to break is thinking of gods and spirits as "out there" rather than "in here." I, being also his storehouse of memories, bring to his mind the words of a Voodoo priest he met several years ago in Miami. "To understand Voodoo, you must *see* the gods and spirits within yourself."

With that in mind, he realizes it's Obaluaye, or Babalu, Saturn, the Great Teacher he's dealing with during this fast. In the Yoruba tradition, Obaluaye is said to "arrive" with a retinue of "twenty-one members of the dead," a mythological way of conveying Babalu's realm of activity. Gover has more than twenty-one residues of civilized living to rid himself of, however, and more than twenty-one angels of Babalu's realm to acquaint himself with.

So tonight as he sleeps I bring him this dream vision: He finds himself in a large old gothic house, which he soon discovers is haunted by a wild assortment of weird and horrible visages. They wander halls, appear in doorways, and float through the air. At first he thinks he's having another nightmare, but these dream creatures show no signs of threatening him, so he clings to sleep and dreams on. The last thing he remembers before awakening is meeting his wife. What are you doing here? he asks. She smiles and shrugs and asks him the same.

Gover: Fourth day of fasting. Lennox drives me far out into the countryside to visit a "preacher lady" from a neighborhood he lived in as a child. I'll call her Mary, for there is a kind of black madonna quality about her. She lives next door to her Baptist Shouter Church and "mourning ground" and is flying Shango flags, which are triangular and of the seven primary colors. Flown in certain combinations, they attract certain combinations of spirits. They are mounted on long bamboo poles that bend in the wind.

The combination of four she flies today is for the person who is in her mourning ground. The mourning ground is a bare one-room building behind the church. One goes into the mourning ground for various reasons but primarily to make closer contact with the gods and/or have a personal religious experience. You decide before going in how long you'll stay and what you'll eat or drink. You might decide to stay for ten days, say, and drink one mason jar of orange juice a day.

The mourning ground has one door and no windows. The orange juice or whatever is slipped to you once every twenty-four hours. You're aware of night and day, for it's not tightly insulated, but otherwise you are completely alone with yourself.

At the end of your appointed stay, the congregation gathers outside and begins to sing, chant, drum. This is the signal that your mourning ground experience is complete. The door is opened and you emerge into the bright daylight. You've been busy with your own consciousness, and if you're a Shango Voodooist, with the gods who compose all consciousness. The flags are flown to protect you from evil spirits while you undergo this ordeal and to attract the deities you seek.

When you emerge, you are, in the Western sense, out of your normal mind. From the Voodoo perspective you have experienced a kind of death, transformation, and renewal, and you are going to come out brimming over with a desire to share your experience with the congregation. You are, to one degree or another, possessed. Perhaps you have acquired possession of the Christos, the Light, the Christ, so it is Jesus who speaks through you when you first emerge.

In any case the mourning ground is a carefully planned and executed ordeal, and its purpose is to achieve a new level of self-knowledge, enlightenment. As part of the process you might break down into utter psychosis, but your friends and neighbors outside will be helping you through that travail with their prayers—not only out of love and generosity but because they too want the benefits of whatever you return with.

The preacher lady jokes about me spending time in her mourning ground, and I give the idea consideration. But I'm an outsider here, a stranger among these people, so it wouldn't be the same. Besides, the idea scares me. Suppose I panicked and demanded to be let out. Or suppose the spirits of these people were on hostile terms with my spirits. Or suppose I went through ten days in the mourning ground and then came out possessed—I'd be speaking American English to West Indians who speak what they call Beewee, British West Indian.

Driving back to the city, I feel a twinge of shame for chickening out of the preacher lady's invitation. For even though it was proffered lightly, it was real enough. Then I excuse myself on the grounds that the fast I'm on and the immersion into this culture—so different from my California surroundings—is mourning ground enough at this point in my life. My purpose is to prepare myself to experience more of the Voodoo reality and bring it back alive, to make it comprehensible to my fellow countrymen. I don't want to dive too deep before I'm ready.

• • •

O. Govi: Good idea. Gover's national soul is ruled by Ogun, and it is well known that Ogun can quickly become lost in the mysterious depths of Olokun (Neptune), who rules the national soul of Trinidad. And although he's not in the mourning ground per se, he feels stranded on a small island surrounded by a vast ocean. The nature of his national soul requires some means of transportation through this Neptunian consciousness so alien to his native culture. It is Lennox who helps him build his ship.

• • •

Gover: Fifth day of fasting. Lennox takes me through the narrow streets around the Old Market to meet a renowned Shango priest. The Old Market is a huge one-story building that sits empty and idle now, replaced by the newer Central Market. But along the street outside the empty Old Market vendors sell their wares—fruits, vegetables, homemade preparations, remedies, bottled essences, and all manner of clothing.

One of these vendors is the Shango priest Allen. At first glance there is nothing special about him—medium height, round face, husky, ordinary clothes, no beads or bangles, skulls, or rooster feathers—nothing to distinguish him from the many other vendors on the streets of Port of Spain. Judging by the lines in his face, he's in his sixties.

Lennox introduces me, then the two of them have a lively exchange in that Trinidadian Beewee I still can't quite understand. As they talk, I notice that Allen has a certain air of attentive preoccupation, as though he is thinking of two or more things simultaneously. And even though he is obviously a poor man, he has the dignity of an aristocrat. He is at once clearly at peace with himself—even here in this crowd, where people continually rub each other wrong or right— and proud. I get the impression that he is also utterly fearless, a man of daring who relishes each nuance of experience.

Lennox tells him of my interest in the Old Religion, avoiding the words Shango and Voodoo. Allen nods approval and asks, "You want to see a Shango feast, eh?"

I try to tell him I'd like to do more than just see it, I'd like to become as much a part of it as possible. That information strikes him as odd, coming from a white man, and I sense a twinge of suspicion growing in him.

"It's a feast for Saint Anthony," he says, looking me over closely. "You know Saint Anthony?"

"Ogun."

"Yes yes, the same. There will be lots of food, dancing, African drumming. . ." He pauses a beat, and I intuit that he wonders what motivates my interest in Shango Voodoo. "Strange things can happen," he adds.

"I'm interested in the Old Religion because it's essentially the same as that of my Native American and pre-Christianized European ancestors," I tell him.

He raises his eyebrows and regards me anew. He knows now that I've at least done some homework on the subject, but centuries of harassment have made him extremely cautious about sharing the inner reality of Voodoo with whites.

"I'd like to write about it," I say in answer to his unasked question.

He nods knowingly, and now his expression contains the hint of disdain. "People won't believe what you write, if you tell the truth. And to learn the truth would take much time. Years." He says that as though he's been approached by journalists, folklorists, anthropologists, and other nonbelievers many times before and has had more than enough of their gross misrepresentations.

"I'm not interested in facts and figures. I want to know the inner reality."

"You yourself are of the Old Religion, then?"

"Well, not formally, but I want to learn all I can about the old gods."

He nods approval. "Okay. Come to the feast for Saint Anthony then. Perhaps he will single you out and touch you."

Then he and Lennox get the time and place of the feast clear, speaking that rapid Beewee I can't keep up with, and we move on.

• • •

O. Govi: At home in Lennox's guest room again, my collaborator is inspired to write ten pages about his slave-owning ancestors, recalling tales his great-grandfather passed along to him about what those times were really like, compared to the official written history of them. After that burst of scribble, he pauses to reflect, wondering if his brief encounter with Allen had anything to do with this sudden bout of ancestor worship.

Of course it did. Allen, being a Shango priest, is deeply concerned with ancestors, both African and European. And perhaps like other priests of the old gods, Allen has found that the ancestral souls of white people withdraw from being "touched" by Saint Anthony/Ogun or any other deity. And also that guiding white aspirants toward the inner reality of Voodoo can be dangerous for the white aspirant, whose ancestral soul—haunted by the Inquisition—shudders with dread as the approach is made, and that can cause massive upheavals among his other eight souls.

Perhaps he doesn't think of it in those terms, but that's the gist of it.

Gover picked up Allen's curiosity telepathically, and that's what sent his attention to his ancestors. And what he was writing is what he would like to tell Allen, the sum of which is that neither of them is racially pure; both are of mixed ancestral souls.

• • •

Gover: Sixth day of fasting. Last night I dreamed I stood at a fork in a road, wondering which way to go. One road led to a very urbane scene, a party of the rich and famous, a lot of glib people exchanging clever quips while standing on a penthouse balcony

overlooking a modern city. Take this road, said the dream, and you'll
find yourself here.

The other road led to a beautiful stretch of unspoiled beach:
invitingly soft, white sand, the sea glistening like diamond-studded
jade, and behind the beach a virtual garden of Eden—coconut palms,
papayas, mangoes, bananas. Take this road, said the dream, and you
will glory in this attunement with nature. I saw myself living in a palm-
leaf-covered hut, amid lovely women and happy children, fishing,
gathering fruit, swimming, and lazing about in delicious sensuality.

But I seemed unable to make a clear choice in that dream.
"Going native" was extremely tempting, yet it would estrange me from
my native culture, those clever people and the commanding vista of
the important events of our time. Do I have an unconscious desire to
withdraw from the urbanized Western world and lose myself
somewhere down here near the Equator on some secluded stretch of
beach? Would I soon be bored with such an "ideal" life? Or is my
search for the inner meanings of Voodoo really a search for the end of
that second dream road?

• • •

O. Govi: I slapped his consciousness with that dream so
smartly it lingers with him all morning. But the dream has more
meaning than he at first supposes. It's not just a choice of
romanticized life-styles. What I'm trying to tell him is that if he
cooperates with me, his astral soul, he'll soon have an amazingly large
range of new possibilities.

• • •

Gover: Seventh day of fasting. Seems I was cooperating so well
with my astral soul last night I participated in the birthing of Lennox's
new baby boy without even being there. I dreamed I watched his wife
giving birth, clearly saw her struggle with her contractions, saw the
other people in the bedroom with her, watched as Lennox gently
accepted his new son in his hands and bathed him in lukewarm water.
I even woke up with a vivid memory of the baby's face.

Then, when I went into the kitchen for my morning orange
juice, Lennox told me I had missed the birth, that he and two friends
had tried to wake me but I was so soundly asleep I refused to budge. I
said, "That's strange, because I dreamed I was there." I even told him

who else was there: a doctor, a photographer, two friends, his mother, and his brother. And they were!

One of the impressions I recall from the dream is that I was helping. Not in any physical way but by adding spiritual force to the whole event. And I felt that I, as the visitor, was somehow responsible for making sure it went smoothly and that the baby was beautifully healthy, because if anything went wrong, I'd feel as though I'd brought bad luck.

The baby's a beauty.

After orange juice Lennox and I go out shopping for a scale to weigh the baby but find there is not one such scale for sale in all of Port of Spain. It's just as well. He weighs in heavy as a blessing and light as a worry, this reincarnating soul of an ancient elder.

• • •

O. Govi: Now he's starting to get the hang of it, this new relationship with me. In the beginning is the word, the intention formed into meaningful sound.

The words of some entities are far more powerful than those of others, however.

• • •

Gover: Eighth day of fasting, and it feels as if the word of Obaluaye is resounding within me with such force it threatens the end of my world. Well, I've accumulated a lot of evil eating companions over the years, and it's time to chase them out. And it feels as if Babalu is down there in my gut somewhere, cracking the whip over those evils—and they don't want to leave. He's lashing them without mercy, and they're screaming and pleading to stay—and all that ruckus is raising hell with my disposition. Some of them are good ol' boys, friends of mine for years—cigarettes, alcohol, coffee with sugar, red meat with all of its chemical additives. Lord Babalu sure doesn't like those chemicals, and he's letting both them and me know it in no uncertain way. Me, I'm inclined to pity the poor devils, hear them out, even consider forgiving them and letting them stay. They've been with me so long, I'm really the only home they ever had. But that mean, lowdown, nasty, cruel, and unforgiving Babalu is far more powerful than I am.

So there's not much I can do except give Babalu some help. I go to the kitchen, squeeze the juice out of a dozen oranges, filling a pitcher. I strain that into another pitcher, then slice a hot pepper in half, drop it into the juice, and stir it around. And when I say hot pepper, I mean hot. I've eaten jalapeños raw, but I wouldn't touch one of these things with so much as the tip of my tongue. I keep the half a pepper in the juice for about sixty seconds, then take it out. What a great cocktail! The orange juice soothes my jangled nerves and the taste of pepper is a big hit with Babalu. He's soon got a bunch of unwanted guests trapped in my lower bowel.

I feel a lot better after moving them out. I feel good enough to do something I've been wanting to do for days: go downtown to the Ministry of Culture and find out who *they* think is the greatest Shango priest in Trinidad.

There I meet a good-looking black lady with a coy twinkle in her eye, and in my sensitized, fasting state I fall immediately in love. And who does she think is the greatest Shango priest?

She sidesteps the question with a toss of her head and tells me she wants to go to the United States and study parapsychology. Soon I'm talking Shango Voodoo and she's talking parapsychology, and neither of us is listening.

I leave with the impression that what interests her most about parapsychology is getting funded. With funding, she'd be delighted to do a parapsychological study of Shango priests. She'd be even more delighted if her tests scientifically proved they were all just a bunch of half-crazed actors, that there are no such things (or nonthings) as gods and spirits, and that the Old Religion is a lot of bunkum.

• • •

O. Govi: I take him far away and show him something. He writes this dream down as follows:

I'm in a strange, foreign country with a lot of people, blacks and Latinos. They're all very friendly but I can't understand a word they're saying. Yet I know what they're saying. Either I'm reading their minds or just know ahead of time what they're communicating to me: "Hey, isn't it wonderful that we're all here together; let's go for a bus ride." We leave the large hut we were in and find ourselves on a high bluff overlooking the sea—sun glistening on the water, colors supervivid, breathtakingly beautiful. Then we're in a bus, bouncing over a dirt road toward a main highway. We seem to be going somewhere important, but I don't know where or why. When we reach the highway, the bus suddenly goes backward and everybody is laughing. I'm disoriented by this backing up, by the landscape going by in reverse. I ask the guy beside me why we're going backward but he only laughs harder. I turn and look out the back window and see the bus hit a basket and knock it rolling into a field. I ask someone else where are we going and he says, "Who cares! We're moving, aren't we?" But I care, and soon we're back where we started—the bluff overlooking the sea, the beautiful vista. The bus stops with its rear end suspended over the cliff, an incredible drop straight down to broiling surf and deadly rocks. One more inch backward and over we'd go, but everyone is laughing and I'm not feeling any fright, because I realize we're all souls, and if we were to go over the cliff, smash on the rocks, and die, we'd go right on laughing—wouldn't we? With that in mind I turn to my companion and we exchange smiles, as if saying, "But of course, we always go back to start, don't we?"

• • •

Gover: Ninth day of fasting. It's market day, and Lennox is waiting when I awaken. I hurry out into the predawn semidarkness, feeling light on my feet and swift, even slightly psychedelicized—a good sign that Babalu doesn't have many more evil eating companions to evict.

We drive to the Central Market and are soon cruising through the crowd amid displays of fruits and vegetables being sold out of trucks, vans, the trunks of old klunkers, pushcarts—anything that's mobile. A great variety of people are shopping here this morning—rich and poor, grocery store owners, street vendors, family providers, and just plain hungry folk with a taste for something earthy fresh this fine day.

Lennox is a very serious shopper. While he's busy comparing qualities and prices, I seek evidence of the old gods in action. The orange vendor Lennox finally chooses to buy from, for instance, is clearly ridden by Shango. He's dandily dressed, fiery-eyed, a magnet to the ladies, and exceedingly headstrong. He's convinced he's got the best oranges today, and nobody can reasonably dispute that fact.

We carry two large sacks of oranges to the car and put them in, then go inside one of the market's two buildings, under its sprawling top of corrugated tin, and we approach a youngish hustler type, who's a horse for Ogun. He sells tomatoes, cucumbers, hot peppers, beans, and onions, and he works at it like there's no tomorrow. He reminds me of Sousa marching music as he moves about behind his stand. He's muscular, singleminded, willful, and he glowers as he handles his produce like a soldier in the heat of battle. Simultaneously, he counts out change to one customer, fills a bag for another, and chatters away at Lennox. "Today my tomatoes are the best, yes sir, you'll find none better." Lennox looks skeptical. "Look, look! Two sizes. All quite ripe." Lennox moves on, unconvinced, or maybe he just wants to get this vendor's goat. I glance back and see the guy watching us like a cop about to make an arrest.

One of my favorites is a lady who specializes in hot peppers. She's so full of Oshun she looks flirtatious just sitting there all alone staring off into space. If you were going to paint a picture of Venus manifesting as a dark-skinned lady in her middle thirties, you'd want her as your model. I don't think she smokes marijuana, but she looks very high and happy, moving with measured, easy grace and speaking in a velvety tone while batting her eyelashes so demurely. I catch her infectious feeling and smile broadly while Lennox selects some peppers and buys.

Then I go off by myself on a mission to buy onions, and Lennox, who seems to zip about like he's possessed by Eshu, returns to the Ogun-dominated tomato man. I come to an old guy who is definitely Eshu-headed and has a big stack of onions before him. With a crafty glint in his eye, he's wheeling and dealing with a bunch of customers, selling garlic, potatoes, and so forth so swiftly, with such deft fingers, it reminds me of a stage magician doing card tricks. I'm instantly suspicious that he's liable to shortchange me, but when my turn comes to buy and I ask for two pounds of onions, Eshu becomes Shango; he looks down at me like a bolt of lightning and fires out, "Is that *all* you gonna buy from me?"

I'm taken aback by this sudden shift. "Yeah, just two pounds of onions," I say. I bought two pounds of onions from him last week—so what's the problem?

"No no," he snaps, "you cannot come here for onions only. Why? Because of the shortage!"

"Shortage?" People are staring at me like I'm a thief.

"Yes yes, the shortage. Don't come to me for onions only, mon. That will never do, no no."

I don't know if this is the Great Trickster Shangoing me as a joke, or what. A shortage of onions in Trinidad? I can't believe it. But while I stand there stunned, wondering what else I can reasonably buy from him, he moves on to other customers. And when he sells one a few garlics only, I move away.

I come to another pile of onions, these in front of a lady who looks very Yemanja. Her round face and eyes remind me instantly of a full moon, and it's clear she is sensitive, intuitive, emotional. Her stall is away from the heavy traffic near the doors, so there's no crowd around her, and she's watching my approach with a look of strong pleading in her big round eyes. When I ask for two pounds of onions, she regards me even more plaintively and asks, "Which kind, sir?" And I notice she has two kinds of onions. I point to the larger of the two kinds, and she carefully drops some in a bag, weighs it, adjusts for weight, and hands me the bag in a manner that suggests she's sorry to part with them. I start to leave, then turn and ask, "Is there an onion shortage in Trinidad?"

"Oh, I don't believe so, sir."

I'm tempted to tell her about that Eshu-ridden vendor who said there was, but she's radiating such emotional power it fairly overwhelms me, so I just stand there a moment, basking in this radiance.

Suddenly Lennox is beside me, looking like he's possessed by a god they call Oshagun in Brazil—the Militant Christ, a mix of Oshala the Sun god and Ogun the Warrior. "Here, I have a Shango lady for you to meet," he says and leads me outside to a gray-haired old gal who is sitting on a folding chair beside a heap of papayas. Lennox introduces us and is gone, and I didn't catch her name in that rapid Beewee, which sounds to me like a bunch of words strung together in one sound.

Her disposition is such that I think she must be harboring Babalu: grouchy, taciturn, unresponsive. She stares out at the parking lot as I nudge a few questions at her, which she doesn't answer. Makes me feel stupid, like I'm talking to the wall. But just when I've given up trying to converse with her and am about to walk away, she begins to speak, still with her gaze focused on the parking lot. She says something about never making animal sacrifices, no sir, never, none.

"Is that not done anymore?" I cautiously ask.

Her eyes go back and forth, looking right, left, right, left, as though expecting calamitous trouble to descend mysteriously at any moment. And the realization hits me: she's been traumatized because of her Shango Voodoo beliefs. She's frightened to talk about Shango with a white man. The Old Religion was ruthlessly persecuted by missionaries like that Pentecostal preacher, and she's old enough to have caught a lot of such hell. I want to say something that will put her at ease but can't think of anything.

Suddenly she winds up and delivers, coming out of her chair with arms waving. Shango isn't what it was in the old days; the purity's gone out of it; it's just a show for carnival people now, a lot of silly dancing on broken glass. In the old days it was pure but no more. It was destroyed by the stinking British, by those hypocritical Protestant bastards and their intolerant henchmen. Shrines were smashed, people put in jail and beaten. Why? Isn't all religion the same? Why did they destroy Shango?

I shake my head. She glowers at me awhile, as if it's all my fault. Then she relaxes a bit, finds her chair and sits down again, heaves a sigh, and says, "But it's the same with the Catholic and Anglican faiths. They are in no better shape than Shango. The young people, they don't *believe*. All they want is money—no Shango, no religion at all, just money."

I lean against the building's wall awhile, wondering what god's realm that outburst came from. I decide it must be from Shango himself. Then, cautiously, I say, "I once heard a story about Shango. He was the most glorious man in the village, the richest, and with the most wives and children. But he was so splendid that some people envied him, even hated him, and this hurt him deeply. One day his youngest wife came running into the village from the forest, crying, 'Shango is dead, he hung himself.' The villagers all rushed out into the forest after her to find Shango. But when they came to the spot where his wife said he'd hung himself, all they could find was a rope with a hangman's noose, no body. And it wasn't long after that another man in the village became possessed by Shango's spirit, and then he became the most splendid man."

After delivering that toward the parking lot, I turn to find her eyes pinned on me, her expression somewhere between anger and astonishment. I step around to her stack of papayas, with her eyes still boring into me, and select a couple. We don't need them, but it gives me a graceful exit.

• • •

O. Govi: This evening he wonders if he's come to the right place at the wrong time. Oil workers and sugar cane workers have gone out on strike, and Trinidad is shut down. Gas stations have closed, and no one knows when more fuel will be delivered. Allen's Shango feast is called off because there's no way to get to the site, which is far out of town.

But what bothers him most is the wall of suspicion his curiosity meets, the old lady in the market being just one instance. I remind him that Voodoo arose in secret, nurtured by slaves who often risked their lives to celebrate their old gods. Some were physically mutilated by Jesus-spouting, narrow-minded, self-righteous Christians. And their offspring are still persecuted, even by the Western meaning of the word *Voodoo*. Is it any wonder that the other side of the wall of prejudice is made of suspicion?

I plant a seed. The radio is playing, and he hears a tune he recognizes but has forgotten the name of. It's a Brazilian-sounding tune. Where, he wonders, has he heard it? Oh yes, it's from a movie, and the name of it is "Bahia."

• • •

Gover: Tenth and final day of fasting. This afternoon I go for a long walk and find myself down at the docks watching a pleasure ship unload several hundred tourists from West Germany. They file down the gangplank in standard sports clothes, and as they step ashore, each is handed a flyer. I walk over to the Trinidadian who is handing out these slips of paper and get one. It's an advertisement for the Miramar Nightclub:

> Miramar presents such breathtaking, blood-curdling African dances as the Voodoo, the Shango, the P.K. and the Watusi. These give real pleasure and excitement to the tourist, expecially when the dancers are overpowered by the supernatural spirit. It's so real—you have to laugh to hide your fear and superstition. You wonder—because native visitors, members of the cult who come for entertainment, very often are overcome by the spirit—to the amazement and amusement of the tourist. . . .

> Fabulous Battle Dance: the midnight dance of the followers of the sacred Shango Cult had its first public preview at the Miramar. The dancers catch the real Shango spirit to the eerie music of African drums. They jump, dance, prance and roll on broken bottles without being cut. Tourists are allowed to supply the bottles for the dance.

I've seen that show. And in Haiti I've seen even more spectacular Voodoo feats. Now here come all these West Germans out of their Protestant Christian background, although most probably are nonreligious now. The ones who read English are translating for the others, and it's clear by their enthusiasm that the Miramar will be packing them in tonight.

Walking back to the house, I find myself humming that tune, "Bahia." It's from a movie I saw when I was five or six called *Road to Rio*. Lennox has mentioned several times that the best place to experience the Voodoo culture in its purest form is Bahia, nicknamed "The Voodoo Vatican."

But I'm not sure what Bahia is, so when I get back to the house I call the Brazilian consulate, tell them I'm thinking of going to Brazil, and ask about Bahia. The Portuguese-accented voice informs me that Bahia is a wonderful vacation spot famous for its fine beaches and its folklore—Condomble, Macumba, Shango, Umbanda, Quimbanda, and other Voodoo cults. He says the principal city of Bahia is Sao Salvador and that Sao Salvador is to Brazil what New Orleans is to the United States—the historic port of entry for slaves arriving from Africa. I ask if the African culture is still strong in Bahia. Definitely, he says. It's stronger there than it is across the Atlantic in Africa. I tell him I'd like to look up some Voodoo priests and talk with them about the Old Religion, and ask if he thinks they'd be open to that.

"Definitely," he says. The Old Religion was not so harshly persecuted in Brazil as it was elsewhere in the Americas, so the Macumbeiros are quite open and willingly discuss all aspects of their practices.

As I pack, Lennox talks about what a great country Brazil is—he lived in Rio for a year or so—and how much he'd like to be going with me. He gives me the name of a Brazilian novelist to contact. I'm worried about the language barrier, but he says not to worry, since many Brazilians speak English.

And it's a good thing I've been fasting, he says, for now I am cleansed and ready to host the higher spirits. And there will be plenty of opportunities for that in Bahia, "a very spiritual place." Then he gives me instructions on how to come off the fast: *gradually*. First some soft fruits and vegetables—avocados, papayas, mangoes, all very cheap and abundant in the street markets.

My intention is to stick to that "soft" diet in Bahia, for it feeds Obatala, and I feel a great need to keep my mind clear as I dive deeper into the depths of Voodoo.

O. Govi: The lack of gasoline and the old gods as nightclub entertainment conspire to send him on this next leg of his journey. He couldn't have timed it better if he had consciously tried. And although he doesn't realize this yet, the farther he travels "out there" in miles, the deeper he'll go "in here" where what he seeks awaits.

3 Conversations with Invisibles

Gover: On the plane I listen to people all around me smacking their lips over cocktails, while I twiddle my thumbs and yearn for green coconut milk. Just before leaving Trinidad I acquired the knack of cutting a coconut open with a machete, and now I wish I'd bottled some coconut milk so I could have my cocktail too.

Presently the hostess serves the standard airline dinner, and I'm in culture shock. It looks and smells so familiar and good I want to wolf it down and ask for seconds. Ah, but that is not the way to come off a fast, so I click into my Voodoo perspective and see if differently. It's been fried, frozen, and fried again. Pressed ham, minced chicken, canned tuna, soggy string beans, wilted lettuce, and a dandy-looking cake of factory products, mostly refined cane sugar. Imitation milk and overprocessed coffee. If the spirit components of this food are still here, they must feel hellishly tortured.

But damn it, I'm hungry. My sentimental attachment to these aromas threatens to overpower my Voodoo perception. The butter, for instance. The wrapper it comes in says it's real. I open the wrapper and sniff, just for old time's sake. Then I spy an interesting-looking piece of French bread and I'm gone.

Two bites of the buttered bread, though, and I click back into Voodoo. I inspect this stuff called bread and butter very closely, and to my fast-sensitized sense of smell it stinks. It reminds me of decaying animal flesh and dances into my mind visions of chemically induced assembly line slaughter in the Chicago yards.

Quickly I grab a plastic cup and peel the foil from its top and drink. Water. I down it in two big swallows. Strange how fasting rearranges your relations with food. I'm hungry but I can't eat this stuff...yet.

• • •

O. Govi: Thus, he pays a tax of willful resistance to the principle of will, his own personal government, Ogun. Some taxes are more easily paid and benefit the whole being. If he is to dine for the spirits of Obatala, as he intends, he'd best remove his attention from airline cuisine.

• • •

Gover: I sit in the front seat beside the taxi driver as we head for the town of Cayenne, French Guiana. Another American, a tourist in his sixties, is in the back seat. I strike up a conversation with the driver, who speaks about as much English as I do French—very little. He jolts me with the news that the plane I was expecting to catch tomorrow for Belém, Brazil, no longer flies. The schedule has been changed, and I will be in Cayenne for three days instead of less than twenty-four hours.

This strikes me as a rotten trick for the fates to play and simultaneously causes me to worry about my mental health. I have physically returned to Western culture, it seems, for here I am rolling along in a taxi in what is still a province of France, feeling wronged by invisible forces because I'll be stuck here for three days. It's the airline bureaucracy I should blame, not the invisibles. But just what the hell are bureaucracies? They're procedures, not people. The schedule change was probably dictated by the airline's computer-directed money sensitizer. Yes, the bureaucracy is an organism composed of people but run by a computer. Well, maybe the computer will cough up my hotel bill, since it's the computer's fault I'll be here three nights instead of one.

Back to business: I ask the driver about the local Voodoo scene. At the sound of those two rumbling syllables he rolls his eyes, acting out a skit of comic fright. He's Afro-French, but he doesn't want to talk about Voodoo, so I use words like *African religion, spiritualists, shaman.* Oh, he says, there are plenty of those. Also, he finally admits with a coy smile, there are some Voodoos, and he will be happy to see what he can arrange for me.

Then the man in the back joins in to tell us he has just returned from a six-day journey through the jungles of Surinam, and has a tape recording of a Voodoo ceremony held by people in a remote village. Plus a conversation he had through an interpreter with the witch doctor, which he'll be happy to play for me the first chance we get.

We're entering the town of Cayenne now, and it's like watching the negative of a film of Paris, shot in black and white. Under a neon sign reading "Vietnam Restaurant" stand a group of black people in Parisian clothes and postures, the men in that typically French-type macho pose and the ladies demurely foxy. African spirits wearing French personalities.

The one European-style hotel in town is full, we learn when we get there. The parking lot is full of Mustangs and English Fords, MGs, Jaguars, Mercedes, and such, all outfitted for road racing. They've just raced down from Paramaribo in Surinam and filled the hotel to capacity.

So we load our luggage back into the taxi and go in search of a non-European hotel. The other American tells me he's a sixty-five-year-old retired marine engineer with a battery-powered heart. He's on a seventeen-day excursion to this part of the world. He's visited eighty-five countries so far and wants to see as many others as he can before he dies. While here in French Guiana, he plans to tour Devil's Island, the famous penal colony, no longer in use but still standing as a tourist attraction.

We wind up in a small pension that has an Arab-style toilet just outside the room they put me in. The lower hinge of the john's door has broken loose, and all night long, when anyone goes there, it bangs loudly, waking me up. Around midnight I give up trying to sleep, turn on the light and read. By three A.M. I am playing host to the spirits of self-pity and depression.

They rush through my mind like Hun raiding parties, hacking at everything I think I should be, taunting, accusing, torturing me with self-regret. While part of me wonders how the hell I allowed myself to be swept away by such a howling rampage, another part of me submits. I think of the people I have wronged in this life, and tears trickle down my cheeks. The trip I've embarked on suddenly seems absurd. Whatever possessed me, a white man, to dive into this stange culture? Who do I think I am that I should want to explore Voodoo and bring back something of it?

I decide my whole life has been a self-delusion. I've wasted it, and it's now beyond redemption. I shed a few tears for my wife and sons. Poor souls, they deserve better than me. To hell with Voodoo, to hell with this trip—tomorrow I will catch the first plane out of here and go home to California.

Then, from a dark corner of the room, a face appears. I blink, shake my head, and tell myself to stop hallucinating. But the face is still there. It's an ugly, brutal face, and I know immediately it belongs to a French convict. But is it really there, or am I imagining it? Why doesn't it blink off and go away? Why is it watching me so intently, or why am I hallucinating that it is?

I turn off the light, hoping that will switch off the vision. But instead it slowly expands until a whole man appears. I feel as though I've just been sent to Devil's Island, and this guy is my cellmate; and I don't belong here, there's been a terrible mistake—but he's laughing now. He is laughing at my anguish, not out loud but with such a sinister grin it sends chills up my spine. I turn the light on again, but he's still here.

What the hell, if I'm this far into insanity, I might as well keep going. So I commune with him, as in a dream, telepathically. He says he's laughing at my self-pity, and that he's been here for most of his life. For what crime? A very minor crime; it doesn't matter. It amuses him that I should feel sorry for myself while he's feeling fine, and I have enjoyed years of freedom while he's been imprisoned most of his life. But, I think at him, you're dead, you're a ghost. He agrees.

No, that can't be possible, I tell myself. Even if there are such things as ghosts, they don't really *appear*. He says, very seriously now, that he's made it his business to appear to me. Why? Because the living and the dead must help each other—isn't that basic to the Voodoo belief? Yes, but. . . Where do you come from, and why do you appear to me? He's been here for many years, he says, and he appears to me because we need each other, as I shall soon learn.

Oh no, I say, this isn't really happening. I get out of bed, put on my clothes and step outside into the dim light of dawn. The vision comes with me like a memory I can't shake. And when I finally find a little restaurant that's open this early Sunday morning, my hands are trembling so much it alarms the lady who serves me coffee. My hands are shaking because the ghost is sitting across the table from me.

O. Govi: On the trail of the Voodoo experience, my man's personal mind has opened a door into Mind. What he sees "out there" is not of his personal mind but of his personal relationship with Mind. You don't reach faraway places of consciousness by airplane or rocketship. At the proper time a bite of bread and butter triggers a switch, and presto, you're there.

Within the Voodoo reality, consciuosness is the Son, the offspring of Father Spirit and Mother Earth. All creatures encountered in consciousness—whether "out there" or "in here"—are real enough. This one comes from that realm of Mind ruled by Obaluaye, of whom it is said, "he comes with twenty-one members of the dead." Babalu is the Great Teacher, and his entourage serves his cause. So our dead French convict is a good omen and will prove valuable if Gover quits his "fear of ghosts" and cooperates.

• • •

Gover: After one cup of coffee, I feel like I'm high.—I grab my bags and taxi to the big hotel on the hill, the Montabo. The crowd of auto racers are departing for the return drive north to Paramaribo, and soon there are very few people around. One is a pretty young girl, who gives me the eye, suggesting she's selling sexual favors. I respond awkwardly, not sure whether to take her up on it or not. I sense the dead convict grinning and imagine I can hear his laughter. In an attempt to recapture my normal senses I go exploring in and around the hotel.

• • •

O. Govi: I show him a worm. He is pacing, feeling trapped, around and around the hotel, when his attention is arrested by a worm. He stops and looks down at this long tropical specimen whose path crosses his own. He bends over and watches it closely, this fellow-creature, and then his mind opens enough for me to remind him that this worm is even more vulnerable to "invisibles" than he is. The worm is at once immune from the perversities of pride and fear and less open to contact with the ancient inhabitants of Mind.

This worm is heading south toward Brazil, he notices. He wishes this little creature a safe journey and decides to persist on his own way, this venture into Voodoo.

Gover: After that encounter the coffee high relents, and I feel suddenly tired, so I go to my room and sleep. No sooner do I close my eyes, it seems, than I'm engulfed in a nightmare. It's like a third-rate horror movie that could be called *Voodoo Kidnapping.* I'm being held captive by a bunch of Devil's Island convicts. It's night and there's a bonfire, and one of these dream convicts is telling me they are going to roast and eat me. I struggle but can't break free. Then I snap awake, look at my watch, and find that I've slept two hours.

While pondering that dream, I feel the presence of my ghost again, and this time he seems less a vision "out there" and more a reality "in here." I can hear his voice, or so I imagine. I don't know if I have conjured this being, or it has conjured itself, or what, but it's taken on a reality of its own.

Yes, it's true, he tells me, that meals in solitary confinement were bread and water. (I hadn't asked, hadn't even thought about it, not consciously. But I do feel stuck in a kind of solitary confinement here in Cayenne, waiting for my "conviction" to Brazil.)

But the bread wasn't as tasty as your airline bread, and there wasn't any butter to fuss over the animal smell of. And when you spend weeks or months or years in this remote part of the world, you learn to free your mind and converse with spirits. You do so to save your sanity, and so you become spiritual. You'd be surprised how psychic some convicts became in this environment. Some could cause amazing effects. Some became as adept as Hindu gurus.

It is, he tells me, because he himself developed such powers that he is able to appear to me with such forceful "reality."

Soon I'm up pacing the floor, trying to shake this vision again. But it sticks in my mind like a TV jingle, so I put on my swim trunks and head for the hotel pool, hoping to mingle with other people and become normal again.

But there's nobody in or around the pool. I dive in and swim lengths. It's a twenty-five meter pool, I judge, and I figure if I swim ten laps, I'll regain my rightful senses. I soon lose track of my count, however, and just keep swimming until the tension eases.

• • •

O. Govi: I wish he'd quit resisting and make himself comfortable in the presence of his newfound friend. There's not much else to do here. Time, as the saying has it, stands still. An hour here is like a month in California. Here meditation isn't a discipline, it's an inevitability. In this ambience he slows to tree-talking speed. Lying in the sun to dry off, he watches the thoughts that come parading through his mind. Good. The convict spirit isn't the last visitor I shall introduce, nor the most informative. Now that he's able both to *have* thoughts and to mark their arrivals and departures, he's ready for bigger and better.

• • •

Gover: I'm about to go back to my room when into the pool area comes an Afro-French lady. She's large, about six feet tall and big-bottomed. She's got a cheerful face and is wearing a print dress, and I'm instantly at ease with her. "You are interested in African culture?" she asks in French-flavored English.

"Yes."

"I have a taxi. You want to go touring?"

"Okay, just give me time to get dressed."

"No hurry. I wait in the lobby."

"Are there any Voodoo priests in Cayenne?"

That word again. Her eyes narrow and she looks into me, through me, beyond me. Finally she says, "Yes. Come, I take you to the best."

I hurry back to my room, eat an avocado, dress, and go down to the lobby to find her ample bottom filling a large easy chair to overflowing. She leads me out to her Renault and she is soon overflowing the driver's seat. A light rain begins as we head out of town, going south along the coast. As we approach the ruins of a stone building, she notices my curiosity and stops. "This was one of the prisons," she says. We take a brief tour of its remains, then resume driving.

I get out my ever-present notebook and scrawl a few thoughts, and the next time I look up, we're on a four-lane freeway. I ask her why the French built such a highway out here in the middle of the jungle, and she says they were expecting big business but nothing has come of it.

Soon we're sloshing back on a muddy road, one lane that cuts into the jungle, and then we're skidding to a squishy halt in a village of leaf-roofed huts. If I didn't know I was in French Guiana, I'd sure think I was in Africa. We're met by a host of dark-skinned people, clearly of African descent but also showing some European and Asian traits.

They're dressed in what look like secondhand Western-style clothes. She leads me deeper into the village, and the crowd follows, sidestepping and hopping mud puddles. The rain has stopped, but the air feels thick with moisture.

She stops at one hut and has a brief exchange with someone inside; then we enter, and she is warmly greeted by an elderly man wearing an African dashiki and blue jeans. While they converse in French, I am startled to hear a familiar voice speaking American English. Looking around for the source of this voice, I spy a TV set on a box in front of the chair the elderly man has been sitting on. An American news show is on. The familiar face and voice are that of TV newsman David Brinkley. This Voodoo "witch doctor" has been sitting here watching the news!

My driver/translator explains that the French built a large disk antenna tracking station near Cayenne, and thus they are able to pick up telecasts from satellites. But where's the source of electricity? She indicates a cord running from the back of the TV set out of the hut and shrugs, as though to say. "One doesn't ask that question."

Then she draws my attention to the old man, saying, "He's the best. If you want to know where someone is, you bring him a picture or a piece of that person's clothing, and he will tell you exactly where that person is and what that person is doing."

Right now he's concentrating on the televised face of the American president. The old man doesn't speak English, yet he watches the president's talking face as though he understands precisely what is being said. His concentration is awesome. What else, I wonder, is he able to do with a person's picture? Can he have an effect on a person from a distance? I ask my translator. "Oh yes, and sometimes he can cause criminals to confess."

We watch with him until the program ends; then he switches off the set, stands, and strides out of this hut toward another. We follow. Outside the other hut is a cluster of people waiting to see him. Some have obvious physical ailments and others appear worried. Judging by the variety of clothing styles, they are from widely different social classes. I notice that now, besides the taxi, several other cars have arrived.

"Now we must wait our turn," says my driver. "Come. I take you for a tour of the village."

The most popular spot turns out to be a soft-drink bar in a hut that doubles as a home. Here a crowd of black people lounge about drinking sodas. All around them on the ground are fallen green coconuts. Someone asks if I'd like a soda, and I indicate I'd rather have some coconut water. The crowd finds that highly amusing, but someone hands me a machete, and I demonstrate the skill I picked up in Trinidad by hacking the top off a choice young nut and slurping the milk without a straw—which brings convulsive laughter to the assembled.

Conversing through my driver, I explain that I'm here because of my interest in Voodoo. Immediately more people show up, expressing interest in him who is interested in Voodoo. To show off and, I hope, gain their confidence, I begin naming the African gods. I pick up a stone and say, "Ogun." They giggle and avert their eyes. I heft a coconut and say, "Eshu." They hoot and hiss and wave. I point to the distant sea and say, "Yemanja." They chuckle and sigh.

Someone brings a drum and begins pounding out a rhythm. Some others begin stepping about, dancing. I point to the sun and say, "Obatala." An old woman comes dancing up to me, smiling toothlessly, her eyes gleaming. Her earth-brown face is wrinkled, her body emaciated with age. She dances barefoot in a tattered one-piece dress and waves her arms merrily, executing some extra-fancy footwork for my benefit. She's being a goddess they call Erzulie in Haiti, the saucy sexpot flirting with a stranger. The others laugh and hoot and urge her on. When her solo ends, a teenage girl steps out, catches Erzulie's force, and channels it through her dancing.

While the drumming and dancing continue, I fall into a daydream: I come to this village to live. I stay here a year, two, three; and when I return to the United States, I have a true comprehension of Voodoo from A to Z.

This daydream ends abruptly when my driver touches my arm. Our turn has come to visit the priest, so we leave the dancing and drumming.

We find the old man sitting at a table of the French Colonial period, wildly out of place in this banana-leaf hut with earthen floor. On the table is a lamp with a fancy white shade. Then I see other lamps and a web of wires feeding them electricity. They are set up to illuminate a shrine, a mix of African and Catholic idols.

My guide and the priest exchange a few words, then he gestures for us to sit by the French Colonial table. He produces a small cloth bag, and from this he carefully takes out his cowry shells and whispers his question to them. He will divine to find out where I'm from and why I have come to see him, I think, for that is fairly customary in the Voodoo culture.

After a few throws, his face lights up, and he speaks. "He says he is happy for you because you suffer no sickness or misfortune." A few more throws and: "He says the gods tell him you are from the western part of the United States, and that you are married and have two sons. He says you travel to Brazil to dress the old gods up in the latest Paris fashions and parade them through the halls of science." His eyes twinkle. "The gods are pleased, and you are on good terms with Eshu, the messenger and traveler. But for the success of your work you should make sacrifice to Obatala."

Then the priest dips his fingers into a bowl of water and flicks at me, spraying my face with wet coolness. He chuckles as I wipe my glasses. I've heard it said that some Voodoo priests steal holy water from the Catholic priests because they find the Catholics very good at blessing water.

"Ogun the pioneer is with you," continues my translator. "Do you know that Ogun is the patron saint of the United States?" I nod and keep writing in my notebook. "He says there are many on this continent and in Africa who are sending Eshu to confuse the war-making Ogun of America. Russia is also Ogun, and Eshu is being sent there too."

I ask, "Does that mean he and the others are practicing Voodoo on the politicians of America and Russia?"

The question gets a belly laugh out of him. "He says he merely asks the spirits to do what they will do in any case."

"Does he work with televised pictures?"

"Sometimes. Many faces enter this village by television."

I had a bunch of questions in mind for a priest such as this one, but I can't seem to think of them at the moment. So I ask, "What place do the old gods have in the lives of industrialized people?"

"He says the gods and spirits are everywhere, among industrialized people as well as here, among these people. But Ogun is not the king, and he should take his orders from the king, Obatala. When Ogun will not listen to the higher wisdom, he must be confused by Eshu. When Ogun is completely confused, then he will listen."

• • •

O. Govi: This interview with a doctor of witches has gotten out of hand, he thinks. Instead of exploring the gods as a map of consciousness, he is listening to a Voodoo lecture on politics. He wonders if he's expected to apologize for his government's activities.

He's missing the point. The priest is not assigning fault; he is saying that if one understands the American nation as dominated by Ogun, the god who rules the atomic programming of the mineral kingdom, you gain insight you would otherwise lack. You understand your national soul. Ogun is sometimes depicted as the sports hero who is either being loudly cheered for winning or loudly booed for losing. At this point in time much of humanity is booing the American Ogun. And this old man is talking gods and politics because politics has become the biggest game in the world. He talks American politics now because he is speaking to an American and because American politics are widely televised and occupy a large space in the collective human mind. This large space is Ogun-dominated, and as a prayer maker this priest must appeal to Ogun. So he wishes America would exhibit the best of Ogun the Pioneer, because then he'd have a better Ogun to work with here in his own village. In other words, he does not separate the consciousness of this village from the consciousness of the world, as Gover does.

Or did. He leaves this interview with the mind-boggling impression that there must be hundreds, maybe thousands of Voodoo priests watching American news shows on TV.

He leaves the priest a hefty sum but scraps his daydream of moving to the village. He is anxious to move on to Brazil and find out if Voodoo priests there watch the talking faces of American politicians on their TVs. But he has two more nights in Cayenne, and I'm not yet finished preparing him.

• • •

Gover: When I get back to the hotel late that afternoon, the pool is crowded. There are only three guests staying in the hotel, so these people are from Cayenne. Lots of girls, all ages, all races, and some spectacular Afro-Asian mixtures. They're definitely not unfriendly, and I'm wondering what it would take to bed one this evening, for I'm suddenly feeling a tremendous rush of sex energy.

One Asian lady in her middle twenties stations herself near me. She looks wealthy, worldly, ready, and is using some very bold body language. Another, a teenage Afro-Asian, is playing with her girlfriends in front of me and keeps turning to see if I'm watching. I am. We exchange quick smiles. Then the older one puts a cigarette between her lips and asks if I have a match. I have a great erection under my towel, but no match! I tender my regrets and the goddess of love salutes herself through our eyes. Then the lady suddenly remembers she has a cigarette lighter and digs it out of her handbag.

• • •

O. Govi: I hate to be a killjoy, but my man's present purpose is the intercourse of Afro-American and Euro-American beliefs, and this purpose would not be served by addressing the cute angel buns of the love goddess incarnate in Cayenne.

In Greek, the word *Voodoo* means Logos. Yes, the Greek word *logos* means *word,* as in the Biblical phrase, "in the beginning was the word," an auditory vibration imbued with meaning. To remain open to Logos (Voodoo) he must forgo the pleasures of Eros (Erzulie). Or to dress the same thought up in other words, his quest for the Voodoo perspective requires he have intercourse with the interface of spirit and matter. So I withdraw the spirit force of eroticism from him and focus his attention elsewhere.

• • •

Gover: There's a handyman working around the pool. He's white, French, and gray-haired but in fine physical condition. I ask the young Asian lady who he is. Through a mix of French, English, and Spanish she tells me he's an ex-convict who fell in love with a local girl, and when his prison term ended, he stayed on in Cayenne.

He's one of the most serene individuals I've ever seen. He moves through this crowd of the local well-to-do, his gray hair lifting in the breeze, with a dignity that is neither revolutionary-threatening nor lower-class-subservient. Although no one speaks to him, all are keenly aware of his presence as he flows like a quiet proclamation of freedom from want through this kingdom of earthly desires. He's the "worker king," the servant of benevolent Obatala, and in some uncanny way beyond legality he owns this swimming pool he cleans and maintains.

• • •

O. Govi: Why have I jumped his attention from sex to death, from the chains of lust to an ex-convict's freedom? Because he has unfinished business with the Silent Majority, that's why.

Gover: Sunday evening alone in my room. Well, not alone, for my ghostly convict is present. And I am overcome by a strange sensation of being in close contact with my own personal death.

Like a mugger out of the shadows it sneaks up on me. It comes from the Kingdom of Oya, goddess of death, transformation, and conception. She also rules the demise of "truths" unable to survive the centuries. The truth of one's personal, physical life usually doesn't survive a century, so one's personal death is a minor figure in Oya's kingdom, but not an unexciting one.

In the Voodoo manner I think of my own personal death as a spirit force, a persona with an existence of its own. And I wonder if, with the help of my friendly convict ghost, I can open communications with Oya. I concentrate on her, listening, waiting for her to speak.

But she doesn't say anything. Or, if she does, I don't hear or understand. Just when I think I have a "live one" I can pump for rare information on this most mysterious of subjects—death—she goes mute and just hangs around like a coy expert, waiting to hear what I have to say on the subject.

Well, I've considered a wide variety of beliefs and myths about death, but I don't know what to believe. My father was killed in an auto crash when I was a baby, so I never knew him personally, but he was such a legend to so many that he came alive in my imagination. He was conjured up by all the stories I heard about him and came to exist as spirit or myth or imaginary being. While I was growing up, I used to have make-believe conversations with him. I'd ask his advice about this or that, and when I got into trouble I'd ask for his help. And I could muster up plenty of evidence to support the belief that he came to my aid.

Now I realize that at a very young age, and quite unconsciously, I was practicing one of the basics of Voodoo: communications with the dead. The Voodoo belief is that you must bring your dead ancestors with you when you move or else suffer loss of individuality. I have been doing that, unconsciously, most of my life, although I never mentioned it before.

It's a very un-Western idea. In Christendom, ancestors reside in heaven or hell, with a large number of Catholic souls in purgatory. There they remain for eternity, remote, out of contact with the living. In America even the elderly are made remote by sending them to nursing homes, where they are depersonalized and prepared for a heavenly oblivion.

I much prefer the Voodoo concept of nine souls and a continuum of living and dead. And there's evidence of national souls, sexual souls, family souls, historical souls. But when we get down to astral souls and personal souls, I've tended to block on what evidence there is. Either there isn't any or I've ignored it—till now.

• • •

O. Govi: I remind Gover that his favorite graffito has for some years been: "Death is the greatest thrill of all, that's why they save it till last." This graffito he has laughed at, but the Voodoo continuum of living and dead spirits of nine different categories deserves serious attention.

Since life is a one-way ticket to death, you'd think he and everyone else would want to know more about it. I insist he forthrightly examine the presence of his own personal death. That's why it's here. He would rather evade it like a draft dodger running from conscription—but we're dealing here with the government of the universe, and there's no possibility of evading that draft.

So I shall persist. I shall see to it that this business gives him some thoughts. It's not a matter of indifference to me, for I am making the trip with him. I have definite ideas on the subject and considerable resources at my disposal. All very reliable, too. It's true that what they say is often misinterpreted or misunderstood or ignored, but whose fault is that? "Thou shalt not kill" is incorrect. "Thou *cannot* kill" is the truth of spirit in matter. The energy (spirit/consciousness) of the universe can be neither increased nor decreased but only transformed.

But, he wonders, is it possible for the living ever to really know?

I recommend he ponder another question: Which aspects of the "energy that is all" look through his eyes, hear with his ears, think with his mind? How much of the energy that is all is it possible for him to become?

• • •

Gover: Okay, I accept O. Govi's recommendation. I'm still pondering the question by sundown. I'm prone on the bed, staring out at a tree. The green leafy body of the tree seems friendly, even protective. In Voodoo, trees are special because they connect earthly matter with heavenly spirit.

As I contemplate this tree outside my window, I become filled with the conviction that it and I are of the same aliveness, the same components of spirit and matter. And I try to establish telepathic communications with this tree. I concentrate, and a powerful sensation grows within me. It's as if the tree swallows me up and transports me to a different dimension. I and my physical surroundings dissolve, and I am overcome with the sensation of flying. It feels as if the atoms of my whole being are flying out of their usual orbits.

When I snap out of that, I'm aware of a huge and compelling presence, far more awesome than the presence of the dead convict. I am not in a state of total possession, for I am still here enough to witness what is happening. But practically everything else has fallen away, and this presence and I have become everything. And what it says, as best I can render it, is roughly as follows:

I am the Kingdom of Sound. Call me Aum, if you like. I am the primary vibration of sound made meaningful. You deal with my kingdom of forces in music and language and word/thought. I am that primary state of energy you deal with when writing. To experience the Voodoo reality—the gods as states of consciousness—and translate this experience into Western terms it is the forces of my kingdom you must use. But even as you do this, you must appreciate why the ancient pagan gods-worshippers have passed down no written scriptures. The meanings of words change over the centuries; new words are continually needed to rediscover the old gods as basic truths.

When you invent a fictitious character, it comes alive in your mind and speaks through you, and some characters linger like friends or visit now and then. I am very much like that, yet I am much more than a fictitious character. Think of me as an essence of nature, for out of my being flows what is called reality, both physical and mental. When a person speaks or writes at his best, he is being visited by my forces, even though he may not think of it that way. Your purpose is to experience Voodoo and write about it, and that is why we are in contact now. Each relationship with a primary state of consciousness is unique, because each individual is unique. You are learning to develop your own unique method of achieving such contact as this.

Do not waste time wondering if this experience is real or imaginary. You understand that energy is consciousness and that everything is of this energy, this consciousness. Now what you must grasp is that imaginings are as real as anything else that impresses your awareness. Since I am able to fill your entire awareness, realize that I am a basic component of your reality. What's important for you to know is how this experience comes about. It begins with your naming it and proceeds with your decision to reach for it. It is furthered by intellectually refining what it is you are reaching for and grows into feeling, emotion, the movement in consciousness of imagined sensation. This feeling then acts as anticipation, which triggers the experience and brings it into your awareness as an event.

In the many languages of the world I have many names. You may think of me as the *Amakua* of Polynesian Huna, the *aum* sound in the Biblical amen, the *aum* of the ancient Sanskrit and Hindu mantra, the sound of the Tao, the *ah* sound that begins your alphabet; or you may simply consider me the origin of sound. Like the color white I am one end of a spectrum, yet like the color black I am also its opposite. You may also think of me as the opposite of light, if you prefer to consider sound and light opposites. All these ways of conceptualizing me are symbolic, however, and I am above all an immediate experience that is at once within you and beyond you. You exist in the human dimension, whereas I exist in countless dimensions simultaneously.

Now the task you have set for yourself often seems impossible to complete, and you fear your trip to Bahia may prove worthless because you don't speak Portuguese. Do not fear; you will succeed, but not in any way you now think of as succeeding.

You understand, in theory at least, that success or wealth is really well-being and that well-being can be represented by money but not purchased with money. Well-being is obtained with intelligent judgment and will. The ten-day fast has left you with increased well-being. Now it's important not to trade that well-being, for it's the brain of your subconscious mind and most necessary for the success of your efforts. Without a finely tuned well-being, you won't be able to capture and convey the Voodoo experience.

The Voodoo belief is that the dead are here among the living, and that is quite true. You serve the dead, whether or not you realize it, and they serve you; for both living and dead partake of the same energy/consciousness. But it is up to you as a living person to choose carefully which of the dead to develop relations with and which you must not entertain. Otherwise, you are not in control of your life and may even be in danger of being pushed or pulled by spirit/thoughts that might destroy your will and harass you into helplessness.

You and the spirit of the dead convict sought each other out. He's a much better guide to the Voodoo of Cayenne than any living person, for he's been here longer. There's no reason to fear him. He needs this relationship with you, and you need yours with him. Your two lives are strangely parallel, for he might have lived a life very much like yours, and you were almost sent to prison at a young age yourself, remember. This and other similarities make it possible for a strong contact to exist between the two of you now. In a dimension beyond your usual time-space-motion reality, the two of you are closely linked. You have read and heard about how Voodoo practitioners feed and care for such spirits—now you are being offered the opportunity to experience exactly what this entails. Feed him vegetables, especially potatoes. Keep him alive in your mind and bring him to Bahia. He'll prove very helpful.

When you get to Bahia, interview as many Macumba Voodooists as you please, but understand that this activity is only the exterior of the work you will be doing, which is your own personal exploration of consciousness and which will be helped by contact with Voodoo priests. Bahia will be an important station on your journey, and it's important to know that the most valuable possessions you bring with you are invisible but nonetheless alive.

Also become clear about what you want to bring back from your journey into the Voodoo reality. Why is it that you and millions of others find industrial civilization unsatisfactory? Become clear about this, because the essence of your trip is to reach back in time for beliefs that have endured and will continue to live as basic truths into the postindustrial future. Indeed, pagan gods are such truths, for they are older than any religious scriptures and more basic than any scientific principles. What modern civilization robs people of is self-knowledge. Knowledge of self means knowledge of consciousness, which is the home of both pagan gods and scientific concepts. It is knowledge of self that motivates your search of Voodoo beliefs and culture, and it is knowledge of self you must acquire in order to understand Voodoo. With that understanding will come freedom from certain conceptual restraints imposed by Western culture and language.

• • •

O. Govi: This experience brings Gover face to face with Ifa—or as he is called in Haiti, Damballah—symbolized by the snake with its tail in its mouth, and with the eternal question: which comes first, creation or the creator? Are the old gods human creations or the creators of humans?

And of course it is I who mediate his mediumship. He proposes, true, but it is I who expand his awareness so that the invisible force he proposes to contact comes into existence. Or to dress the same thought up in different words, I am his personal envoy, his go-between, his connection between personal subjective reality and the subjective reality of all and everything.

He is feeling at the moment like an antique collector pawing around at a garage sale of knicknacks from the Heavenly Mansion. He doesn't quite realize what a good bargain he just scored.

I remind him that theory preceeds discovery of evidence, that you can't find something you cannot conceive of or name. The name Aum thus becomes an important theoretical addition to his accumulation of self-knowledge.

• • •

Gover: That evening I meet the American with the electronic heart stimulator who has a tape recording of a Voodoo ceremony held in the jungles of Surinam. We go to his room and try to listen to it, but his recorder, mysteriously enough, isn't working. So we chat. I'm still feeling light-headed from my visit with Aum when this retired engineer says, "My lifelong hobby is sound."

Sound? Yes, he has a passion for sounds of all sorts, he says, and a large collection of recorded sounds. For instance, he has the original version of the Orson Welles "War of the Worlds" radio drama that caused such an uproar back in 1938.

I like this guy, and except for one other person, a forestry consultant, we are the only guests in the hotel. So when he asks about the trip I'm on, I'm so relaxed I make a terrible mistake. I use the word *Voodoo*. I tell him frankly that I'm attempting to make Voodoo understandable in Western terms. After that he's sure I'm crazy.

"God and gods and all that are just bull droppings," he says. Oh, he believed such nonsense when he was a child, but when he became a man he put away childish things. Now, even though he's a nonbeliever, he serves on the board of two churches in Florida—only because he's "civic-minded," he says.

I ask what then does he have faith in? He taps the battery that powers his heart and spreads his lips to reveal a fine set of dentures. "Engineering," he says.

"We don't need to learn anything about Voodoo," he says; "it's they who must learn our technology."

He continues this rap as we dine together, the only two people in a very large dining room. His chatter makes me suspect he's loaded on some interesting pharmaceutical. There's no use my trying to debate the subject with him, for his is the prevailing Western belief, and it's hard as a rock. I marvel anew at the power the word *Voodoo* has—for it set off an avalanche of verbiage.

Well, I also feel irked and frustrated and am tempted to practice a little Voodoo by sending Eshu the Mischievous into the electronics of his heart stimulator. But I'm afraid I might succeed, so instead I focus on his bright white artificial teeth as they bite off chunks of meat.

This reminds me of the toothless old lady I met in the village earlier. I guess they're about the same age, and I wish I could pose the pair of them side by side and take a color photo and insert it right here, to show what absolute opposites they are. His thing-oriented culture has provided him with a battery-powered postponement of death. Her spirit-oriented culture has provided her with a secure place in the land of the dead, from which she may be summoned and consulted by the living.

• • •

O. Govi: I remind him that Voodoo occurs in the interface between spirit and matter and that one must assume responsibility for the well-being of the gods who compose all things, including one's fellow diner. To prevent the bull droppings of Western ignorance from mucking up his meal, I suggest he remember that he eats for more than just himself.

• • •

Gover: Oh, the French convict—potatoes. My fellow diner's diatribe against Voodoo distracted me. Now I hail the waitress, and between her little English and my petite French I obtain a potato salad.

So here I sit, bombarded by this lecture on the glories of Western technology, feeding a ghost potatoes.

• • •

O. Govi: Our visitor from the Silent Majority is pleased. He agrees to go with us to Bahia, provided we drop him off here on our return trip. Good. It's always nice to have a helpful ghost around.

• • •

Gover: I go to bed that night feeling a forlorn uncertainty. I'm tossed and turned by nagging questions. What good is Voodoo in this modern, urbanized, standardized, industrialized age? What reality can the old gods have to nine-to-five office and factory lives? To people dependent on mass production for food, shelter, and clothing? To a society that will soon be largely run by computer? Why do I subject myself to Western prejudice and Voodoo suspicion? Have I gone over the edge into utter madness?

For help in this storm I stare into the leafy body of the tree outside my window and feel myself again gradually absorbed by it. Soon a great calm comes over me, and I'm again in contact with Aum, who proffers the following:

Industrialism has people living in an unnatural rhythm. The clocklike precision of the machinery of mass production is out of sync with nature's rhythms. It has people dancing the same daily jig— summer, fall, winter, and spring. The human being is not designed to function to merely a mechanical beat, and doing so causes tremendous stress. Much of the world's human population now lives according to the industrial rhythm—up at seven, on the job by eight, coffee break at ten, and so forth, through prime-time TV, with "the long weekend" and "blue Monday."

If people did not live for the demands of the industrial machine, they would pace themselves according to the rhythms of the seasons. Even each day has its unique rhythm, which has been upset by the demands of mass production. In fact the whole planet now vibrates with this banging monotony. And what is the source of this mechanized monster that now controls so many lives? The one-right-way standard one-God concept.

People are the brain cells of the planet Earth. If you had such a painfully monotonous pounding in your head, wouldn't you try to get rid of it? Well, despite the present scientific belief that the Earth is an unfeeling *thing*, it is very much alive, aware of and sensitive to its brain cells—humanity. Will Mother Earth find a way to cure her headache?

As for the value of Voodoo to modern, urban people, that will grow as people discover it to be a refuge from the postindustrial chaos. Its origins are remote, but they have been refined by the first victims of American mass production. Its polytheistic system and values are built into the genealogical makeup of all people. It is currently a threat to the established order because it provides the means for each individual's unique discovery of ancient gods and spirits. Industrialism requires standardized minds to design, produce, and consume its products—even diseases became standardized concepts during the rise of industrialism. In the old pagan reality, each person's dis-ease is unique, since each relationship with all manifestations of aliveness is unique.

When people find unnatural standardization intolerable, then the ancient gods will be rediscovered through whatever people and cults have kept them alive. Only then can the current Western meaning of Voodoo really change. Its beliefs will assume a new importance, for it is the beliefs of Voodoo that have maintained mankind's proper place in the ecology of consciousness. The one-god-for-all concept is a historic aberration and cannot last. Pantheism, the Old Religion, will arise from the ashes of monotheism.

By developing this rapport with me, an area of consciousness beyond your usual, you are practicing the Old Religion. Once you become familiar with the process, you can conjure and relate to other gods and spirits, other shapers of energy/consciousness. This is how you expand your mind to contact the gods—of Voodoo, of your pre-Christianized European ancestors, or of your Native American ancestors.

Do not fool yourself, however. Keep a record and be as consistent as a dog trainer in your dealings with the invisibles. They can, and routinely do, produce spectacular results on both personal and collective levels. Science calls its gods theories and has developed a disciplined priesthood to record physical evidence. Become just as scientific in your personal dealings with the unseen entities, and they—we—will serve you.

When visited by such doubts as those you entertained tonight, remember they are not inseparable from your mind. In the one-god concept of consciousness they are considered inseparable, but in the polytheistic reality such demons are dealt with as separate entities. It's not quite possible for individuals to deal successfully with the one-god notion of absolute evil, the Devil. But it is possible, and rather easy, to deal with a whole bunch of little devils, for they are relatively less harmful, less powerful, and far more responsive to your worded intentions.

• • •

O. Govi: Two days later, as he flies over the Amazon River's vast network of outlets to the sea, Gover wonders if he should write about his conversations with Aum or keep them to himself. If he is to make the Voodoo perspective comprehensible to the Western mind, how can he present a voice he heard in his mind as an expert on the subject?

Well, as he will soon learn, there are many such invisibles at large in Bahia. Their advice is considered expert in the best sense of the word. They are solidly in the ancient pantheistic tradition, and no Voodoo priest would be without his own contingent of them. They are regularly summoned up by whole cults, and over the centuries they have proved to be the most reliable of all experts. Besides, it is mainly through such communications that the Old Religion can be acquired, the old gods rediscovered.

Gover will find he is unable to understand the language, dance, ritual, and paraphernalia of Brazilian Voodoo and that his best expert on the whole subject is Aum. He will also find that his best protector from the suspicions of some Voodooists is his French convict friend.

4 Receiving the Spirit

I'm in Maria's home in Sao Salvador da Bahia de Todos os Santos—the City of the Savior on the Bay of All Saints. It's a balmy Friday evening, and a ceremony for the Voodoo Christ is about to begin.

Maria's home is also her *terreio* where she holds her *candombles*. She's a *macumbeira*, although to call her that tonight would be like calling the president of the United States a politician during wartime. The word *macumba* is as loaded with contradictory meanings as the word *Voodoo*, and both mean the same for all intents and purposes. Maria is addressed as *Mai de Santo*, mother of the saint, and the Catholic saints are understood here as Christian depictions of the ancient African gods, the *orishas* (pronounced oh-ree-*shahs*, spelled *orixas* in Brazilian Portuguese).

Maria is a round, radiant woman of medium height with milk-and-coffee-colored skin. She appears to be in her middle thirties, but I'm told she is certainly older. She could easily support herself as a *macumbeira*. I've seen her waiting room full of clients, and she's packing them in now for her *candomble*. But this morning I encountered her in the Afro-style market near here, behind her charcoal brazier, selling tasty treats.

This evening she is very much the Voodoo priestess, assisted by a host of helpers as she prepares to guide this ceremony.

I've been to more than a dozen *candombles* since arriving in Bahia a few weeks ago, but this one is especially interesting because it's for Oshala, the Voodoo Christ, the spirit that visited Jesus of Nazareth for three whole years.

Oshala is spelled *Oxala* in Brazil, and like *orixas* is from the Yoruba language, from what is now Nigeria. Some Brazilians believe— as does Efuntola in South Carolina—that *Oxala* is a corruption of the Yoruba word *Orixanla,* the Great God. There's a lot of disagreement about such details within the Voodoo culture, and your mind could get badly twisted trying to make sense of it all. But like the guests arriving here this evening, I am concerned only with the basic beliefs of Voodoo, so I'll stick with phonetic spellings and the fact that Oshala is equated with Christ and is expected to bring great blessings when he arrives tonight.

• • •

O. Govi: My collaborator is trying not to indicate the trepidations he is experiencing. Although he is not a church-going Christian, he has been molded by a culture that considers Jesus of Nazareth the one son of their one and only god. His culture also takes a dim view of what is here called receiving the spirit. A good Christian can worship Christ, be born again, and have Jesus come into his life, and so on, but to have his entire being utterly taken over by the Christ spirit, even temporarily, is unthinkable. And to have this happen at a Voodoo ceremony in Brazil is worse than unthinkable, it's heretical.

Moreover, many of the faithful in Brazil do not believe it's possible for anyone to receive Oshala's spirit. "Oshala does not descend," they say. But others dispute this, and assure Gover that Oshala does descend but only at the purest and most carefully prepared and conducted *candombles.*

So he is wondering what will happen here tonight. Will this *candomble* turn out to be an occult fraud? Or will someone here receive Oshala, the Christ?

He has seen some Brazilians who are seemingly able to acquire temporary possession of their spirits practically anywhere, at any time, under any circumstances. Sometimes such performances are awesomely authentic; sometimes they're embarrassingly bad acting jobs.

Assuming there are some authentic mediums of Oshala here tonight, he wonders how it will be possible to recognize the Christ spirit as a Brazilian Voodoo god. The French Caribbean Legba, known here as Leba, or Eshu, is regarded by many Brazilians as a more devilish spirit than he is in Haiti. Complicating it all is that there are so many different Eshus, or different "lines" of spirits from Eshu's realm. Some of these Eshu spirits are difficult to equate with the French West Indian Legba. So how will he recognize the black Brazilian Christ? What evidence will there be? And if such an event occurs, how can he explain it to his Christianized and rationalized countrymen?

These are worthy questions for our scribe. After all, many Christians believe in Christ, worship Christ, pray to Christ, and weep for the Christ crucified, but who among them would have the audacity to become Christ? Such a psychic triumph could easily be rewarded with electric shock and other medical attentions. This being the case in Christendom, how dare these "heathens" court possession of the Christians' only son of God?

But African and Native American people have been courting and gaining possession of this god for centuries. These "heathens" can locate and call forth this god from their own consciousness and from the aliveness of plants, animals, minerals, planets, solar systems, and so on, to the endlessness of pure energy. Besides being inspired by stories about this god, they are able to invoke it, make it manifest as a presence through the beings of one or more of them, and thus confront it personally.

Modern travel technology has brought Gover so quickly and easily to the physical reality of these "heathens" he's wondering if it's possible to go this final leg of his journey just as easily. And the answer to that is no, not so easily.

• • •

Gover: I have, by now, met well over a hundred Voodoo priests of various cults but none more warmly hospitable and helpful than Maria. She immediately intuited why I had come (as did many others) and she suggested that I just hang around and watch her work. I watched her heal mental illnesses, treat physical maladies, make charms, remove hexes, and transform expressions of worry into smiles. And it seemed at times that I could almost "see" the spirits she used as clearly as I "see" my friendly French convict.

Regarding spirits, Brazilians are 180 degrees distant from most Americans and Europeans. I'm told the all-time best-seller here is *The*

Book of Mediums, originally written in French by one Hippolyte Leon Denizard Ravail under the pen name Allan Kardec.[27] It's not very well known in Europe or America, but here it is treated as something of a Bible. When I read the English translation, I realized why, for it describes the invisible world of Voodoo in European terms. In this part of the world, Kardec's spiritism is white collar Voodoo, so to speak, practiced and supported by westernized, educated Brazilians, many of whom are too genteel for the more roughhouse version, *Macumba.*

In Brazil that word seems to mean any ceremony that courts spirits. Rita, my translator, says it's probably from the Bantu language, but whether you call it Macumba or Voodoo it's all the same. No one seems to know the origins of the word *candomble,* which Rita translates as "a dance party." Rita's a great help, even when her English renderings startle.

The other day I told her about the book *Chariots of the Gods*[28] and how in it the gods are defined as prehistoric astronauts from outer space. That news gave her a belly laugh, and since then when we attend *candombles,* she jokes, "Here comes another astronaut," as someone is about to receive a spirit. This evening she and Maria exchanged smirks about Oshala as an astronaut from outer space, and I think Maria got the idea that this is how I think of gods, which bothers me. But it seems to have tightened Maria's determination to deliver the living experience of the old gods to me in a very personal way.

But I'm still wondering, as we wait for the lead drummer to arrive, how to recognize the Christian Jesus as a Voodoo god if it arrives tonight.

• • •

O. Govi: Has he forgotten that the Jesus of the Oral Roberts singers is not the same as that of the Catholic priests, which is not the same as the Baptist, Methodist, Presbyterian, Anglican, and other Christian versions of the Christ? I remind him that this is just another example of how different gods can wear the same name, or that different names can signify the same god. Christian cults consult the same scripture, but each has its own interpretation of this same "objective evidence."

---

[27]Allan Kardec, *The Book of Mediums* (York Beach, ME: Samuel Weiser, 1970).
[28]Erich Von Daniken, *Chariots of the Gods* (New York: Putnam, 1974).

I bring him a telepathic communique from Maria: all these different interpretations fall into seven primary categories, corresponding to the seven visible planets of our solar system. There is the Martian "warrior" Christ, the Venusian "loving" Christ, the Mercurial "messenger" Christ, the Jupiterian "king" Christ, the Saturnian "teacher" Christ, the lunar "inspirational" Christ, the solar "enlightened" Christ, plus the earthly dead hero Jesus, as pure spirit who suffers in material form.

Maria's Christ concept, Oshala, is far more encompassing than any one or all of the Christian cults. Instead of being a particular individual who came and is rumored to be coming again, Oshala never left and lives in every person and every thing. Oshala is also the son of Olodumare and the father of all other gods and goddesses, people, plants, animals, and minerals.

As Maria told Gover through Rita earlier this evening, "No one can ever see God, Olodumare, but Oshala is God's first reflection." So he put it down in his notebook that Oshala is the light of God, as the sun is the light of our solar system.

• • •

Gover: Maria's house is a labyrinth of indoor and outdoor rooms. Concrete steps bring you up to her front door but when you step inside you're on dirt floors until you reach the far end, the concrete floor of the *candomble* room. Between one end and the other, there are three shrines, with statues, pictures, African-type wood carvings, and other items containing the forces of the gods. And there are two consultation rooms. Her house also doubles as this impoverished neighborhood's psychiatric clinic. Or more likely, she accepts mental patients from all over the city. When I first met her, she had four or five in various states of derangement, and a week later they were all gone and she had four or five others. One of the things she invited me to watch was how she and her *iaos* (female initiates) heal mental illness. The crazed spirit possessing the sick person is transferred to one of Maria's assistants and then spoken to through Maria by a healer spirit; and eventually the crazed spirit is taken away to be cured. The human patient is dazed but quickly recovers his rightful senses.

A year ago I would have blocked on the possibility of such a happening as this. Now it seems as natural as rain. And here in Bahia just about everyone believes in spirits, good and evil. Even the waiter at the Grand Barra Hotel understands that I have the spirit of a French convict along and that he likes potato salad.

It's a good thing I have him too, because not every *macumbeiro* is friendly and harmless. I met one from Nigeria who specializes in offing people. You pay him half the money down and the other half when your enemy has been eliminated. And if something doesn't happen to the victim within a month or six weeks, you get your down payment back. This *macumbeiro* drives a Mercedes and dines in the finest restaurants, but I doubt that he has many friends, for taking care of his psychotic killer spirits is a full-time job.

Our visit with him was brief and angry. He said nothing, letting his wife do all the talking while he stared out the window as if he were hiding from the police. I had eye contact with him for about one moment, and it was like a glimpse of hell. I immediately conjured up my French convict and put him on the job. As soon as I did that, this *macumbeiro's* wife and Rita got into a loud argument. Seems the man wanted five thousand dollars just to talk about what he does.

We left, and I could "see" my convict beating off the attacks of his maniacs. Rita was in a terrible state of upset and anger until we met our next interviewee, a *mai de santo,* who immediately ran her hands up and down both our bodies, blessing us with holy water from a rusty tin can and ridding us of the evil ones who, for lack of anyone else to bedevil, were trying to have at us. She said she could see I had a protector but that we shouldn't visit any more *macumbeiros* who specialize in evil. We didn't. Rita makes it a point to check out the health and well-being of people in a village or neighborhood to determine the benevolent powers of the local priest. If what she sees does not gladden her heart, we move on.

Maria's village, for all its poverty, is full of happy, lively people, who seem anxious to do anything they can for Maria and for this stranger who has come to learn what he can from her. The only prohibition, it seems, is photography. I tried to document Maria's mental healing on film, but that attempt went quickly awry when I had to reload and the film leaped out of my hands and unraveled on the *terreio* floor. It was the third roll of film that had been ruined by uncanny means. Rita advised that I give up trying, because the secrets of Voodoo do not wish to reveal themselves to strangers.

What I was trying to capture on film were the physical effects, not the spiritual causes, but I gave up anyway. Besides, cameras are not allowed at *candombles,* and even tape recorders are prone to malfunction.

O. Govi: It's just as well. There's no shortage in America of pictures about Voodoo. What's lacking is insight into the Voodoo reality of gods and spirits. And they, being invisible, cannot be documented.

• • •

Gover: Half of the *candomble* room is now full of people, but where's the lead drummer? From what I've learned about Brazilians, he's probably making love and will prolong the pleasure as long as possible. Well, that's worth delaying a *candomble* for, because it's important that the lead drummer is relaxed and feeling fine.

The name of this impoverished neighborhood is Alto da Ubarana. It is built on terraces that step down steep slopes into a ravine and half way up the other side. The paved road ends at the edge of this neighborhood, and its earthen streets are lined with ruts so deep you're in over your head if you miss a step.

From what I can gather, the city surrounds this neighborhood, and yet here you are out in the country, where people raise pigs and chickens, grow most of their food, pick wild fruits, and catch fish. Not much money moves in or out of this village within the city. And I get the impression that these people would not want their streets to be paved. They believe the Lord of the Earth, dirt, is Obaluaye (Babalu, Saturn), and Babalu would much rather feel the tickle of human feet than the hot chemicals of road surfacing.

There are many such villages in and around Salvador, and there is much traffic across the Atlantic between Bahia and Nigeria. As the desire grows in Africans to rediscover the beliefs of their precolonial ancestors, more and more West Africans find their way to Bahia, where the African tradition has been preserved more purely than in West Africa. Or so it is claimed by some.

Although the old gods and ancestral spirits are triumphant here, there is little agreement about which *candomble* maintains the tradition in its purest form. Certainly not Maria's. But that's not her intention. Her intention is to work effectively, and from what I've seen, she succeeds. The details of purely Yoruba theology she leaves to others.

One of the others—an anthropology student I met at a party—remarked that in the Old World the Dahomean and Yoruba peoples had been bitter enemies, so the word *Voodoo* should never be used in connection with the *orishas*. Someone else told me Macumba is black magic and I should leave it alone, attend Umbanda ceremonies only, and become an initiate in order to protect myself. And someone else told me that because I'm white and educated, I should travel south and consult only with spiritists steeped in the teachings of Allan Kardec, who are also predominantly white and educated.

But I have been heeding the advice of Aum and of my French convict spirit. They assure me it's not part of my task to become involved in theological squabbles, which are the works of Eshu, the one who makes life seem so full of contradictions. My job is to sort through it all and get to the basic elements, for everything is the work of the one Great God acting through His agents, the gods.

Anyway, I feel comfortable here at Maria's *candomble,* in this country village surrounded by the city of Salvador. And I'm at ease with this particular type of black paganism. These people live at the interface of urban and rural life-styles. They know both the western ized world of mass production and standardized ideals and the world of sacrificial goats and spiritual forces. I like to think they have rejected the standardized in favor of maintaining their own uniqueness, but I'm not sure of that. In any case, despite their deep poverty, they appear clean and well fed and ready to welcome Oshala.

Now the lead drummer arrives, working his way through the crowd with a sheepish grin, one tooth missing from his front uppers. Rita draws my attention to the room just off the *candomble,* where various sacred objects have been put in readiness. She wants to acquaint me with each thing—garment, necklace, weapon, tool—and its meaning, and the meanings of each color and consecrated day, each amulet and talisman, plant and animal. I stand patiently by while she points, names, and explains, but not much registers. I have long since given up trying to sort through each cult's exotica and remember its details.

• • •

O. Govi: I applaud my man's determination to keep his focus on the basic beliefs common to all Voodoo cults instead of the exotica peculiar to each. When we first arrived in Bahia, he filled a notebook with Brazilian, African, and Indian names for the old gods and descriptions of each. But the result of all that was a sea of confusion. To make matters worse, a prominent Brazilian anthropologist, whose first name is Vivaldo and whose last name he didn't catch, shook a forefinger at him and scolded that he would "learn practically nothing" until he had mastered Portuguese, Yoruba, and Bantu.

Fortunately, his many interviews with *macumbeiros* convinced him otherwise: that the learning he seeks is an inward process, and that process is stimulated by contact with people like Maria. As the first *macumbeiro* he visited told him, the information he seeks will come from dreams, visions, flashes of insight. And it will come in American English so he can understand it.

His purpose here is not to accumulate information *about* the gods but to become informed *by* the gods. And the gods are not found in the babble of strange words but on the most subtle levels of being. It's all very well for him to tape-record and scribble notes from Rita's translations of Portuguese to English. What's needed most, however, is a translation from Voodoo culture to Western culture, and from ancient to modern.

For this task we have helpers at the ready on the intuitive level of mind. Each is demanding an audience, and all have something worthwhile to say. I do my best to keep them waiting, but they haven't got all week. Being mercurial types, they're restless by nature. I strongly urge my collaborator to pay attention, so these visitors can make their messages manifest and be on their ways.

• • •

Gover: Speaking of visitors, I'm not the only outsider here tonight. Besides my translator, Rita, and my lively taxi driver, Viarney, there are six Israeli students and a Brazilian poet.

The poet lived in San Francisco for a few years and speaks fluent English. We've had some very spirited conversations about the Old Religion during the past week. But I think the fact that I'm an American is a slight embarrassment to him. They say that Brazil is mixed racially, whereas America is a racist society. Yet the upper stratum of Brazilian society is white and westernized, whereas the poorest among them fall into the classification of black, and their culture is Afro-Brazilian.

Well, Rita and Viarney don't treat me like an American tourist, and they tell me to ignore anyone who does. And America's reputation here is no obstacle in dealing with *macumbeiros*. They welcome my interest in Voodoo, and my desire to make it understandable to Americans delights them. When my tape recorder broke down,

Viarney took me to a friend who is a disc jockey, who lent me the radio station's recorder. We tested it out by recording from Viarney's Volkswagen radio a Christian-sounding hymn to Oshala, played here every day at high noon.

I've been averaging three interviews a day and about four hours of sleep a night because of going to so many *candombles*. My day usually begins with breakfast at seven in the Grande Hotel da Barra's outdoor restaurant. I read over yesterday's notes, then meet Viarney at nine. We drive a couple of blocks and pick up Rita in front of her apartment building, then head out for our next *macumbeiro*. Sometimes we hit the freeway connecting Salvador with Brasília to visit villages in rural Bahia. And sometimes we are up past midnight attending *candombles*.

I think of Rita and Viarney as gifts from the gods. Rita I met an hour after landing at Bahia Airport. I went to Bahiatursa, the state tourism agency, in search of a translator, feeling that with Eshu's blessings I would find an American student interested in Brazilian Voodoo. But the official I was supposed to meet there never showed, and Rita was waiting to see him too. She introduced herself as a freelance journalist from Rio, in Bahia to conjure a TV documentary about Macumba. Since our missions dovetailed, she voluntarily assumed the job of translator.

Rita's English is heavily accented. When she first told me her name, I wrote it out phoentically as *Hayeeeeeta*. Ethnically, she tells me she's half Egyptian and half Italian. She's a lively woman and quite attractive. Frankly, I'm not sure I believe she's a freelance journalist working on a TV documentary about Macumba, but what the hell, she's pleasant company and does her best to help me sort through the profusion of Bahian cults and make sense of Macumba.

Our biggest problem was transportation. Rita doesn't have a car, so we were catching taxis—or missing taxis and having to walk long distances. That problem was solved the third day when we hailed Viarney's taxi on our way to the next interview. Viarney was delighted by the idea of visiting *macumbeiros* and *candombles*, so he took the taxi sign off his VW and we struck a deal.

Neither of them belongs to any particular cult. Both are intrigued by my effort to comprehend Voodoo/Macumba and write about it. They have endless tales about the old gods, about *macumbeiros* with miraculous powers, and about people who receive spirits.

I estimate there's an average here of one *macumbeiro* per city block, more or less. Almost everyone is happy to deal with any questions I ask through Rita, who is sometimes so overwhelmed by the answers that she forgets to translate. We don't call ahead for appointments, since few people have telephones. We simply show up, and if there are other visitors ahead of us, we wait our turn to be ushered into the consultation room. Each *macumbeiro* usually divines with cowry shells, Tarot cards, beads, or whatever to find out who we each are and why we've come.

Their divining methods vary, but most are contacting the Yoruba Ifa, god of all that is, was, and will be. And although they often speak mythologically, I'm amazed at how many are so accurate. Some call Ifa Damballah, and one discussed my relations with my wife and the pattern our arguments often take and why. Since it is Shango who "sits on her head" and Damballah who sits on mine, I'm inclined to feel *burned* by her at times and she to feel *bitten* by my sarcasm. My purpose for being here is expressed in various ways: "He says you come to take the African *orishas* out of blackface," or "she says you come to put the *orishas* in a scientific book," or "he says your *odu* [personal destiny] is to rediscover the old gods of your own ancestors.

During this preliminary exchange, with Rita translating, Viarney and I get the tape recorder plugged in and working. If there's no plug-in, it runs on batteries. Rita then reads my opening statement, which says that I'm interested in Voodoo as a very ancient and time-tested map of consciousness and/or the anatomy of pure energy. But that fetches such a variety of responses, from laughter to frowns, that I've stopped using it and just let Rita improvise. Viarney leans forward and listens closely, and I lean back, put myself into a light trance, and examine the effect of our subject's presence on my thoughts and feelings.

• • •

O. Govi: Later, back at the hotel, when he sits down with Rita and she translates each *macumbeiro's* recorded response, Gover finds his inner-viewing has often provided him with essentials of the information imparted. Yesterday, while listening to Rita and Maria talk, he wrote in his notebook: "Modern science is the old gods rediscovering themselves in new symbols. Voodoo and science are both forms of magic. Both are based on theories that find evidence of themselves." Later Rita translated Maria: "She says science no different than Macumba. Science has its *orishas* and Macumba has its *orishas,* and all, all are *orishas.* Science *orishas* talk through books; Macumba *orishas* talk through people. But...same *orishas* always talking, everywhere."

Thus, Gover finds he can often learn his Voodoo lesson before the lecture has been translated.

• • •

Gover: Which, after interviewing Maria, was a good thing, because on the drive back we tried to play the tape, which we had so carefully set up and tested, and found that after Rita's opening statement we got only one word from Maria: *"Bon."* After that, there was a hissing, snaky sound that made Viarney stop the car and get out. Rita got out of the back seat, and the two of them walked in opposite directions awhile, then returned and said they weren't sure we should continue this business. They got back in the car, and while I tried to figure out what had gone wrong with the recorder this time, Viarney ate some coconut meat and flipped the shell out his right front window. It immediately jumped off the ground, flew back into the car, and landed on my foot—which set off another round of hooting.

That wasn't the first time the recorder had failed or that strange things had happened. The first night I was here Rita and I were strolling down a street when an old lady came waving and shouting to us, telling us her *macumbeiro* was waiting to see me, expecting me, knew why I had come, and said I should leave my tape recorder behind because it wouldn't work in his presence. He said he would set up his own machine and give me a tape. So we got his address from the lady and went to see him the next moring. And sure enough my recorder didn't work, and his big reel-to-reel job was ready. He hyperventilated to receive Damballah or Ifa and cut short the questioning by delivering more answers than we had questions for.

A few days later when we went to the oldest mission in Salvador to meet a priest, Frei Eliseu, who is reputed to be notorious in the Vatican for lauding Macumba in written broadsides and moonlighting as a *macumbeiro,* there was a more dramatic confrontation between old gods and new electronics. Frei Eliseu, a robust cleric in his seventies, first advised it would be best to use his own personal tape recorder, then had to perform an exorcism to free its devils and make it work. First he stood over the thing, reading from the instruction book, while Viarney and I, Rita, and a half dozen others fingered it according to this litany. When we could find no mechanical or electrical oversight, the priest did a spirit exorcism on the thing, and then it worked. Rita said there was a temporary malfunction because the recorder was a Catholic, but Frei Eliseu assured us it was not that, and even if the thing were a Moslem it would still have trouble with the local spirit population. We then taped the interview, stopping now and then to replay and make sure the thing was still working, and it was— only to find, when we played the tape on my recorder, that what we had sounded like a speeded-up squabble of Mickey Mice.

As for the troubles with camera and film, the doorman at the hotel explained it this way: Because Macumba services were harassed by the police in the old days, many of the ancestors had become over-protective. And the less enlightened among them, not realizing my intentions were benevolent, were not going to allow me to bring any photos home.

One warm, muggy afternoon we parked the VW at the end of the paved road and walked into a mud-floored village, completed our discussion with a lovely old white-haired *macumbeiro,* and were returning to the car when we discovered we were lost. But how could that be? It wasn't a large or complex village, and we had found our way in easily enough. Why couldn't we find our way out? As we rounded a bend and came upon a kind of suburb of the village, we heard the first drumming and chanting of what turned out to be an impromptu afternoon *candomble.* We laughed, switched on the recorder, and spent a couple of hours watching people receive Shango. After that, we found our way back to the car with no further disorientation.

By the night of this *candomble,* which I will describe presently, strange coincidences and mysterious happenings have become commonplace. And in Bahia spirits are blamed or thanked in all such cases, and that's that—there is no other explanation. Hardly a day has passed without something "impossible" happening, but since none of these events has caused injury of any kind, we have learned to take them in stride. I've even stopped grousing over the loss of photos and the misbehavior of tapes. If the local spirits don't want me to come away with such audiovisual records, so be it.

• • •

O. *Govi:* This loss of records that rankles him is a blessing in disguise. The ancient ones have sent Eshu to free him from such distractions. Instead of fumbling with mechanical buttons, he is now free to play with the buttons of mind and spirit.

Besides, the audiovisuals he sought would convince no one who is not already open to the possibility that the Voodoo belief in gods and spirits is logical, valid, and verifiable. It's high time he stops banging his head on the Western wall of prejudice and come on over to the Voodoo reality, where the audiovisuals will be more than enough.

• • •

Gover: It's 8:30, and this *candomble* is still delayed. The drummers and ogan (iron clangor) player are warming up, but the dancers and chanters are having a powwow or something in the kitchen. People are still arriving. The room's full, though, so they are gathering outside and peering in through the door and windows.

I wonder if this delay is because of the six Israelis and myself. Maybe these people don't like tourists watching their religious rites.

I strike up a conversation with an Israeli girl in her early twenties. "Are they ever going to *do* anything?" she asks. She's bored and weary and anxious to return to her hotel and sleep. "I've seen all this in movies. It's a lot of superstitious nonsense." She's bought a tourist booklet printed in English and reads aloud to pass the time:

"The name Candomble is applied to the place where the Brazilian Negroes perform their characteristic religious feasts. Elements from various African religions and remnants of the Brazilian Indians' cults are sometimes combined in the Candomble cult. The Candomble's temple walls are always made of clay, and its floor of brick or cement; the initiated must dance barefoot...."

The poet interrupts to let me know, in no uncertain terms, that he has grown suddenly restive too. I thought I had become accustomed to his sudden whims, but this one really surprises me. After coming here with Rita, Viarney, and me, and after waiting around for the ceremony to begin, he has decided the whole thing is "most impure."

"A celebration for Oshala after dark on Friday," he scoffs. "Such a fiesta is for the dead. I want no parts of it. I'm leaving."

The Israeli girl wants to catch a ride with him, but he tells her he's not going in her direction.

As if the poet's departure is the signal for the ceremony to begin, Maria appears carrying an incense urn and gets to work on the first order of business: prohibiting any interference from Eshu.

"It's all so counterproductive," says the Israeli girl, as we watch Maria fill the room with smoke.

"Counterproductive of what?" I ask.

"Look at them, how poor they are. Have you ever seen worse poverty? What good is all this superstition? Did you see the ruts in the road outside?"

I almost fell into one arriving this evening—had to sit down in the mud to stop the slide that would have landed me in a rut I'd have had to walk the length of to get out.

"Their roads need to be paved," says the Israeli, "and they need electricity, running water, flush toilets. They're probably all protein starved too. But instead of doing something to improve their wretched condition, they hold this silly *candomble*. It's awful. I hate it here."

She pleads with the others of her group to go, but now that the ceremony has begun, they want to watch some of it. She stands there tapping her foot impatiently, frowning, as onto the *candomble* floor come ten women ranging in age from teens to seventies, all dressed in the traditional white satin and lace skirts. While Maria continues to shoo away Eshu, the drums and clanging resound, and the ladies begin their dance of invocation.

It's a very serious undertaking but not approached in the somber, solemn mood common to religious services among Moslems, Jews, and Christians. Spectators are free to chat and joke, smoke and drink *batida*, come and go as the spirit moves them. Children squeeze in and out of the crowded doorway and scamper about as though at a picnic. And all this sideline commotion is guaranteed to buttress the Western notion that such Voodoo ceremonies are heathen and heretical. The way the Israelis are gawking at it all, I'm sure it's the first such spectacle they've ever seen—and they will come away more convinced than ever that it's just a lot of primitive superstition.

Maybe that's why the poet suddenly fled. From what he's told me, the *candomble* he belongs to would never tolerate the gawking of nonbelievers.

The group of dancers seem one round and whirling blur of white as they circle the yellow star and green cross painted in the middle of this concrete floor. Maria is chanting and walking about with a jug of *batida,* a liquor made from sugarcane and fruit juice, and a plate of meal. She's still stalking Eshu, I think, to make sure he won't disrupt in any way. Maybe the spirit she's addressing is trapped in the girl who is feeling trapped in this room, with darkness and deep ruts outside and all this "superstition" inside.

Maria puts the jug and plate down on the cross and star, raises her arms and sings her chants heavenward. The dancers circle her, shuffling a kind of slow two-step, wooing Oshala. Maria leaves the circle and walks about the room, still chanting. She stops in front of me to say, through Rita, that she is sending Eshu the Confuser away and that this is very important, especially at feasts for Oshala the Elder.

Then she apparently senses Eshu's presence has entered to enjoy the food and drink she's laid out for him, and she runs to the center of the room, picks up the jug and plate, and carries them out the door. With a loud "Ayeeee!" she throws the liquor and meal to the night, wipes the plate clean, and returns. Now Eshu is surely outside, so the ceremony can proceed without worry that old Oshala will suffer any hanky-panky from the celestial rascal.

Great clouds of yellow smoke engulf the room as Maria walks about with another urn of incense. She "feeds" this smoke to everyone and everything in the room—people, plants, walls, drums, designs, and invisibles. After blessing all, she sits in a queenly chair, and one by one the dancers approach her, and each, according to which *orisha* rules her, salutes her.

I glance at the Israeli girl, who says, "It's just a lot of hypnotism."

Indeed, the drums, the rhythmic clanging of the ogan, the dance, and the incense—it is hypnotic. It seems to reverberate in my flesh and bones, echo about inside my skull. The drums are as rhythmic and complex as the atoms of the body's cells, and the dancers whirl like planets around an invisible sun. When next I glance at the girl, her lower jaw is hanging and she looks slightly entranced. Her fellow students are also slightly agape, although they keep snapping each other out of it with quips, jokes, chuckles.

But here comes the head drummer again, pushing his way in through the door and walking across the floor. I guess he left briefly to relieve his bladder. A boy has taken his place, and now the boy slides off the stool as the head drummer slides on, and picks up the beat without missing a single thump in this very complex polyrhythmic invocation. With the head drummer back, the sound takes on a more compelling quality, adding a new dimension to the dancing and chanting. Maria smiles at him as she leaves her chair to join the dancing for awhile. She leads them into a slightly new pattern, more a snaking around the center than a circling. The youngest dancer looks like she's ready to receive, for she's glassy-eyed and a mite wobbly. An occasional child scoots across the floor, ducking between the dancers' legs. Now and then a little one steps out and imitates the dancers' movements.

I begin to feel that electrical tingle I get when a Voodoo ceremony is creating itself. From the hitherto chaotic patterns of people's comings and goings, a cohesive whole begins to form. This phase of it reminds me of hunting, for a Voodoo ceremony is a kind of hunt through subtle regions. The gods and spirits are both remote and immediate. And each is sought along an invisible path that has been tried and tested down through centuries. It is this dazing polyrhythmic sound that cuts the path, and it seems to me that everyone present is involved in this hunt, although the Israelis are unaware of their involvement. And I find myself wondering if Oshala will arrive before these tourists depart.

The Voodoo hunt for contact with a deity is not unlike the scientific hunt for knowledge. Theory precedes discovery of evidence; you can't find what you're not looking for. Watching the pattern made by the flowing white dresses of the dancers reminds me of peering into a microscope at the activity of a cell. In both cases the parts adhere to some central principle.

And while I'm seeing it that way, another correlation comes to mind: Not only do these dancing women duplicate the planets circling the sun and the body's cells clinging to their central principle, but they also behave like a corporate board of directors at a conference table, whose words dance out and orbit a central subject, circle and crisscross, conjunct, and occasionally bump each other in passing.

• • •

O. Govi: The Voodoo ceremony, I wish to interject here, is also an abstract construction made from a carefully planned design. What this construction will house is the presence of a god. Everyone who stays to welcome Oshala will, like laborers building a house in the physical world, each contribute according to his skills, and all will have reason to stand back and admire their handiwork.

The few who sacrifice their beings for the deity to manifest will be supported by everyone present, and all will be affected by the presence of the god. The complex rhythm, endlessly repeated by drums and ogan, chants and dancing, costumes, lighting, ikons—it's a total assault on the senses that works like acupuncture on the subtle levels of body/mind. One does not participate in this event by listening and watching, but rather by absorbing sound and sight with the bone and fiber of body and the genealogical memory of unconscious mind. These carefully designed pulsations reach to remote depths of the mind like long, invisible arms. And those sound-fingers send a message to every cell and get each molecule spinning to the beat. Then, from the very atomic programming of the being, one of the programmers leaps forth into the human dimension and communicates through words and actions.

Gover has told his Brazilian friends he would like to experience receiving a spirit but doesn't think it's possible for him to do so at a *candomble,* mainly because the language and ritual are foreign to him. The truth is much simpler. He has seen the look of fright that springs from the human face when a god "mounts his horse," and he has rightly speculated that the experience must be terrifying. He's afraid.

But he's also feeling quite at home here at Maria's *candomble* and rightly speculates he'd be safe in her hands if, per chance, a deity should choose to knock him over and inhabit his being. And when Rita asks, "Would you like to receive the spirit tonight?" he replies, "Yeah, I would, but I don't think that will happen."

"Why not?" she says coyly.

"I don't speak the language."

"You don't have to, the spirit speaks through you."

"Well, why don't you receive the spirit here tonight?"

"Maybe I will, who knows?"

• • •

Gover: I flash on science and religion as both rhythmically performed rituals devoted to a common cause. In the lab, the common cause is called truth. At this *candomble,* it's called a god. But these are two different words for the same thing, it seems to me, because both gods and truths are basic beliefs that have endured. We seek to verify these basic beliefs through scientific and religious ritual. Both gods and truths are creations of human mind, I suppose, yet able to be demonstrated. This ceremony is attempting to demonstrate a god, a truth, a basic belief that has persisted over many centuries. Now, to bring the god through requires a lot of persistence.

• • •

O. Govi: And cautious discrimination, for there are some confusing untruths lurking about, and they're much easier to summon than the eternal truths. Even modern science gets possessed by some half-truths that barely survive a century. Some don't even make it through a decade. Many scientific cults unwittingly court possession of untruths, and even Voodoo ceremonies have been known to fall prey to such entities.

Great discrimination is needed to work with both the deeply messaging drumbeats of Voodoo and the clickety-clack of laboratory electronics. The truths who wish to discover themselves in the human dimension at this *candomble* are merely different aspects of the gods who seek discovery through scientific endeavors. But the ancient truth, the god, is often surrounded by a lot of tricky detractors. To guide the drumming to its target, one must be able to recognize the difference in a visceral way. That is Maria's specialty.

• • •

Gover: A week or so ago, at another *candomble* (for Oshun, Mother of Waters), I got into a discussion with an educated Brazilian about whether the theory of relativity is from Oshala or Olodumare. I thought it must be from Oshala. Wasn't the word *Oshala* a contraction of Orisha-nla? "Oh no," he said, "Oshala was originally Obatala in Africa, or Obatala's female counterpart, Odudua. Relativity must be from Olodumare." But after thinking that over a minute, he said, "No, relativity must be from Ifa (Orunmila), the knowledge of past, present, and future."

We both agreed the quantum theory is from Eshu, but we never came untangled concerning relativity. Recalling my interview in South Carolina with Efuntola and how he ascribed relativity to Orunmila (Ifa), I decide to stick with that deity as the father of relativity.

The problem is, the names for the gods went through changes down through the centuries in Yorubaland, and then in crossing the Atlantic to the New World. And in *candomble* they were strongly flavored with the names of the same gods from other African traditions. Now it's difficult to figure out which one corresponds to the Christian God, the original creator. Olorun and Olodumare are two names associated with the original creation, yet Ifa (Orunmila), and in the French West Indies Damballah, are also thus associated.

In Bahia, when you first walk into a *terreio* to meet a new *macumbeiro,* you don't know which name he applies to the Great Creator, God. And I've had some tell me the Great Creator is too remote to be named and is therefore nameless.

I have yet to learn how Maria correlates her gods with the Christian pantheon, and from what she has said, I suspect she makes no such correlation except for Oshala and Christ. But she describes Oshala as the grandfather, whose wives, sons, and daughters are the gods and goddesses. Eshu, being the youngest, is sent by the others on errands, but as often as not he gets his messages confused or plays pranks on his elders. His unreliability is the reason he is associated with the devil in Brazil, but this is only because to the Christian eye he appeared devilish.

One is often uncertain about the truth or untruth of Eshu's gifts, yet some of his best works come into our reality seeming illogical, cryptic, or nonsensical, and it is only later that we learn the hidden meanings that make divine sense.

Ah, but when Oshala comes through, his presence shines the bright light of clear understanding, dispelling ignorance and mystery.

No one here has received the spirit yet, and I'm beginning to wonder if it will happen. Then in fairly quick succession the Israelis troop out into the night and are gone, the drums change their rhythm slightly, and the dancing and chanting picks up the new tempo, and the whirl of white dresses and brown skin intensifies. Then a slim young lady in her early twenties, with long, loose black hair cascading down her copper-tan back, closes here eyes as she dances. With her eyes shut tight, she steps and bobs, turns and weaves, in and around the others. Maria spots her and is at her side in a flash, guiding her off the floor.

They are gone briefly, then they return and Maria leads her to a place near the other dancers but out of their way. The young woman stands with her arms extended, making a cross. She appears to be in a kind of catatonic trance, totally immobile. Her body has become like a statue of Christ crucified. I watch her eyelids closely and they don't blink or flutter. I can't even detect any breathing.

O. Govi: This has Gover slightly disappointed. He'd been expecting a more communicative spirit. In other Voodoo services, the gods and goddesses who came through were quite eloquent at times, in both words and deeds. The other night an old lady received Eshu and through Rita's translation has a lot to tell him. He has also been addressed by Ogun and Oshun and has seen Shango perform amazing dance feats. But never before has he seen a possession such as this seeming catatonia.

I beg his patience. There's more to come.

• • •

Gover: The mother of the saints stops by to ask if I'd like to join her for a taste of her own *batida*—raw rum with herbal or fruit additives. I'm already feeling lightheaded, but with Rita and Viarney I follow Maria into the small room just off the *candomble*. I really don't want any *batida* (any more than I wanted the Brazilian-style chitlins that made me throw up at another *candomble*), but her invitation indicates I'm welcome here, even though I'm an outsider.

I feel as though I'm walking and standing on a carpet of sound, and I realize I must appear tranced out. Maria pours the *batida* into three plastic glasses, then we toast; and while Viarney proclaims something in Portuguese, Maria looks very deeply into my eyes, filling me with something between a chilling foreboding and awesome wonderment.

She has poured water for herself. Now she downs it in one swallow and is gone back to the *candomble*. Viarney is pumped up with enthusiasm and is trying to tell me something, but Rita is not translating. She's looking at me with a smirk, as if to say, boy, are you in for a surprise!

There's no point asking what Viarney's enthusiasm and Rita's smirking are all about. The boom-booming of the drums is too loud for such an exchange of words, and Rita looks too flushed with excitement to speak. But why is she looking at me that way?

• • •

O. Govi: Because she thinks it is time Gover received a spirit, and she is suggesting he will tonight at this *candomble*. But he can't imagine such a thing happening to him.

I remind him that Oshala and all the other gods are always his possessions, for they are what compose the aliveness of pure energy. To become a medium for the Oshala spirit, all he has to do is cooperate with the mood the drums and chants create, for they are designed to separate this one god, Oshala, from the congress of his aliveness.

But, he protests, he has no desire to go into catatonic trance and stand like a statue of the crucified Christ. It looks like a psychotic episode rather than the reception of a Voodoo spirit. Indeed, it is what psychiatrists call psychotic but mystics call divine. Such divine psychosis, he thinks, is not for him.

Yet he has to admit he's never felt so close to the edge. So he buckles his mental safety belt as he downs the last of his *batida* and returns to the *candomble.*

● ● ●

Gover: A second woman has received Oshala and is standing next to the first. The second one is just as catatonic as the first, but her arms dangle from the elbows and her head hangs slightly to one side.

Momentarily, I wish the Israeli students had stayed to see this. I'd like to hear what that girl would say, for it would help me keep my distance from it. But it wasn't until the Israelis left that the spirit descended. It's the custom here that no one is barred from attending a *candomble,* which doesn't mean the spirits will arrive while nonbelieving tourists are present.

I glance at Viarney, who gives me the thumbs-up sign and departs for another *batida.* I glance at Rita and am surprised to see her eyes at half-mast, staring off into spaces other than normal. When I look back at the dancers, a third woman has received Oshala and has been positioned with the other two. This third lady appears to be in her fifties; she stands with her arms extended slightly upward, as though her body is sagging on the cross.

Abruptly the drums stop. For a moment there's a deafening silence, then people turn to each other and talk, children scamper about letting off steam, and the dancers wipe perspiration from their faces. The drummers stand and stretch, then walk into the adjoining room for *batida.* The three entranced women remain immobile, catatonic.

Rita is chattering into my ear, but I'm not hearing what she's saying. I can't seem to separate her sounds into English words. And I feel a need to relieve my bladder, so I extract myself from her as politely as I can and head for the door. It's pitch-black dark outside. The air is cool and moist.

• • •

O. Govi: As he walks over the soft, damp earth in search of a little privacy, I remind him of the dream he had last night. I do this by the brown faces that watch him as he walks out the door into the darkness. "Aztecs," he mutters.

In the dream he is living with an Aztec tribe and has been selected to become the annual human sacrifice. This means his heart will be cut out and offered to the proper god, but he hasn't been told when this will happen or which god is involved. He supposes it's the sun god, but he doesn't know the Aztec name for this one and feels remiss in his research.

Then the dream skips to much partying and fondling of pretty girls, and he learns he's become the collective tribal ego and is expected to act out everyone's collective lusts in preparation for the sacrifice. This news makes the partying seem interminable, but he sticks to it doggedly to fulfill his duty.

Then the dream skips to when he's prone on a flat rock on top of a pyramid under a clear sky and a blinding sun, with the priest's arm raised over him, holding a long knife. The priest chants and the crowd below waits, and Gover feels ready to die, which surprises him. Why does he feel ready to die? Oh yes, because he knows his spirit will be welcomed as a gift to the sun god. At last the knife goes into his chest. He feels neither pain nor pleasure. "Maybe I've been drugged," he thinks.

Gradually he feels himself becoming pure spirit and rising up, spreading out, then showering down like a fine mist of sunlight on the waiting crowd. He feels he's gone light years away and returned instantly, all in a time-motion dimension that is divine. Now he comes down as this shower of pure light, into the cells of these people, where he immediately becomes part of the tribal whole. He sees himself looking out at himself through everyone's eyes. As they look at each other, each pair of eyes has something of him in them. He is also present in their voices, and he is able to leap instantaneously from the senses of one person to another. And all this feels quite pleasurable except for one thing: Why, he wonders, has he, a white man, become part of this tribe of Aztecs?

Now, as he urinates, I remind him there are other questions he might ask of that dream. For instance, when he woke up to write that dream down, all he wrote was, "I dreamed I was dead and seeing through the eyes of others, who were Indians." Then he fell asleep again. So the question I now suggest is, When people receive the spirit at a Voodoo service like this *candomble,* whose eyes do they see through? Their own or others? Or do they go blind for the duration of the possession?

And of course there's only one way to find out for sure.

• • •

Gover: Back inside the *candomble,* it suddenly occurs to me that I walked in that utter darkness over some ruts that are deeper than I am tall. And very slippery, for this is the rainy season, and the ground is rarely dry. Even coming down here in daylight I had trouble keeping my footing. How did I walk diagonally across those ruts, totally forgetful of them, without so much as the least little slip?

• • •

O. Govi: The Christian Jesus, in full possession of Oshala, is said to have walked on water. Is it any wonder that a light entrancement by the same spirit conveyed Gover over ruts?

• • •

Gover: I have read and heard it said that two or more people cannot receive the same spirit at the same time. And there are those who believe that no one ever gains possession of Oshala, Obatala. But that is certainly what has happened here tonight, isn't it?

I move in close to inspect these three Oshalas. None of the three ladies has moved a muscle, even with adults, kids, and one stray dog moving around them. I suppose they are breathing, but I can't detect any sign that they are. Are they suspended somewhere between life and death?

The phenomenon baffles me. There's no way they can be faking. It's impossible for a person in his right mind to stand perfectly motionless for such a long time.

I saunter over to Rita, hoping for an explanation. "This is the Christ crucified," she says, "but soon Oshala will arise from the dead and serve us food."

"But those women aren't even breathing. Are they dead?"

"Of course they're dead. But when the time comes they will live again."

"But how long can they remain like this?"

"Don't worry, Maria has everything under control."

Now the drummers return to their stools on the raised platform in one corner. A cigarette dangles from the lips of the lead drummer as they resume, the booming and clanging echoing off the walls and external to me now. It will take awhile for their pattern of rhythm to find its way into my flesh and bones again.

The dog is removed, and the dancers begin stepping around again. But this time each seems to be into her own movements. And there's one, about as wide as she is tall, whose movements are exceptionally vigorous, even downright rough. I hadn't noticed her before and wonder now how she can possibly acquire Oshala with such movements as these.

I'm about to ask Rita when suddenly this squarely built woman's left foot plants and she shoots forward, reels, nearly falls, then lets out a supernaturally loud and masculine shout: "Ayeeee! Hey-eeeee-ayeeeee!"

What's this? An unscheduled visit from Ogun or Shango? Someone hurries out of the back room and hands the woman a wooden sword, and then she does something truly incredible: leaping like a ballet dancer and brandishing this sword, she hurls her approximately three hundred pounds about twelve feet through the air. From takeoff to landing she covers what I estimate to be twelve feet. She leaps again, and again, all about this very crowded room without knocking anyone down. She leaps around and between the other dancers, lands, squats, hisses, yells, turns like a warrior ready for battle and leaps again—all in time to the drums and ogan.

"Oshagun," says Rita. Oh, the Militant Christ, the one who throws the money changers out of the temple. But is Oshagun's arrival on Maria's agenda tonight? She's hard at work trying to subdue it, or harness it, or something. She follows Oshagun about the room, her arms outstretched, fingers reaching, until she makes an invisible contact with the back of Oshagun's neck. Then, as if lassoed, Oshagun is drawn backward by Maria, who carefully guides the spirit and his "horse" out of the *candomble* room. From elsewhere in the house, we soon here "Ayeeee!" and other sounds that indicate this spirit is still very much here. But the sounds are decreasing, losing their angry intensity, and a few minutes later Maria returns with Oshagun, who now wears a helmet and carries a shield as well as the sword. He strides onto the floor and does a stiff, heavy-footed, bellicose dance, more like an Indian war dance than a military ballet.

Except for the other dancers, all attention is now fixed on Oshagun. He strides to the drummers and, still moving with dancelike steps, lays down his sword and shield in front of the musicians. Then, beginning at that end of the room, he steps his way around, giving each and every one a big bear hug, executed in a quick, stiff way and accompanied by a shout, "Ayeeee!" Even the three Oshalas receive this quick bear hug and shout, which does nothing to disturb their trances. When my turn approaches, I get an urge to flee into the other room. The woman's eyes seem to be focused on some distant star, and it is definitely an Ogun-type character that shapes her face. I stand my ground, receive the hug, and feel a jolt of electrical bliss, a shock of pleasure that leaves me sucking in deep breaths of air. Then gradually I feel loosened, soothed, slightly intoxicated.

The round of hugs completed, Oshagun departs, and the lady is left sprawled on the floor. She is helped to her feet and looks about, as though wondering how she got here. Gently she is guided by two women in long white dresses out of the candomble room to the cot in the adjoining room, where she will lie down and rest until she's recovered.

• • •

O. Govi: What my esteemed partner fails to mention is that Oshagun's hug leaves him with the fearful sensation that it is possible for him to be inhabited by this force. Some Voodoo ceremonies he's attended have risen to such frenzied heights of spirit possession, such wild and impossible shouts and behavior, such a tangle of spent "horses" dazed and recovering, he knew (or thought he did) he could never participate. He felt alien, separate, detached from it all. Then there were ceremonies in which either the possession was so light, or the acting so poor, it was obviously a fraud.

But Maria's candomble is neither frenzy nor fraud, and even though he doesn't know the language, nor understand the meaning of all the various symbols, he feels at one with the spirit of the proceedings, and that scares him. He is not unfamiliar with the King

James New Testament version of the Oshala myth, but these people have a quite different version of that myth. So how, he wonders, is it possible he can feel at one with the spirit here tonight when it has never been possible for him to receive the Biblical Jesus? I respectfully request he flip back in his notebook and read the latest dictation he received from Aum.

• • •

Gover: "To appreciate the basic beliefs of Voodoo, you must step beyond the beliefs your culture conditioned you with; one of which is that the unscriptured religions of illiterate people are inferior to the scriptured religions of literate people; and another of which is that primitive, illiterate people are fast becoming extinct.

"Recall what the Navajo medicine man you once visited said: that species that seem to have become extinct are merely migrating. When the cause of their discomfort departs their natural habitat, they return to physical manifestation again, as spring flowers blossom after winter thaws. So it only *seems* that 'civilization' is causing the extinction of 'primitive' people.

"Literacy does not confer superior intelligence. And scriptured religions are no improvement over unscriptured. Enlightening as scriptures can be, the negative possibility is to constrict the intuition with literal meanings. It is the expression of mind through intuition that distinguishes humanity from other earthly forms.

"The 'distance' between a human being and the source of his aliveness is not bridged by literacy and scripture. If it were, the scriptured religions would provide their faithful with possession, god-realization, yogic oneness. Instead it is the faithful of the unscriptured religions who have access to this experience and are skilled at sharing it. And oneness with one's god is exactly what Voodoo is all about.

"Oneness with one's god may not be possible for those who believe in scriptured 'facts,' however. Rendered into words on paper, the religious experience no longer exists, for it can only exist as a firsthand experience. Solidly lodged in the mind of the literate, scripture blocks experience. Any scripture's god is an energy force, but such a force cannot take up residency in a human being filled with the heavy furniture of the written ecstasies of long-gone ancestors.

"Scripture causes the old gods to migrate and seemingly become extinct. The literal meanings scripture produces poison the psychic ecology, making it uninhabitable for those primary spirit forces known as gods. Only when one casts out the literal meanings of scripture and deals with the mythological meanings does the ecology begin to clean up.

"To gain possession, you must not only contact your god, you must also make yourself available as a medium. This act of surrender may seem frightening at first, for one isn't dealing with a mundane therapist, one is dealing with a far more rapacious force. Surrender to such a force takes courage. Some gods leave their 'horses' feeling like losers in a barroom brawl.

"And possession is not to be undertaken for selfish reasons. The self is absent during possession and does not necessarily benefit from it later. It is the collective self of the group that is served when one of its individual selves offers a god access to the human dimension."

• • •

O. Govi: Maria, who has been monitoring activities on the inner plane, has a plan. And I, the guardian of Gover's interface between spirit and matter, am at the crux of that plan.

It takes one to know one, as the saying goes, and Maria is one who knows a likeness in Gover. She has reached the turning point in the *candomble,* for she now has six crucified Christs lined up against her south wall and must begin resurrection ceremonies soon. But she still has time to invite another spirit, and she plans to use Gover to do just that.

She has noticed him reading his notebook out of the corner of her eye. Now she approaches. He is sitting in one of the few chairs here and has closed his notebook. He looks up to find her standing over him, smiling. She takes his hand and guides him onto the floor. But he's wearing shoes, a violation of *candomble* protocol. Through Rita, she asks him to remove his shoes. He does. He removes his socks voluntarily.

In the manner of a courtly eighteenth-century gentleman, Maria leads him into the dance. If he didn't have such complete trust in her, he would flee. But she stares him in the eye, and what he reads from her intense concentration disarms his fears. She's as subtle as an unknown virus invading his body and as harmless as pure water.

By her actions she lets him know she expects no fancy footwork. The dance she gets him doing is a simple two-step shuffle.

And to take his conscious mind away from the fact that he's a stranger here and the only male who has danced tonight, she keeps him facing the six Oshalas. They line the south wall, as immobile as death. Dancing with his attention fixed on them, Gover screws up his courage to receive a spirit. But as he is about to learn, one cannot be one's courageous self and an invading spirit at the same time. He feels as if he's being pushed over a cliff, and he turns to Maria for a moment, for consultation. Maria smiles and says, "*Sim,*" yes, and directs his attention back to the six Oshalas. He feels caught between the vices of vanity (feeling foolish) and pride (the determination to see this experience through to its natural limits).

He struggles to hang on and prevent the fall into this bottomless space, but he is helplessly swept away by an oceanic momentum. These people haven't seen a gringo taken by a spirit since they can't remember when.

Now he's falling away in a terror. It reminds him of what astronomers have called "the black hole." He blanks out, is without personal awareness. He feels forced out of life, into some other dimension.

As his astral soul, his dreamer, I register bits and pieces of the experience. As though seen under a strobe light, I catch glimpses of his physical being leaping about the *candomble* floor, the "horse" of Oshagun. I can tell it's Oshagun because he has a sword in his hand, a shield, and a helmet—the same set that adorned the three-hundred-pound lady. But he isn't doing exactly what she did—those twelve-foot leaps in ballet style. I'm not sure what his body is doing or how to describe it to his conscious mind. His movements are no less acrobatic than the other "horse" of Oshagun, and they are seen as a holy spectacle by the crowd. As a parked ego with blanked perception, he is gone and knows nothing of this.

He will later recall the impression that life as a parked ego wasn't half as terrifying as he'd expected. And the impression that, "seen" from this other dimension, life is a wriggling, squirming, exciting dance of interlocking organisms. Another impression he will recall is of his vocal cords resonating. Was Oshagun screaming? No, for the sound comes from his solar plexus and is rough, gruff, and rowdy, like the hoarse-voiced bellow of a wounded warrior.

Well, it's a blessing that he is unconscious and knows nothing of how his body is being manipulated. It is moving to the rhythm of the drums, but as everyone here knows, these jumps and strides, squats and leaps, would be quite painful if he weren't parked in this other dimension, feeling nothing. As the spirit withdraws and he gradually regains consciousness, he realizes he's received a spirit at a Brazilian *candomble,* and he wishes he knew more about what has happened. He tries to cling to this intermediate state and with the dawning of fleeting awareness to gather impressions of himself possessed. He wants to bring back something from this horrendous experience, something he can scripture in words on paper. Is it like a scary rollercoaster ride? No, because it's devoid of physical sensation. It's more as if his head had been chopped off and caught only a few strobe-lit glimpses of his body hurtling about, "seen" in suspended slow motion. One huge solar cell wriggling in slow motion.

Later he will remember making some dream connection between the faces of the six Oshalas and TV commercials—advertisements betraying the Christ who revolts violently against the practice of usury, excessive interest for loaned money. Is that what Oshagun's message was? That true values cannot be loaned at interest? Perhaps. But what about the six Oshalas? What they speak of tonight cannot be reduced to words, to sounds made meaningful, he thinks as he gropes his way back to consciousness. What they say can only be understood in a moment such as this, when the sound—the drums and clanging—resound through hundreds of centuries into a moment in modern time.

Done as a TV commercial, this moment—if he could capture it in words—would destroy Western civilization, would cut off its stalk and reduce it to its roots—this experience of the Christ consciousness captured and *shared,* as compared to captured and restrained, subdued, transformed into docile obedience to *The Church.* No church is this, this barbarism, this decapitation of sanity in the hunt for ancient mysteries...banished long ago from consideration by the offspring of Inquisition-haunted Christians.

And he, suspended here between life and death, can only wonder at the absurdity of all religious beliefs and faiths, and marvel at how this experience makes faiths and beliefs irrelevant.

Now the bare electric bulb hanging from the ceiling over the cot he rests on looks dim compared to the radiance he recalls. What happened? Hypnotism? Or de-hypnotism? He decides quickly. Hypnotism is normal. De-hypnotism is when your normal self is replaced by something far more powerful. Removed from your normal awareness, "you" do not exist. Well, nonexistence, like New York City, is a great place to visit but you wouldn't want to live there.

• • •

Gover: After resting for half an hour or so, I struggle to my feet. Once, a few years ago when I was living too fast, I fainted dead away. I feel now much as I did then when I recovered from that faint. I shuffle sheepishly back into the *candomble* room, just in time for a round of divine refreshments.

While I was recovering, Maria led her six Oshalas off the floor, down six steps, and into her outdoor kitchen. Now, Rita tells me, they are preparing food to be shared by all.

In the meantime, kids are leaping about, imitating Oshagun, while the drummers share a joint and sip *batida*. People stroll about, stretch, chat, step outside for a breath of fresh air. Several approach me and remark on my reception of the spirit. Others give me the thumbs-up salute.

Well, I'm happy to have had the experience, but I'm still so dazed I don't know what to make of it. A stranger here, I feel like a wanderer who has come back and found the familiar strangely changed.

Presently a female chorus is heard from inside the house, and people hurry back to their places in the *candomble*. Someone turns out the electric lights, and now the scene is bathed in the softer hues of candlelight. Up the steps and into the room come the six Oshalas, singing and carrying large trays and bowls on their heads.

At first I think they must have lost their possession and are now doing a theatrical. But when they pass me and I get a close look at the glazed, gone look in their eyes and hear the hymn breathing itself forth from mouths that hardly move, I know Oshala inhabits this whole line of bodies. Their serpentine togetherness, their long dresses swaying in precise rhythm, could not be achieved by the most talented acting. What they are doing is delivering a gift from the Christ.

They walk majestically to the middle of the *candomble* floor, form a circle and kneel, lift their trays and bowls from their heads, and place them gracefully on the floor in a particular arrangement around the star and cross. Then one by one their heads bob forward and snap back, and this whiplash action of the neck seems to alter their trance and prepare them for the next round of activity.

Two Oshalas dish out a thick white liquid from the cut glass bowls into individual glasses. Two others serve these to the assembled. There aren't enough glasses to go around, so the other two take emptied glasses to the kitchen, wash them and return them to be filled again. This is coordinated with such precision that the Oshalas dishing out the liquid never miss a beat.

It's a tasty drink that reminds me of tapioca. Aware that the spirit of Oshala has been involved in its making, drinking it fills me with a sensation of light and love. It also brings up a distant memory: When I was three or four, my grandfather took me to a church—Methodist, I believe it was—and I had this same feeling then. I remember standing on the church's front steps, entranced, lightly possessed by this same god.

• • •

O. Govi: The gods are both the same by different names and different by the same names. But by whatever name, when summoned from their natural habitat, a god summoned is a lot rougher to handle than the same god worshipped from afar.

Gover can't help feeling that possession of such heavy-handed spirits as the Militant Christ, Ogun, Shango, Eshu, and some others should be for karate black belts only. And even they might feel afterward as though they'd just stepped off a torture rack.

Well, it's been a long day, and he feels a sudden letdown. Exhaustion sets in. His feet are cold, and that chills the rest of his body. He's anxious to return to his hotel and sleep, then bid farewell to Bahia and fly home.

The bowls and glasses have been cleared, and the Oshalas have walked as one body to their previous stations, but their stances are not so rigid now. Their eyes are closed and they are motionless, but their arms dangle at their sides. Christ has been taken down from the cross, and Maria's chant now calls for Oshala to speak.

But they will speak an African language, so he and his two friends prepare to leave. Just before they do, Maria takes his hand and walks him briskly past the Oshalas, then gives him a quick hug that seems to communicate everything the risen Christ will say.

Glossary
of Voodoo
Gods

Rather than attempt a comprehensive listing of all the gods and goddesses extant in all the various Voodoo cults in the Western Hemisphere, this glossary is limited to those I have found to be most widely known. I have included their astrological correspondences so that anyone familiar with the ancient Hebrew Kabala and its astrological correspondences can place this pantheon on the Tree of Life design. Those who are familiar with the Hindu pantheon can compare the Voodoo gods with those deities. The same holds true for Druid, Celtic, Hawaiian, American Indian, or any other pantheon: the key to comparing deities is their astrological correspondences. This is so because the planets were named for the ancient gods of Western civilization.

The pronunciation of the name of each Voodoo god is included, although such indications can be only rough approximations, because the same names are pronounced differently from place to place. I have also tried to render the gods' names spelled as they are pronounced in American English.

Babalu: see *Obaluaye.*

Chango: see *Shango.*

Damballah: see *Orunmila.*

Erzulie: see *Oshun.*

Eshu, or *Legba:* (Aye-shoo, Leg-bah). Mercury, messenger of the gods, go-between for gods and mankind, ruler of communications and the marketplace, source of fortune and misfortune. Youngest of the gods, sometimes called the Great Trickster.

Ifa: see *Orunmila.*

Legba: see *Eshu.*

Obaluaye, or *Babalu:* (Oh-bah-loo-why-eh, Bah-bah-*loo*). Saturn and Earth, the Great Teacher, bringer of lessons to be learned in this life, and finally bringer of one's final lesson: death. Sometimes referred to as the fact that spirit suffers in material form. The only god one never asks any favors of.

Obatala, or *Oshala:* (Oh-*bah*-tah-*lah,* Oh-shah-*lah*). Sun and Jupiter, the Christ spirit, source of light, warmth, creativity, and enlightenment and begetter of earthly forms.

Ogun: (Oh-*gon,* Oh-*goon,* Oh-*gum*). Mars, ruler of the mineral kingdom, of martial force, war, and pioneering effort.

Olodumare, or *Olorun:* (Oh-lo-du-*mah*-ray, Oh-lo-*roon*). The godhead, source of all and everything; in some cults called *Orisha-nla.*

Olokun: (Oh-low-*kun*). Neptune, ruler of oceans and mysterious depths of consciousness, the subconscious, and distant places in consciousness.

Olorun: see *Olodumare.*

Orisha-nla: see *Olodumare.*

Orunmila, or *Ifa:* (Oh-*roon*-mi-lah; Ee-*fah*). The firstborn of Olodumare; the Zodiac; the knowledge of past, present and future. Priests who commune with this deity specialize in divination. Some correlate Orunmila with the Haitian *Damballah.*

Oshala: see *Obatala.*

Oshagun (Oh-sha-*goon,* Oh-sha-*goom*). Sun conjoined (conjunct) with Mars. Oshala and Ogun combined. The Sun god's Martian ray. Ogun acting at the behest of Oshala, or Obatala.

Oshun, or *Erzulie:* (Oh-*shoon,* Er-zoo-*lee*). Venus, source of love, beauty and the arts, of justice and celestial legality.

Oya: (Oh-*yah*). Pluto, goddess of the netherworld, of death, transformation, and conception; sometimes call Shango's warrior wife.

Shango, or Chango: (Shahn-*go, Chang*-go). Jupiter, until the discovery of Uranus. Ruler of fire and electricity, source of genius, sometimes called "the heir apparent to Obatala's throne."

Yemanja: (Yeh-mahn-*jah*). Moon, Mother of Waters, source of emotions both subtle and violent.

Contents

Michael Frayn

1933 8 September: born in North London. He lived first
      in Mill Hill, in a flat above a Victoria Wine Stores.
      His father, Thomas Allen Frayn, was a sales rep for
      Turners' Asbestos Cement, a roofing materials firm.
      His mother, Violet Alice Lawson, studied as a
      violinist at the Royal Academy of Music. She later
      worked at Harrods, where she occasionally modelled
      clothes. The family moved to Ewell, a suburb in
      South London.

1940 Attended 'hideous' private school in Sutton, a
      Dickensian establishment with bullying and beating.

1945 His mother died from a heart attack, aged forty. His
      father had to get a housekeeper and was no longer
      able to afford the school fees. Frayn went to
      Kingston Grammar School. 'It was my good fortune
      to be sent there because it gave me a good
      education.' Frayn swung between being a 'diligent
      little swot who was frightened of everything' and 'an
      obstreperous clown'.[1]

1948 After a brief religious phase Frayn became a
      militant atheist, communist and 'cultural snob'.
      Wrote poetry, stories and plays. As a sixth-former, 'I
      had a very lordly view of life.'

1952 National Service. Trained in Cambridge as a
      Russian interpreter. The playwright, Alan Bennett,
      was on the same course. (They became close friends
      and would later live opposite one another in
      London.)

1954 Attended Emmanuel College, Cambridge, on a state
      scholarship. Read Russian and French in his first
      year and Moral Sciences (Philosophy) for the second
      and third years. His supervisor for his last year,

Jonathan Bennett, recalled: 'I sharply remember his saying at one session – his face expressing a kind of happy earnestness – that when he had read the opening sentence of Wittgenstein's *Tractatus Logico-Philosophicus*, "The world is everything that is the case," it made him "want to dance".'[2] Edited *Granta*. Wrote May Week Footlights revue, *Zounds*, which 'fell into the stalls like unrisen sponge cake'.[3] His contemporaries included Frederic Raphael, Bamber Gascoigne, Jonathan Miller and Leslie Bricusse.

1957 Reporter on the *Manchester Guardian*. His beat was the north of England. (He also covered Harold Macmillan's trip to Russia.)

1959 Columnist on the *Manchester Guardian*. His 'Miscellany' column appeared three times a week.

1960 Marriage to Gillian Palmer.

1962 Columnist on the *Observer*. *The Day of the Dog* (articles reprinted from the *Guardian*).

1963 In one column Frayn introduced his famous distinction between ambitious meritocratic 'carnivores' and well-meaning *Guardian*-reading 'herbivores'. *The Book of Fub* (articles reprinted from the *Guardian*).

1964 *On the Outskirts* (articles reprinted from the *Observer*).

1965 In his first novel, *The Tin Men*, computers take over human tasks. Winner of the Somerset Maugham Award. P. G. Wodehouse calls it 'brilliant'.

1966 *The Russian Interpreter*, about a love affair conducted through an interpreter. Winner of the Hawthornden Prize.

1967 *Towards the End of the Morning* ('the only fiction set in Fleet Street that can bear comparison with *Scoop*' Christopher Hitchens). First published in the United States as *Against Entropy*. *At Bay in Gear Street* (articles reprinted from the *Observer*).

1968 *A Very Private Life*, a novel set in the future and written in the future tense. First television play, *Jamie, on a Flying Visit*, broadcast. (The story came to

Frayn in a single sleepless night.)

1969   Second television play, *Birthday*, broadcast.

1970   *The Two of Us* (Garrick Theatre), four one-act comedies, with Richard Briers and Lynn Redgrave, attracts hostile reviews. 'All right, they laughed,' said Frayn of one audience, 'but why didn't they laugh until they fell helpless on the floor?'[4]

1971   *The Sandboy* (Greenwich Theatre). A newspaper dispute led to only one review appearing: a 'shattering dismissal' from *The Times*.

1973   *Sweet Dreams*, a novel about a man, waiting at the traffic lights, who finds himself transported to heaven – an attractive modern city which offers unexpected challenges to the modern liberal.

1974   *Constructions*, a non-fiction volume of philosophical reflections.

1975   *Alphabetical Order* (Hampstead, then Mayfair Theatre), with Dinsdale Landen and Billie Whitelaw. Winner of *Evening Standard* Best Comedy Award. An assistant librarian has an unexpected impact on a provincial newspaper library. *Imagine a City Called Berlin* (first of a series of documentaries). Frayn's subjects included Vienna, Jerusalem, Prague, Budapest and the London suburbs.

1976   *Donkeys' Years* (Globe Theatre) with Penelope Keith, about a reunion night at an Oxbridge college. *Clouds* (Hampstead) with Nigel Hawthorne and Barbara Ferris (then Duke of York's, 1978) with Tom Courtenay and Felicity Kendal. A journalist and a novelist travel round Cuba reporting for rival magazines.

1978   *Balmoral* (Guildford), a farce set in a royal residence after the Revolution. 'It was terrible. I withdrew it and completely rewrote it.'[5]

1979   *Liberty Hall* (Greenwich), the rewrite of *Balmoral*, with George Cole. Reviews were 'lacklustre'.

1980   *Make and Break* (Lyric, Hammersmith, then Theatre Royal, Haymarket) with Leonard Rossiter and

Prunella Scales, about a British building components firm at a trade fair in Frankfurt. Winner of *Evening Standard* Best Comedy Award.

1982   *Noises Off* (Lyric, Hammersmith, then Savoy), with Patricia Routledge and Paul Eddington. A farce about actors putting on a farce, it ran for four years.

1983   *The Original Michael Frayn* (articles reprinted from the *Guardian* and the *Observer*).

1984   *Benefactors* (Vaudeville) with Patricia Hodge and Tim Piggott-Smith. The play drew on Frayn's experience when, with his wife and three daughters, he was involved in a housing initiative in Blackheath. (The house was designed and built as part of a small community.) In *Benefactors* an architect finds opposition to his new scheme in unexpected quarters. Winner of four Best Play awards. *Wild Honey*, after Chekhov (Lyttelton, National Theatre) with Ian McKellen.

1986   First screenplay, *Clockwise*, a comedy about a luckless headmaster (John Cleese) en route to give the keynote speech at a head teachers conference.

1989   *The Trick of It*, an epistolary novel about an academic who marries the female novelist who is his main academic subject. Marriage to Gillian Palmer dissolved.

1990   *Look Look* (Aldwych), a farce about audiences, with Stephen Fry as the playwright in Row H of the stalls. Panned by critics, the production ran for 27 performances.

1991   *A Landing on the Sun*, a novel about the death of a civil servant who has been working for the Ministry of Defence.

1992   *Now You Know*, a novel about free-speech campaigners with secrets of their own. The events are narrated in turn through the eyes of each of the eight characters.

1993 *Here* (Donmar), about a couple moving into new accommodation. Married Claire Tomalin, biographer and critic.

1995 *Now You Know* (Hampstead), a play based on his 1992 novel, with Adam Faith. *Speak After the Beep* (articles reprinted from the *Guardian*).

1998 *Copenhagen* (Cottesloe, Royal National Theatre). Winner of *Evening Standard* Best Play of the Year and Critics' Circle awards. *Alarms and Excursions* (Gielgud), short plays and sketches, with Felicity Kendal and Nicky Henson.

1999 *Headlong*, a novel, shortlisted for 1999 Booker Prize. An art historian obsessively pursues a missing Bruegel painting.

2000 *Copenhagen* opens Royale Theatre, New York. Winner of Tony Award (Best New Play). *The Additional Michael Frayn* (articles reprinted from various publications). *Celia's Secret*, co-written with David Burke, a non-fiction account of how David Burke (Bohr in *Copenhagen*) deceived Frayn with forgeries that supposedly related to events in *Copenhagen*.

2002 *Spies*, a novel about two boys during the Second World War. Winner of Whitbread Novel of the Year. Frayn's *Spies* and Claire Tomalin's *The Unequalled Self*, both nominated for Whitbread Book of the Year. (The winner was Tomalin.) Frayn received the Heywood Hill Literary Prize.

2003 *Democracy* (Royal National Theatre).

2007 *The Crimson Hotel* (Donmar Warehouse).

2008 *Afterlife* (Royal National Theatre), based on the life of theatre impresario Max Reinhardt.

[1] www.guardian.co.uk/saturday_review (14 August 1999)
[2] Ibid.
[3] *Observer* (1 April 1984)
[4] Ibid.
[5] *Frayn Plays: Two* (Methuen, 1991), p.viii

Plot

Copenhagen has a non-realistic setting. Three characters exist in an 'afterlife' from which they revisit events in the past. Without any changes in costume or make-up the characters move between periods in their lives. Time and place are fluid as the dialogue locates the action.

Act One

The play opens with the Danish physicist, Niels Bohr, and his wife, Margrethe, considering the events that occurred on a single evening during the Second World War. At the time Denmark was occupied by the Germans. In September 1941 the German physicist Werner Heisenberg, a former pupil and colleague of Bohr's, visited the Bohrs' home. Why? The visit was the end of the famous friendship between these two Nobel prizewinners. In the 'afterlife' setting of *Copenhagen*, Heisenberg agrees with the others to make one more attempt to explain his reasons for the trip.

The action flashes back to September 1941. Heisenberg arrives in Copenhagen and Bohr and Margrethe agonise over whether to invite him to their home. Bohr promises not to talk to him about politics but to stick to physics. Heisenberg struggles to remember the details of the trip. As he approaches the house the Bohrs speculate on why he wants to visit them. Bohr welcomes Heisenberg warmly. Margrethe remains detached and sardonic. The pressures of the war make social pleasantries extremely awkward. Heisenberg fails to grasp the depth of the Bohrs' hostility towards Germany. Bohr is half-Jewish. Heisenberg is working for the Nazis as director of nuclear fission research. They all know that the Gestapo are probably monitoring their conversation. Heisenberg asks if Bohr has been in touch with mutual friends, scientists now working in the Allied countries. Bohr resists Heisenberg's advice about staying on good terms with the German Embassy.

The conversation flashes back two more decades to the first time Bohr and Heisenberg met. At the end of one of Bohr's lectures, the twenty-year-old Heisenberg had challenged the famous physicist over his maths. They recall their intense competitiveness, whether they were discussing theoretical physics, playing table-tennis or poker, or skiing. Heisenberg was the quick, impulsive one, Bohr moved slowly and carefully. Heisenberg recalls the headlong manner in which he had met and wooed his wife. There's a momentary silence. Heisenberg knows that the Bohrs are thinking about their children, two of whom died young. Bohr remembers the boating accident in which his eldest son was killed.

Bohr and Heisenberg decide to go for a walk so that they can talk. What Heisenberg has to say is treasonable. As they leave, Margrethe recalls the vast amount of time these two physicists had spent walking and talking. Within ten minutes, the two men have returned. Bohr looks furious and Heisenberg soon leaves. Margrethe wants to know what Heisenberg had to say.

The three of them realise that they cannot agree on the simplest details concerning that evening. Heisenberg says he was asking Bohr if a physicist had the moral right to work on the practical exploitation of atomic energy. Bohr thought Heisenberg was trying to provide Hitler with nuclear weapons. Bohr knew that an explosive chain reaction could never be achieved using natural uranium. Heisenberg knew that uranium could be turned into neptunium, which could be turned into plutonium. At this moment 'the bomb' goes off in Bohr's head.

Heisenberg insists that Bohr had always misunderstood the conversation. He'd told people variously that Heisenberg had tried to pick his brains about fission and the Allied nuclear programme, that Heisenberg was hoping to persuade him that the Germans had no nuclear programme and that Heisenberg had tried to recruit him to work on it. They agree to go over the conversation one more time. They also agree to discuss it in plain language so that Margrethe, a non-scientist, can follow it. Heisenberg says that he tried to explain to Bohr that the future of the atomic bomb lay in the hands of scientists. Both sides would have to desist from building it. What should Heisenberg tell the German government if they came to him asking if it would be possible to produce nuclear weapons? Heisenberg is a patriot. He loves his country. What if the Allies were building an atomic weapon? Bohr says he can tell him nothing about the Allies' programme. Margrethe scorns the suggestion that Bohr should persuade the scientists, driven out of Germany because they were Jews, to stop work on a bomb to defeat Hitler. In September 1941 it looked very likely that Germany would win the war. Heisenberg's scheme would favour the Germans.

Heisenberg says that he didn't try and build the bomb. It wasn't until after the war, when he was detained with other German scientists in a house near Cambridge, that he heard the news about the exploding of an atom bomb. He couldn't believe it. During the war, Bohr worked at Los Alamos, where the atom bomb was developed. Yet after the war, Heisenberg was the one who had to live with thirty years of reproach. Margrethe refuses to let Heisenberg off the hook. She says that he had told the Nazis that he could produce an atomic bomb. Heisenberg insists that when he met with Albert Speer in June 1942 he was able to sideline the atomic project. Bohr scorns the research that Heisenberg had been doing at the end of the war. The three characters agree that after the war their friendship never recovered.

In the silence that follows, the question resurfaces. Why did Heisenberg go to Copenhagen in 1941? They agree to try another draft. For a second time Heisenberg approaches the Bohrs' house. As Bohr opens the door, Margrethe reflects that from these two minds the future will emerge, which cities will be destroyed and which will survive.

Act Two
We see Bohr and Heisenberg on a walking holiday in Denmark in 1924. These are the early days of their friendship and collaboration. The discussion moves to the three years they spent together working on quantum mechanics, the 'uncertainty principle' and 'complementarity'. By following the discoveries they made in theoretical physics other parallels emerge. Their work led to the realisation that there can be no precisely determinable objective universe. Margrethe challenges their memory of making their discoveries together; in fact the most important ones were made alone. She also points out that the one person you can have no objective view of is yourself. It is therefore no good asking Heisenberg why he came to Copenhagen. Heisenberg's motives, she says, have not always been admirable. Perhaps in returning to Copenhagen he wished to show off his success to his old mentor. Perhaps it was fear of failure that stopped him obtaining large resources from Speer. Later she asserts that Heisenberg didn't build the bomb because he didn't understand the physics. Though Bohr suggests that if Heisenberg had known how close he was he might have made a bomb, Heisenberg maintains that he was never trying to build one. If he wasn't trying to – the question comes up again – why did he go to Copenhagen?

For the third and final time they go through the evening's events. This time round the three characters concentrate on what it was that they were thinking and feeling. Margrethe states that Heisenberg wanted Bohr to understand him and that Bohr's final act of friendship was to leave Heisenberg misunderstood. Heisenberg describes how he survived at the end of the war, when he was nearly shot as a deserter by an SS officer, by offering him a packet of cigarettes. It was a simple solution to a life and death problem. Bohr says that uncertainty and knowledge are inextricable. Heisenberg agrees that the meeting at Copenhagen might have gone a different way and history been very different, there is a final core of uncertainty at the heart of things.

Commentary

The playwright's themes

Of the many successful playwrights and novelists working in Britain, some of the playwrights have written a novel and some of the novelists have written a play. Only one writer has achieved notable success in both fields. By 2003 Michael Frayn had written ten novels and fourteen plays, winning literary awards for his novels and theatre awards for his plays. As one reviewer put it, 'Nobody since Chekhov has been as good at both plays and fiction, or as productive.'[1]

How has Frayn achieved this double act? There is only one tip about how to be a successful writer that Frayn has so far volunteered, and that is 'to write the same thing over and over again, changing things very slightly and going on delivering it until people accept it. Very simply, people want reliability and continuity in a writer. If you buy cornflakes you want cornflakes.'[2] When Frayn made this suggestion he was not speaking about his own work. He was referring to more commercially successful novelists whose books are a recognisable brand. No one has ever accused Frayn of writing the same thing over and over again. No one till now, that is.

In fact, Frayn has been praised and censured for doing the opposite. When *Copenhagen* opened at the Royal National Theatre in May 1998 the *Evening Standard*'s theatre critic welcomed the play as 'the most astonishing departure in Frayn's theatrical career'. The *Daily Telegraph*'s critic was not so keen on the change of direction: 'It is impossible not to mourn the fact that Frayn has, temporarily I trust, mislaid his sense of humour.'

As a playwright Frayn had been pigeon-holed in the category marked 'sophisticated light comedy'. He had

written the most successful farce of the eighties. In *Noises
Off* actors mislay sardines, hide whisky bottles behind
radiators and present bunches of flowers to the wrong
person. It seems worlds apart from *Copenhagen* in which two
physicists discuss neutrons, photons, fission and wave
equations. And yet, when these two plays are seen in the
context of Frayn's career, evidence can soon be found of
reliability and continuity. The subjects and the genres vary
wildly but a closer inspection reveals many similar
ingredients. Frayn has been following his own advice.

Even before he had the idea of *Copenhagen* we could have
listed some themes that we would have expected to see:

- how we shape the world through work
- how we describe the world
- how subjectivity affects that description
- how versions of events conflict
- how memory works
- how we mask our thoughts from others
- how descriptions of events are always subject to
  rewrites
- how this complexity affects our moral judgements

Frayn's philosophical interest in these questions has been a
constant feature of his writing. *Copenhagen* is one more stage
in a long line of enquiry that stretches back to Cambridge
in the 1950s, if not further still, to his London childhood in
the 1940s. Michael Blakemore directed the Royal National
Theatre and New York premières of *Copenhagen*. He has
also directed six other plays by Frayn. 'I think good
writing,' Blakemore says, 'mostly comes out of the
preoccupations of a lifetime.'[3]

The spark that first set Frayn thinking about a new
subject for a new play, one that would provide a startling
and illuminating focus for his interests, came in the mid-
nineties when he read a recent book by the investigative
journalist Thomas Powers. The title was *Heisenberg's War:
The Secret History of the German Bomb*. A hundred pages in,
Frayn found his subject.

Copenhagen is the story of two physicists who meet for a conversation during the war. After the war neither can agree on what was said. Within this tight framework Frayn investigates questions that he has been considering since he was an undergraduate at Cambridge. These philosophical questions revolve around what we know, feel and think and the uncertain foundations upon which we base these perceptions. In philosophy this area is called epistemology.

As theoretical physicists, Niels Bohr and Werner Heisenberg are involved in unravelling the enigma of the atom. Yet they are unable to agree on basic facts as to what took place during the course of a ten-minute walk. As Bohr's wife, Margrethe, says: 'You reasoned your way, both of you, with such astonishing delicacy and precision into the tiny world of the atom. Now it turns out that everything depends upon these really rather large objects on our shoulders' (p. 76).

The focus in *Copenhagen* narrows down, even further than this, to a particular branch of philosophy known as the epistemology of intention. This examines what we think we are doing and why we think we are doing it. It's a very basic question. The play states it in the opening line. 'But why?' asks Margrethe. Her second line gives the question its context. 'Why did he come to Copenhagen?'

Copenhagen concerns the uncertainties that surround motivation. Every actor knows about motivation. It is what actors ask over and over again in rehearsals. Why am I doing this? At drama school actors are often trained to motivate a line of dialogue with a single *action*. The character is doing this or that action because of this or that *objective*. The actors also learn to motivate the *arc* of a character's journey. They do this by thinking of a *super-objective*. The idea underlying this approach is that an audience won't believe in what the character is doing unless the actor believes in what the character is doing. In a well-rehearsed production each line the actor delivers, each move the actor makes, will appear to be logical and intelligible. In this respect, theatre is quite unlike real life, where people are often unable to clarify their objectives, arcs and super-objectives.

Why did one of the world's leading physicists make a particular journey? The answer that Frayn provides in *Copenhagen* takes the audience on a challenging journey of its own. It explores nuclear physics, philosophy and history. For scholars and students each of these academic disciplines has to be approached on its own terms. To discover what goes on inside an atom and what goes on inside the human mind requires separate investigative and analytical skills. A playwright is allowed to take more liberties. A playwright has the licence to play with ideas and subjects and to highlight parallels, analogies and metaphors that fall outside the academic approach to subjects. 'One of the things about the theatre, and fiction, is that you can play,' Frayn told an interviewer. 'You can actually investigate situations that don't exist, and you're not bound by the actuality of the world.'[4]

In *Copenhagen* Frayn plays with the idea of Bohr, Margrethe and Heisenberg meeting up in an 'afterlife' and holding the conversation that they never had during their lives. This situation allows Frayn to combine his interests in philosophy and physics. These two disciplines have been transformed during the twentieth century as our understanding of what goes on inside atoms and what goes on inside the human mind has been revolutionised. More than that, the developments in the first area influenced the developments in the second. Since Frayn explores the relationship between the two in his work, it is worth taking a step back to consider how far-reaching these developments were.

The modern world is often said to have begun in 1905, when the twenty-six-year-old Albert Einstein, a clerk in a patents office in Berne, published 'On the electrodynamics of moving bodies'. This paper became known as the Special Theory of Relativity. Einstein's astonishing revelation was that when one goes at very high velocities (approaching the speed of light), lengths contract and clocks slow down. Einstein rapidly followed up his discovery with the quantum theory of light (which proposed that light was composed of 'wave-packets' called photons), for which he won the Nobel Prize. That very same year, his research into Brownian motion provided a powerful argument for the existence of atoms. Although his work had a profound effect on the twentieth century, he couldn't possibly have foreseen what some of these consequences would be. Einstein was dismayed when he realised that his work had paved the way for the invention of the atomic bomb. 'It starts with Einstein,' says Heisenberg in *Copenhagen*. 'It starts with Einstein,' agrees Bohr (p. 71).

Philosophy had undergone its own revolution in the first quarter of the twentieth century. In 1911 a young aeronautical engineer from Vienna had gone to Cambridge to study mathematics and logic. Three years later he had to return home to fight in the First World War. During the war, in which he fought on the Russian and Italian fronts, Ludwig Wittgenstein completed his masterpiece, the *Tractatus Logico-Philosophicus* (1922). The book overturned the way we think about the mind and the body, inner and outer experience and how we differentiate between our knowledge of ourselves and others.

In 1929 Wittgenstein came back to teach at Cambridge. His impact was immense. One area in which he was highly influential was his analysis of private experience. He attacked the idea that the mind and the body were separate entities. He denied that we always know what mental states we are in. He stated that introspection is not the same as perception. He could no more look into his own mind than he could look into the mind of someone else. Introspection does not grant us a privileged access into our own minds. Introspection is a form of self-reflection: 'the calling up of memories; of imagined possible situations, and of the feelings that one would have if . . .'[5]

Wittgenstein's ideas significantly affected the idea of motive and intention – the theme in *Copenhagen*. If we can be certain about *what* someone has done and *why* he or she

has done it, we can be fairly confident in describing the
intention and the action as either a good thing or a bad
thing. That's easy enough. But if we don't know exactly
what that person was doing or why they were doing it – or
to take this one stage further – if we can't be sure that
they knew exactly what they were doing or why they were
doing it, we would have to think a lot harder before
describing the intention or the action as good or bad.
Those questions relate to the epistemology of intention.
They lie at the heart of *Copenhagen*.

  Wittgenstein died in 1951. Two years later his second
masterpiece, *Philosophical Investigations*, was posthumously
published. One Wittgenstein scholar writes: 'His thought
dominated Anglophone philosophy for the next quarter of a
century.'[6] In 1954 Frayn went up to Cambridge. In his
second and third years he read philosophy. The one book
of philosophy that Frayn has published, *Constructions*, pursues
many of the questions that Wittgenstein raises. It discusses
the nature of perceptions, dreams, memories, love, ambition
and belief. It examines these concepts through elegant
discussions of photographs, toy cars, clouds, animals, Punch
and Judy, Robinson Crusoe, masks, alcoholism, audiences
and writing. In a humorous column he wrote for the
Observer Frayn finds himself watching a literary quiz game
on the television. He despairs as he realises how many
books he hasn't read compared to the members of the
panel who appear to have read almost every book that has
been mentioned. His wife cheers him up: 'Anyway, you
know all about all sorts of things they don't. You know
about Wittgenstein, and – well – Wittgenstein . . .'[7]

The playwright's career

When Frayn was a fifteen-year-old schoolboy at Kingston
Grammar School he wrote poetry and stories. He was also
a communist. His enthusiasm for communism was short-
lived, but his interest in Russia and Russian remained.
(Frayn's Chekhov translations have been highly acclaimed.)

Before he went to university he had to do his National
Service. The fifties was the height of the Cold War, when
British foreign policy was dominated by a deep distrust of
the Soviet Union. Frayn went on a course to train as a
Russian interpreter. It was based at Cambridge and the
recruits wore civilian clothes. The playwright Alan Bennett
was on the same course. Frayn and Bennett became close
friends and put on revues together. Frayn also shared a
billet with someone who was passionate about theoretical
physics and his enthusiasm sparked Frayn's interest. 'If you
study philosophy,' Frayn said, 'you have to be interested in
quantum mechanics, because quantum mechanics has so
many philosophical implications, very difficult implications,
for philosophy.'[8]

The day after he completed his National Service he went
to university – back to Cambridge. As an undergraduate he
wrote a column called 'Saturday Sermon' for *Varsity* and
guest-edited an issue of *Granta*. The writer and broadcaster
Bamber Gascoigne was a contemporary. 'He was almost
exactly the same man then as he is now,' Gascoigne
recalled. 'His quality is as a cool observer and he is
interested in seeing life happening and then turning what
he sees either into humour or drama.' Gascoigne's memory
of Frayn touches on a theme that would surface in
Copenhagen. 'He is essentially a thinker and an observer and
if you make too much noise as an observer it kills it as
people start observing you.'[9]

Frayn also wrote the Footlights May Week Revue.
Unfortunately this was the only time the Footlights Revue
didn't go on to the West End. Frayn's disappointment with
the Cambridge Footlights dampened his interest in theatre.
It was only after thirteen years as a journalist and novelist
that he returned to the theatre. His first professional stage
production, *The Two of Us*, was an evening of four short
comedies. In the second of the four, Frayn manages to slip
in a little physics and philosophy. In this one-act play, *The
New Quixote*, Kenneth explains to Gina that he organises his
love life round the principle that nothing is what it seems.

'But it's not just people, you see, Gina. It's everything! It's a general theory for understanding the whole universe! You look at this, and you think, this is a chair. But you look into it more closely and you'll see it's not a chair at all. It's a mass of tiny spinning particles! And what about the particles? Are they really and truly particles? Of course not – they're not particles at all! They're electricity! They're energy! Matter is energy!' 'You're a nut,' replies Gina, 'on top of everything else.'[10]

Frayn had played with scientific and philosophical ideas four years earlier, in his novel *The Russian Interpreter*. There he had raised the problem of reaching any precise measurement of either people or particles. The main character, Manning, has gone on a group expedition to the countryside. In the forest he has been kissed by a beautiful, flirtatious Russian woman called Raya. Manning reflects on what curious organisms human beings are. 'How odd and unfamiliar were the relations between them, like the interactions of half-understood particles beneath the microscope.'[11] The pleasure of the kiss soon mingles with an element of uncertainty. Raya might be a Russian agent. It is a moment that combines three of Frayn's interests: Russia, physics and philosophy.

An idea that concerns both scientists and philosophers is the relationship between the observed and the observer. In physics this is called the Uncertainty or Indeterminacy Principle. In *Copenhagen* Heisenberg explains how a problem arose when what was seen during an experiment didn't match his theory. When an electron was detached from an atom and sent through a cloud chamber it appeared to leave a track. According to quantum mechanics this should not have been possible (p. 65).

In 1927 Heisenberg realised that the track that was visible was not made by the electron but by the collision between the electron and molecules of water vapour. It was the molecules that were leaving the track. 'And that's what we see in the cloud chamber,' Heisenberg says. 'Not a continuous track but a series of glimpses – a series of collisions . . .' (p. 66). By colliding with the electron the molecules also affected the electron's behaviour. This led to one of Heisenberg's major insights: *the instrument of measurement affects that which is being measured.* Heisenberg showed that it wasn't possible to establish the momentum and the position of a particle at the same time.

Frayn uses Heisenberg's Uncertainty Principle in a range of ways in *Copenhagen*. During their wartime meeting both Bohr and Heisenberg know that their conversation is probably being monitored by the Gestapo. When they are in Bohr's house on that September evening their conversation remains circumscribed by the hidden microphone. The observers have changed the behaviour of the observed. On a more general level characters are impossible to describe precisely because they behave differently with different people. In *Constructions* Frayn asks himself why he chooses to be enthusiastic with one person and sceptical with another. He gives the answer that it is the same reason that champagne manufacturers sell dry champagne in England and sweet champagne in America. That's where 'the markets are'.[12]

The hardest person to observe accurately is the one person that we can never see. Ourselves. Any estimation that we make about our own behaviour has to take into account that it is not objective. For this reason our account of our own actions may not necessarily be any more accurate than someone else's account of our actions. As Bohr says about Heisenberg, 'He sees me. He sees Margrethe. He doesn't see himself' (p. 87).

Frayn provides a very funny example of this problem in his novel *Towards the End of the Morning.* A journalist, Dyson, takes part in a discussion programme on TV. Before the show he has a few drinks and during the broadcast he thinks that he is giving a sparkling performance. Later that night he wakes up with an uneasy feeling. The events from the previous evening replay in his mind. In the space of a couple of hours Dyson has gone from thinking his performance was a triumph to realising it was a disaster.

He has swapped one subjective reality for another.[13]

After Cambridge, Frayn joined the newsroom at the *Manchester Guardian*. The cosy atmosphere of newspaper offices in the late-fifties, the rolltop desks, portable typewriters and tea-trolleys, has vanished. The problems of good reporting remain the same today. Frayn's time as a journalist introduces an important theme into his work in general and into *Copenhagen* in particular. This is the subject of language: how the observer chooses to describe the observed. In *Constructions*, Frayn writes, 'Language is not the world talking about itself. Language is you talking to me about the world.'[14]

During the 1960s Frayn had won a reputation as a journalist and novelist. In the mid-1970s he established himself as a playwright. After *The Two of Us* Frayn wrote *The Sandboy*, which flopped. And then, in the space of two years, three full-length plays appeared: *Alphabetical Order* (1975), *Donkeys' Years* (1976) and *Clouds* (1976). The third one directly addresses the subject of journalism. In *Clouds*, a newspaper reporter, Owen, finds to his dismay that he has to travel round Cuba with Mara, a female novelist. Owen explains to Mara how the demands of his job are quite unlike the demands of hers. 'Proper reporting involves getting quotes down accurately. Spelling names right. Checking. Then checking again. Boring, meticulous skills that you don't learn by writing fiction. It also involves coming face to face with the real world, a very muddled and overcrowded place where nothing has its name on it, and everything is somehow the wrong shape to be expressed in language.'[15]

In *Copenhagen* Niels Bohr insists that everything has to be expressed in plain language. 'You know how strongly I believe that we don't do science for ourselves,' Bohr says, 'that we do it so that we can explain to others . . .' (p. 38). 'Plain language, plain language!' Heisenberg reminds Bohr, when Bohr uses the phrase 'indeterminate recoil' (p. 68). Science does not lend itself readily to plain language. Bohr once said that in important questions, one might speak clearly or accurately, but never both, and neither easily.[16]

It is no easier for writers. 'When you have to describe some real thing,' Frayn told an interviewer, 'it always turns out to be hideously complicated. Nothing will tie together. It won't make a story. It won't make a plot. It won't tie up. And that is the difficulty of the world from the point of view of the writer. It's not in words. It's tree-shaped and cloud-shaped and room-shaped. It's not word-shaped.'[17]

After two years on the *Guardian*, Frayn took over its 'Miscellany' column, which appeared three times a week. In 1962 he moved to the *Observer* where he wrote a column for six years. His columns included pastiches of nature notes, election broadcasts and childcare manuals, satires of fashionable attitudes and comic transpositions in which modern manners were placed in an historical context. Frayn's journalism also revealed an affection for the overlooked aspects of everyday life. As he put it, 'the really basic stuff'.[18] For instance, Frayn liked home movies, slides and holiday snapshots. In an article titled 'Private Collections' he praises the 'modesty of snapshots – the fact that they make no claims, imply no principles, demand no reactions'. Frayn quotes an observation of Wittgenstein's from the *Tractatus*: 'The mystical thing is not *how* the world is, but *that* it is.'[19] These snapshots, Frayn writes, show us that 'things are what they are, and that they are significant in themselves, for their own sake'.

Thirty years later Frayn returned to this theme in his novel *Headlong*. The narrator, Martin Clay, tells a neighbour about the book he is writing. His subject is a group of medieval painters in the Netherlands who had been influenced by 'nominalism'. They liked the really basic stuff too. Clay explains that these painters placed tremendous concentration upon 'individual, ungeneralised objects, on things that offer themselves not as indications of abstract ideas, but as themselves, as nothing more nor less than what they are'.[20]

In another *Observer* column titled 'In the Superurbs', Frayn confesses to the reader that 'For a long time now

I've nursed the vague project of writing a guide-book to my native London suburbs'. Frayn has the idea of 'actually *describing* the suburbs, without either laughing at them or moralising about them'.[21] Frayn did make a celebrated documentary about the suburbs. He has a keen sense of *milieu*, the mental atmosphere that thrives in a particular time and place. He has also made documentaries about two cities, Vienna and Berlin, that were hothouses of intellectual, artistic and political thought. In the introduction to *Towards the End of the Morning*, Frayn says that Fleet Street was a place which was also 'a way of life with its own style and philosophy'.

It is characteristic that in *Copenhagen*, as in his documentaries, Frayn's instinct is to describe the complexity of the subject rather than to moralise about it. After *Copenhagen* had opened in London and on Broadway, Frayn gave a lecture to the Royal Society in London. 'I didn't really want to get into the morality of atomic weapons,' he told his audience, 'I wanted to get into the question of how we know why we do what we do. We can't come to any moral judgements of people or ourselves until we can make some estimation of motivations. The difficulties of doing this points to a fundamental difficulty in making moral judgements.'[22]

To make some estimation of motive you need to know the facts and people frequently disagree about facts. In *Copenhagen* Margrethe challenges Bohr about the way that he remembers the past. Margrethe thinks he turns it into a story: 'it all falls into place, it all has a beginning and a middle and an end.' When her memory takes her back, what she sees is confusion, rage, jealousy, tears and 'no one knowing what things mean or which way they're going to go' (p. 73). For Margrethe, the sheer amount going on was appalling. This is a major theme in Frayn's work. The first entry in his book of philosophy, *Constructions*, states it clearly. It is also reproduced in large type on the book's back cover.

[1] The complexity of the universe is beyond expression in any possible notation.

> Lift up your eyes. Not even what you see before you can ever be
> fully expressed.
> Close your eyes. Not even what you see now . . .

The point is, there's just so much out there. The way we
deal with this overabundance is to filter, classify, narrate,
organise, arrange, prioritise and label. It's a full-time job.
As Lucy, the resident librarian in *Alphabetical Order*, says,
'I'm worn out with the sheer hard labour of seeing any
sense in anything.'[23]

There is a philosophical theory about the nature of facts,
developed by Bertrand Russell and Wittgenstein, called the
doctrine of logical atomism. In this theory everything gets
broken down to its irreducible constituents. The empirical
essence of this theory is stated by Wittgenstein in the first
proposition of the *Tractatus*: 'The world is everything that is
the case.' In *Alphabetical Order* a rumpled, erudite journalist,
John, visits the library and challenges this idea. Newspapers
appear every day. Readers are presented with more events,
more stories, more facts. 'At each moment more and more
is the case, so that if the world is everything which is the
case, then the world is in a state of continuous expansion,
or perhaps, more properly in a state of continuously
increasing logical density.'[24]

A newspaper is one way we control the flow of
experience. Memory is another. Frayn's next play, *Donkeys'
Years* takes place on an Old Boys' reunion at an Oxbridge
College. It is a companion piece to *Alphabetical Order*: one
deals with how we consciously interpret the world, the
other with how we unconsciously interpret it. In *Donkeys'
Years* men in their forties return to the scene of their
student days, drink vintage port and recall their youth.
They remember events as if it were yesterday. The MP,
Christopher Headingley, says, 'I feel as if I'd never been
away.'[25] The way that the past and the present coexist is a
theme in *Copenhagen*:

> **Bohr** A curious sort of diary memory is.
> **Heisenberg** You open the pages, and all the neat headings and

tidy jottings dissolve around you.

Bohr   You step through the pages into the months and days themselves.

Margrethe   The past becomes the present inside your head. (p. 6)

Memory can be unreliable as it skips, selects and blurs. An event's significance is not reflected in the quality or quantity of what is remembered. Our memories can only be partial recollections of what one person thought was happening. In *Clouds* the journalist and the novelist travel round Cuba with an American academic and a local guide. During the day they bump along dusty tracks looking at sugar mills and fertiliser plants. In the evenings the sound of typewriters mixes with the sound of cicadas. The guide presents one version of Cuba, Owen and Mara write up two others. They are both writing pieces for rival Sunday supplements. (These were the days when there were only two Sunday supplements.) Owen suggests that they find some way of dividing up the material between them. Mara sees no need: 'The clouds you see aren't the clouds I see.'[26]

When Heisenberg meets Bohr in September 1941 he has to be very careful about what he says in case their conversation is monitored. 'I think you must assume that you and I aren't the only people who hear what's said in this house.' They go out for a walk. They still can't be sure that they won't be overheard. Heisenberg has to speak to Bohr that evening about an extraordinarily delicate and dangerous matter. To discuss nuclear research was an act of treason. So he phrases what he says in a tantalisingly vague way. 'I didn't say anything about anything!' says Heisenberg. 'Not in so many words. I couldn't!' (p. 36). In effect, he presents Bohr with something distinctly cloudy. The tragedy is that they do not see the same cloud.

Frayn's plays have plenty of empty spaces. There is the blue sky in *Clouds*. 'Cuba' reads the opening stage direction in *Clouds*. 'Or, at any rate, an empty blue sky.' There are the blank pages that roll through Owen's and Mara's typewriters and the blank pages in *Copenhagen* on which the

three characters try to work out what happened. 'One
more draft, yes?' (p. 86). There is the empty room in
Frayn's play *Here*. The opening stage direction reads 'bare
floor, bare walls, no furniture'. This is the room which a
youngish couple, Cath and Phil, have to decide whether or
not to rent. If they choose it, this is where their lives will
unfold. Emptiness stimulates the imagination. In *Benefactors*
the architect, David, tells his neighbour about the best part
of his job, 'I'll tell you what's really magical. A bare
building site . . . Amazing emptiness, like the emptiness of a
conjuror's hat, because you know that marvels will come
out of it.'[27] A cloudless sky, a blank page, a bare building
site, an empty room and a conjuror's hat: these are all full
of possibilities. They are points of departure. In the final
line of *Clouds* Mara looks up at the sky and sees a new
beginning: 'Not a cloud in sight. Pure light. Pure
emptiness. Everything.'

These empty spaces present a challenge to Frayn's
characters, who strive to fill them. In *Benefactors* David is
designing two tower blocks. He has been persisting with
this frustrating building project in the face of considerable
opposition. 'Because if I can get these two towers up that
will be something fixed. Two pieces of space will have an
outline . . . They won't melt into different shapes.'[28] His
work as an architect allows him to shape the world around
him. Frayn has written about librarians in *Alphabetical Order*,
academics in *Donkeys' Years*, journalists in *Clouds*, salesmen in
Make and Break, actors in *Noises Off*, an architect in *Benefactors*
and free-speech activists in *Now You Know*. 'I like to write
about people doing real jobs,' he said in an interview. 'Too
many dramatists write about characters who are idling,
whose engines are not connected to the road.'[29]

These real jobs share a common quality. They all
involve interpreting the world and giving it a shape. Take
the example of the salesman. He isn't selling a product,
he is selling the perception of a product. 'These are not
brushes, madam, they're eco-friendly, fuel-efficient cleansing
tools.'[30] If there is a single group that, perhaps more than

any other, has changed the way the modern world is interpreted and shaped, it is scientists: the ones doing the real jobs in *Copenhagen*.

Background to the play

Imagine a city of 250,000 people. On a clear sunny August morning the city's inhabitants are finishing breakfast, glancing at the paper, hurrying out of the home to go to work or to school. It is nearly 8.15. A minute later a pinkish light bursts in the sky and more than half the city is destroyed. Eighty thousand people are killed instantly. Tens of thousands more die from the effects of the explosion. Two minutes later, the pilot of the plane that has dropped the bomb looks down from 33,000 feet. 'Where before there had been a city,' he recalled, 'with distinctive houses, buildings and everything that you could see from our altitude, now you couldn't see anything except a black boiling debris down below.'[31]

It is a grim irony that the exhilarating discoveries made by physicists in the first four decades of the twentieth century led to Hiroshima on 6 August 1945. The uranium 235 fission bomb that exploded over the eighth largest city in Japan had the impact of 20,000 tons of TNT. The fireball was almost 110 yards in diameter. Two days later, Radio Tokyo ended its first full report by saying that the United States had used methods which 'have surpassed in their hideous cruelty those of Genghis Khan'.[32] The Americans had only recently got hold of the method of 'hideous cruelty' that would end the war. If a handful of physicists had been working for other countries, or the physicists in other countries had made other calculations, this bomb might have been in other hands and have exploded over other cities. 'London, presumably,' as Bohr says to Heisenberg, 'if you'd had it in time' (p. 84).

How did the Americans get there first? The quickest answer takes us back two and a half years to the desert of New Mexico, USA. In the early 1940s a boys' private school was converted into a massive science laboratory. The location had been chosen because it was sparsely populated, it was away from the sea, and it had a reasonable year-round climate. This was to be the main part of a massive industrial, technical and scientific programme called the Manhattan Project. The school became the centre for the development of the bomb. In the early forties Los Alamos became a self-contained town with barbers' shops, laundries and gas stations. Carpenters, metalworkers and plumbers moved in. In February 1943 the scientists arrived. Many were refugees from Nazi Germany. As Margrethe says, 'The Germans drive out most of their best physicists because they're Jews. America and Britain give them sanctuary. Now it turns out that this might offer the Allies a hope of salvation' (p. 45). The influx of Jewish scientists from Germany has been called 'Hitler's Gift'. The converted school was filled with an extraordinary intellectual buzz. One scientist spoke of Los Alamos as having 'a spirit of Athens, of Plato'.[33] It was an academy with a daunting sense of purpose. This was spelt out in one group of lectures collected in *The Los Alamos Primer*. 'The object of the project is to produce a practical military weapon in the form of a bomb. . .'[34] Many scientists went to Los Alamos with the specific aim of working on a bomb that would defeat Hitler. Regrettably, it was never going to be possible to drop an atom bomb on a single person. After Niels Bohr escaped from Denmark in 1943 he also went to work at Los Alamos. Heisenberg challenges him that the plan was to drop an atom bomb on the Germans. 'You were dropping it on anyone who was in reach . . . my fellow-countrymen. My wife. My children. That was the intention. Yes?' Bohr replies, 'That was the intention' (p. 43).

This aim ceased on 30 April 1945 when Hitler committed suicide. On 7 May Germany surrendered and the war in Europe was over. But that was only half of the war. As one historian neatly summarises it: 'Two separate wars made up the "Second World War": a European war and a Far Eastern war. After 1941 the United States and the United Kingdom took part in both, while their enemies waged separate wars.'[35] With Germany's surrender, all attention switched to the Far East.

Before Hitler's suicide a number of Allied scientists had signed a petition that was sent to the American President asking that the atomic bomb never be used. The petition was disregarded. The scientists were not in control of their research. Senior Allied strategists had known for several years that they would need the bomb to defeat Japan and to defy Russia. The ethics of bombing had changed during the six years of the war from an early position, when it was considered wrong to bomb civilians or private property, to a later position, when German and Japanese cities were mercilessly bombed in an attempt to destroy each nation's morale. On 16 July, at the Trinity site in New Mexico, the Los Alamos scientists successfully exploded the first atom bomb. The explosion could be seen from 180 miles away. Its significance was not lost on those present. The director of the test, Kenneth Bainbridge, said, 'Now we're all sons of bitches.' The man in charge of the Los Alamos project, J. Robert Oppenheimer, quoted from *Bhagavad-Gita*, 'I am become Death, destroyer of Worlds.'[36] Its significance was not lost either on those who soon heard about it. The American President Harry S. Truman noted in his diary, 'It seems to be the most terrible thing ever discovered, but it can be made the most useful.'[37]

The Potsdam Conference took place over the next fortnight. Churchill, Truman and Stalin were meeting to discuss plans for the post-war world. Churchill noticed a decisive change in the American President's manner. When Churchill learnt of the test in New Mexico he realised the reason for Truman's behaviour. 'He told the Russians just where they got off,' Churchill observed, 'and generally bossed the meeting.'[38] America had seen the future. Three weeks after the test explosion, the first atomic bomb was dropped on Hiroshima. Three days later, a second bomb was dropped on Nagasaki. Japan surrendered immediately.

The bombs ended the war and changed the way post-war generations perceived the world.

In Britain, 6 August was a bank holiday. It had been a day of sunshine and thunderstorms. A record crowd at Lords had seen Australia make 273 for 5 wickets.[39] The nine o'clock news on the BBC began: 'Here is the news. It's dominated by a tremendous achievement of Allied scientists – the production of the atomic bomb.' The announcer went on to say, 'There's no news yet of what devastation was caused.' Among those listening to the broadcast was a group of German scientists. They had been captured at the end of the war and spirited back to Britain to keep them out of the hands of the Russians. They were kept as detainees in Farm Hall, a country house near Cambridge. This group included Nobel prizewinners, Nazis and non-Nazis. The scientists were stunned by the announcement on the BBC. When they first heard the news they thought it was a hoax. 'We sit up half the night,' Heisenberg tells Bohr, 'talking about it, trying to take it in. We're all literally in shock.' (p. 46).

What these scientists didn't realise was that their conversations were recorded. The British secret service had installed microphones in the rooms and transcripts of the conversations were regularly typed up and sent to officials in London and Washington. Nearly fifty years later the Public Record Office in Kew released the transcripts. It was now possible to follow the scientists' thoughts as they discussed how an atom bomb might be built. The transcripts made clear exactly how close the German scientists had got to building an atom bomb. They were nowhere near. The transcripts raise a number of questions. Did the Germans not build the bomb because they thought it could not be done or because they tried to build it and failed? Or did they refrain from making the attempt? This last question raises two further ones. Did they consciously sabotage any efforts to build the bomb or did they merely lack the zeal to pursue the science because, subconsciously, they didn't want to?

Thomas Powers, the author of a Pulitzer Prize-winning
book about the CIA as well as books that cover the
Vietnam War and National Security, was one of the first
historians to make use of the Farm Hall transcripts. In
1993 he published *Heisenberg's War: The Secret History of the
German Bomb*. Powers was not the first person to write about
Heisenberg, but he emerged as one of the most
sympathetic. He set out to answer the question: why had
Nazi Germany failed to build an atom bomb? In 1939, the
Germans had been well ahead. 'Nuclear fission had been
discovered in Germany,' Powers wrote, 'Europe's only
uranium mines were controlled by Germany, and in May
1940 German armies seized the world's only heavy-water
plant, in Norway.'[40] According to Heisenberg's biographer,
David Cassidy, 'The German research effort seemed poised
for early success in the autumn of 1941.' Heisenberg
himself said, 'It was from September 1941 that we saw an
open road ahead of us, leading to the atom bomb.'[41] What
happened?

Frayn read Powers' 'wonderful' book soon after it was
published and came across the story of Heisenberg's trip to
Copenhagen to meet Bohr. Accounts of this visit had
appeared in other books, but Frayn read about it here.
'The problem is that there is no agreement about what was
actually said,'[42] Powers writes, adding four pages later, 'The
two versions of the conversation reported that night . . .
could hardly have been more different.' The exact purpose
of Heisenberg's visit has never been clear. Powers'
description of the meeting appealed to Frayn for its
philosophical implications. 'I immediately thought that this
crystallises the whole problem of knowing why people do
what they do,' Frayn said, 'because there is this very
practical question about a really quite striking event.'[43]

Heisenberg was a patriot, he was not a Nazi. He knew
that it would be disastrous to develop a bomb that Hitler
could use. He also knew that the Americans might be
driven to invent the bomb out of fear that the Germans
would get there first. It was his colleague Carl Friedrich

von Weizsäcker who suggested that Heisenberg visit his old mentor, Niels Bohr, and discuss the situation. Heisenberg had a 'vague hope' that the international community of scientists might agree to halt the development of the atomic bomb. Two years earlier his plan would have stood a better chance. As Heisenberg later said, 'In the summer of 1939, twelve people might still have been able, by coming to mutual agreement, to prevent the construction of atomic bombs.'[44]

On Monday 15 September 1941 Heisenberg arrived in Copenhagen. He had a lecture to give on the Friday evening. On Wednesday night he met – very probably went to dinner – with Bohr. It was a fraught occasion. In the two chapters in *Heisenberg's War* that deal with this event Powers shows how an ambition of far-reaching significance foundered because neither person began to understand the other. Bohr's suspicion of Heisenberg's motives prevented him from seeing Heisenberg's point of view. Heisenberg's underestimation of Bohr's anti-Nazi feeling made conversation almost impossible.

The situation was remarkable: a man attempts to halt the development of the atom bomb and fails because he cannot make himself understood to a highly intelligent man who knows him extremely well. An unbridgeable gap existed between the reason Heisenberg thought he was making the visit and the reason Bohr thought Heisenberg was making the visit. This is the psychological confusion at the heart of Powers' description. It is a story about indeterminacy in which the main character is the man who invented the Principle of Indeterminacy. 'If I hadn't been interested in indeterminacy,' Frayn recalled, 'and hadn't been interested in human motivation, it probably wouldn't have helped to have read that story.'[45]

What did Heisenberg hope to achieve from this meeting? It was never clear. Perhaps he wanted Bohr to acknowledge that the physics was possible. Or he wanted Bohr to accept that Heisenberg was right to continue working on the project. Or he wanted Bohr to speak to the scientists working for the Allies. Or he simply wanted Bohr's absolution. No one knows. No one knows if Heisenberg really knew. It was the situation's opaqueness that appealed to Frayn. 'It suggested a way of coming at various problems I had been thinking about for many years in human motivation,' Frayn said. 'Why people do what they do. Why one does what one does oneself.'[46] For Frayn, reading Powers' book had been a piece of luck. But luck itself has its own rationale. As Frayn told one interviewer, 'All luck is usually a combination of external circumstance and some sort of internal situation.'[47]

The advances in physics had created many problems for philosophers. But the advances in physics also created many philosophical problems for physicists as they found themselves facing extraordinary ethical dilemmas. 'It is one of the great ironies of nuclear physics,' Frayn told an interviewer, 'that when it began, it was a subject, like theology or Egyptology, with no practical application. It's almost impossible to imagine your way back to that world: it's like the story of the Garden of Eden.'[48]

Scientists had belonged to a remarkably open international community. They studied in each other's countries. They attended conferences, published papers and followed up on each other's breakthroughs. Niels Bohr catches this innocence early in *Copenhagen*: 'Heisenberg is a theoretical physicist. I don't think anyone has yet discovered a way you can use theoretical physics to kill people' (p. 10). Physics had always attracted highly competitive people. Bohr and Heisenberg were highly competitive about most things: from skiing and table-tennis to poker. Physics could never have made the progress that it did if physicists had not been intensely aware of each other's work. Before the war the prize they were after was the Nobel. During the war, the prize they were after was victory. All the rules had changed.

When Fritz Strassmann and Otto Hahn achieved fission in 1939 they published the breakthrough in the journal *Nature*. The screenwriter Bruce Robinson, who wrote *The*

Killing Fields and *Withnail and I*, also wrote the screenplay
Fat Man and Little Boy about the American atomic
programme. 'If you're about to start a war,' says Robinson,
'and you're looking for a nuclear weapon it's not too smart
to put what you've discovered in an international science
magazine.'[49] When the war broke out, scientists realised
that science, which had always been based on the speedy
dissemination of knowledge, had now become steeped in
secrecy. 'You discover penicillin and within five minutes the
information is everywhere,' says Robinson. 'It isn't like that
any more, and The Bomb is one of the reasons it isn't.
That's where all this stuff started, keeping discoveries
secret.'[50]

Play *v.* novel

Frayn is often asked how he decides if an idea is a play or
a novel. The answer he gives in the Introduction to *Plays: 3*
is that 'the matter decides itself'. In a novel the reader has
access to the private and unspoken thoughts of the
characters. In a play, Frayn writes, 'One sees only as much
of each person as he or she chooses to reveal – or fails to
keep concealed.' In an interview Frayn states this principle
from another angle. 'I think the crucial difference is that
it's very natural in the novel to be inside the head of a
character, or all the characters if you like. In the theatre,
it's most natural to be outside the head of the characters.
Again, you can have characters talk about their thoughts,
soliloquise, address the audience directly. But the natural
mode of theatre is dialogue.'[51] Frayn knew *Copenhagen*
needed an audience. It was essential to the story, to the
way he wanted to tell it, and to the answer to its riddle.
One clue to the motive behind Heisenberg's visit can be
found in *Constructions*, where Frayn wrote: 'You're a cloud,
and you rely on me to see a face in you.'[52]

   At first Frayn had thought of writing about the scientists
while they were detained and closely monitored at Farm
Hall. 'The story of Farm Hall is another complete play in

itself' (see Postscript, p. 115). He also thought of having
other actors playing characters who were listening to the
three characters when they were meeting in Copenhagen in
1941. 'I knew that both men would probably be under
surveillance by the Gestapo, and Heisenberg was certainly
under surveillance by British Intelligence later on. So I
thought I would have the Gestapo and the British
Intelligence listen in on the conversations and tell the
audience what was going on. But then gradually I thought
"do we need these people? Do we need these extras just
sitting in in the darkness listening to what's happening.
We've got an audience already, why not use them?" So in
the end that's what I've done. I've made the audience who
sat in the theatre the audience for the conversations of
Bohr and Heisenberg.'[53]

In 1990 Frayn had written *Look Look*, a play about an
audience. The stage showed the cross-section of the stalls,
with a dozen members of the audience, an usherette and a
playwright watching the playwright's play. 'Really what
Copenhagen is about is what *Look Look* is about,' Frayn told
me. 'It's about audiences. It's why in *Copenhagen* we have
the audience right around the stage. To know what you're
thinking yourself, you need a reaction from other people.
That's why, in the end, Heisenberg goes to Copenhagen.
To have an audience.'[54]

Look Look offers its own stark example of the gap between
what one group thinks it is doing and what another group
makes of it. 'I remember with *Look Look*,' Frayn said,
'everyone in rehearsals thought it was wonderful. Michael
Codron [the producer] came to the last run-through in the
rehearsal room and I said, "What notes have you got?" He
always has lots of scratchy notes. And he said, "None.
Marvellous. Wonderful." And we got in front of the first
preview audience at the Aldwych and we all knew it was
dead. There was no way we were ever going to breathe life
into that corpse.'

After six weeks' rehearsing *Copenhagen* the cast at the
National were saying that what they needed now was an

audience. They needed to find out what it was they were doing. 'That's just what the play's about!' Frayn told the *Copenhagen* cast. 'Heisenberg was seeking an informed sympathetic audience, for whom he had done plays before, as it were. To try out this play.'[55]

Heisenberg and the Nazis

Heisenberg's biographer, David Cassidy, posed a large and testing question about Heisenberg's behaviour before and during the war:

> How was it possible that Werner Heisenberg, one of the most gifted of modern physicists, a man educated in the finest tradition of Western culture, who was neither a Nazi nor a Nazi supporter, how was it possible that such a man would not only choose to remain in National Socialist Germany for its entire twelve years of existence, but also actively seek a prominent academic position in Berlin at the height of the war, a position that included the scientific directorship of nuclear fission research for the German Army at war?[56]

It's a question, obviously, that is asked in hindsight. When considering Heisenberg's actions we have to remember to distinguish between what he knew at the time and the full horrors of the Nazi regime that emerged at the end of the war. We also need to remember what he knew and what he might have been able to do about what he knew. There was always the hope, among many Germans, that the virulent anti-semitism would subside, that the Hitler hysteria would blow over, or that Hitler would be deposed or assassinated. (There were thirty-one attempts on Hitler's life.) The position for many 'good Germans' was that they wanted Germany to win the war and Hitler to lose it. During this period their loyalties were torn. 'It would be another easy mistake to make,' says Heisenberg in *Copenhagen*, 'to think that one loved one's country less because it happened to be in the wrong' (p. 42).

But we also have to remember the nature of the events

that were unfolding in Germany in the 1930s and 1940s. Heisenberg would certainly have witnessed the national boycott of all Jewish shops on 1 April 1933. He would have known about the burning of hundreds of thousands of 'un-German' books (including ones by Einstein, Freud and Thomas Mann) in thirty cities around Germany on 10 May 1933. He would have known about the introduction of the Nuremberg Laws, which relegated Jews to second-class citizenship on 15 September 1935. He would have known about the looting of 7,000 Jewish shops, the burning of hundreds of synagogues and the arrest of 20,000 Jews on Kristallnacht, the night of broken glass, on 9 November 1938.

Heisenberg knew that his Jewish colleagues were barred from posts. Many colleagues had left the country. As the war progressed he knew that colleagues and relatives of colleagues had been sent to concentration camps. During his captivity in Farm Hall after the war ended he admitted this to another of the detainees. Yet Heisenberg still went on trips abroad, as a cultural ambassador for his country, and worked as scientific director of nuclear fission research. By any standards he was severely compromised.

Some distinguished Germans actively endorsed the efforts of the Nazis. In May 1933 Germany's most distinguished philosopher, Martin Heidegger, spoke encouragingly of German students committing themselves to the service of the *völkisch* state. In June 1934 Hitler ordered the murder of his enemies within the Nazi party in the 'Night of the Long Knives'. A law was subsequently issued that legitimised the murders. The country's leading constitutional lawyer, Carl Schmitt, published an article in support of these steps that was (unbelievably) titled 'The Führer Protects the Law'.

There were many prominent figures in German cultural life who never endorsed the Nazis' actions. The charge that is still made against these figures is that they lent legitimacy to the Nazi regime by not leaving the country or actively opposing it. For instance, in his biography of Hitler, Ian

Kershaw writes that the composer Richard Strauss and the conductor Wilhelm Furtwängler 'continued to bestow distinction on German achievements in music'.[57]

The issue of how educated, apparently 'decent' Germans carried on working in Nazi Germany has become a subject of increasing fascination for British dramatists. Their interest in these grey areas of ambiguity, contradiction and divided loyalty has been fuelled by substantial new works of scholarship. Michael Burleigh's recent book *The Third Reich* takes as its central theme 'this assault on decency'. In his introduction Burleigh notes 'a growing interest in the choices made by individuals of the time, with compelling new biographies of Heidegger, Heisenberg or Speer, among the major figures'.[58] Burleigh mentions Gitta Sereny's biography of *Albert Speer: His Battle with Truth* and Powers' *Heisenberg's War*. David Edgar's play *Albert Speer* is based on Sereny's book, which also inspired Harold Pinter's play *Ashes to Ashes*. Powers' book on Heisenberg inspired *Copenhagen*. Burleigh also cites two important new biographies about Heidegger. Perhaps the next play about the moral choices made by a brilliant German in the thirties will centre on this controversial philosopher.

The question that each of these subjects poses is twofold. One: what exactly did he do? Two: what would we have done? Plays do not set out to present characters as either good examples that we should emulate or bad examples that we should avoid. In his Afterword to *Albert Speer* David Edgar writes that the response most great drama demands of us is neither 'yes, please' nor 'no thanks' but 'you too?'. It is a version of 'there but for the grace of God go I'.[59] As we watch these characters on stage we identify with their predicaments. Most of us will never have to face moral choices of this magnitude. It is unlikely that most of us would behave as heroes. The chances are that we would look for a compromise, a way out, a balance between what we ought to do and what we think we can do. As Frayn writes about Heisenberg, 'Why shouldn't he try to juggle principle and expediency, as we all do?' (p. 138).

The subject of the 'good German' is explicitly explored in C. P. Taylor's play *Good*, where we see an ostensibly decent man, Halder, an academic, husband, father – gradually become a Nazi. *Good* explores, in Taylor's words 'how a "good" man gets caught up in the nightmare of the Third Reich'.[60] The strength of the play lies in making the gradual shifts from an understandable position to an utterly malign one appear barely perceptible.

The architect Albert Speer was as active in promoting Hitler's cause as it was possible to be. Even he claimed not to know what exactly was going on. David Edgar's play *Albert Speer* shows how Hitler's favourite architect, and later his Minister of Armaments, managed to conceal from himself the full horror of what was happening in his country. Speer would see crowds of people waiting for evacuation on the station platform. 'But he'd never speculated,' says Pastor Casalis, who became his confessor figure, 'what would happen to them at the other end.'[61] In the play's climax Speer confronts the possibility that what he had always believed about his own life (that he never knew what was going on) was a lie. Speer says, 'If I "turned away", I knew.'[62]

There was a strong desire not to know: to keep your head down, protect your family, career, and – when possible – help colleagues. In Ronald Harwood's play *Taking Sides*, Furtwängler, conductor of the Berlin Philharmonic Orchestra, is cross-examined immediately after the war. Furtwängler's compromises were not untypical. He helped Jewish members of his orchestra. He also conducted at Hitler's birthday. His interrogator after the war is a tough, sceptical American officer. Major Steve Arnold challenges Furtwängler about why he stayed in Germany at all and he answers that he could not leave his country in her deepest misery. 'After all, I am a German. I – I stayed in my homeland. Is that my sin in your eyes?'[63]

In *Copenhagen* Heisenberg explains his patriotism to Bohr. 'Germany is where I was born,' he says. 'Germany is where I became what I am. Germany is all the faces of my childhood . . . Germany is my widowed mother and my impossible brother. Germany is my wife. Germany is our children' (p. 42). Heisenberg was not a Nazi sympathiser. He had been attacked as a 'white Jew' for his teaching of theoretical physics and had been interrogated by the SS. 'He was a rather romantically patriotic German,' Frayn explained in an interview, 'and that seems to me to be no less acceptable than to be a romantically patriotic Englishman or American. There are moral drawbacks in all those cases, and for Germans in the Nazi period to find any decent way to behave was very, very difficult.'[64]

Frayn discusses in the postscripts to *Copenhagen* the views of a number of scholars who take exception to his version of Heisenberg. Professor Paul Lawrence Rose has complained about 'subtle revisionism' in the 'denigration' of Bohr and the 'exalting' of Heisenberg (p. 133). Frayn's position is humane in that it acknowledges the extent of the predicament facing Germans during this period. 'I am astonished by the ease with which British and American commentators have condemned him,' Frayn said. 'People who were never called upon to make any great moral decisions in their life find it so easy to condemn Heisenberg for not taking a heroic stand. I think you can admire people who are heroes, but you can't *require* people to be heroes – otherwise there's no point in admiring them when they *are* heroic.'[65]

To approach *Copenhagen* as a play that asks us to give either the thumbs-up or the thumbs-down to Heisenberg is to miss many of the levels on which it operates. It does not deny the need for moral judgement. But Frayn's primary interest is in describing what happened. That has to come first. 'I am not making a case either for or against Heisenberg,' Frayn said. 'What I'm saying is that it is extremely difficult to know what his motivation was and this is an example of what applies to all human motivation – this difficulty of knowing why people do what they do.'[66]

This is, finally, the point where Frayn's professional interest in philosophy intersects with his lay interest in physics. In *Copenhagen* he shows that there is a theoretical barrier beyond which it is impossible to know precisely how a particle is behaving. You can only see it from one point of view at a time. In the same way we can only understand human actions from individual perspectives. Those who have disagreed with Frayn's portrayal of Heisenberg, for instance, do not agree with each other about how Heisenberg should be portrayed.

The best answer that the play gives, as to why Heisenberg made that trip to Copenhagen, was that he wanted to see his own reflection. 'We can understand many complex things,' Frayn had written twenty years before in *Constructions*, 'but not our own complexity!'[67] Heisenberg wanted to know what it was he was doing by talking it through with Bohr. But perhaps, in one final twist, he wouldn't really have wanted to find out what it was that he was doing. In one of the most important speeches of the play Margrethe says to Bohr:

> That was the last and greatest demand that Heisenberg made on his friendship with you. To be understood when he couldn't understand himself. And that was the last and greatest act of friendship for Heisenberg that you performed in return. To leave him misunderstood. (p. 89)

The characters

The emotional currents between the three characters in *Copenhagen* give the play its questing energy. They are not debating a dry academic question. The characters have something to prove to one another. The central relationship in *Copenhagen* is the complex one between Bohr and Heisenberg, which resembles that of a father and son. As with many father–son relationships there is a shift in power. These two characters are well-contrasted. Heisenberg often led the way, working at great speed. Bohr followed, making sure the ideas worked. The contrast can be seen in the way they skied. Heisenberg hurtled down slopes at breakneck speed. Bohr went so slowly he nearly ground to a halt. In the fable, one would be the tortoise, the other the hare. Bohr's wife, Margrethe, injects a strong sense of conflict into the trio. She supports her husband against his protégé. Her presence ensures that these conflicts are made explicit.

Werner Heisenberg (1901–76)
German theoretical physicist. His childhood in Munich ended with the outbreak of the First World War. As a schoolboy Heisenberg had to crawl through enemy lines to scavenge for food for his family. When he was twenty he met Niels Bohr at Göttingen. Bohr was one of the most celebrated physicists in the world. Heisenberg was the 'cheeky young pup' who jumped up at the end of a lecture that Bohr had given and told Bohr that his mathematics was wrong. That same afternoon Bohr and Heisenberg went for the first of many walks. On the walk Bohr told Heisenberg that *atoms were not things*. This news, Heisenberg said, was the start of his real scientific career. Heisenberg completed his doctorate when he was twenty-two and went to join Bohr in Copenhagen. At this point Heisenberg was shy, arrogant and anxious to be loved. After a year Heisenberg had invented quantum mechanics. After another year he had come up with the Principle of Uncertainty. The year after that Heisenberg left Copenhagen to take up the professorship at Leipzig. He was twenty-six – the youngest full professor in Germany. In 1932 he was awarded the Nobel Prize for Physics. Five years later he met Elisabeth Schumacher, got engaged to her within two weeks, and married her within three months. (They would have seven children.) That same year Heisenberg was viciously attacked in an SS magazine, which called him a 'white Jew' for teaching relativity. The SS interrogated him in their basement headquarters at the Prinz-Albrecht-Strasse. It took a year for his name to be cleared. He was

warned not to mention Einstein in his lectures. Before the
Second World War broke out Heisenberg turned down job
offers in America. During the war he was put in charge of
the German nuclear reactor programme.

In September 1941, when the meeting in *Copenhagen* takes
place, Heisenberg was nearly forty. The humble assistant
had become a middle-aged professor. He was the leading
scientist in a nation that had conquered most of Europe
('our tanks are almost at Moscow'). What Heisenberg had
to say to Bohr that night was treasonable and could have
led to his execution. Nine months later Heisenberg had a
meeting with Albert Speer, the Minister of Armaments, in
which he convinced Speer that an atom bomb could not be
produced before the end of the war. As the Allies' bombing
of German cities increased, Heisenberg witnessed terrible
scenes in Berlin, with people burning to death in the street.
He left Berlin, taking his scientific equipment south, to a
little village, Haigerloch, in the Swabian Jura. In the final
weeks of the war he managed to escape shooting as a
'deserter' by offering an SS officer a packet of cigarettes. In
April 1945 he was captured by the Allies and taken to
Farm Hall near Cambridge as a detainee. In early August,
while still a detainee, he heard on the BBC the news about
the atom bomb. After the war, Heisenberg faced thirty
years of reproach and hostility from scientists around the
world. He visited Bohr in Copenhagen in 1947. It became
clear that their friendship was over. Heisenberg revisited
America in 1949. Many physicists refused to shake his
hand.

Heisenberg was a patriot. He had wanted to save the
honour of German science. He never claimed to be a hero.
(At times, during the war, he showed considerable courage.)
He had a restless combative nature. He took little pleasure
in paradoxes and contradictions. He sailed, skied fast and
played the piano. (He could play chess without a
chessboard.) In *Celia's Secret* Frayn writes that Matthew
Marsh, who originated the role of Heisenberg, had

totally 'embodied the ambiguity and deviousness of Heisenberg'.[68]

Niels Bohr (1885–1962)
Denmark's leading theoretical physicist. He was half-Jewish. Bohr inspired love. He was a father-like figure to many younger physicists. (His pupils called him 'the Pope' behind his back.) Modern atomic physics began in 1913 when Bohr realised that quantum theory applied to matter as well as energy. He was thirty-eight when he started his three-year collaboration with the young Heisenberg. By 1941, when Heisenberg visited Bohr in Copenhagen, Denmark was occupied by Germany and Bohr was under surveillance. Bohr escaped from Denmark in 1943, crawling along the beach in the darkness on his hands and knees. A fishing boat took him across the Sound as two freighters arrived with orders to ship the Jewish population east. He had escaped the Holocaust. Bohr went to America and worked on the Allies' atomic bomb programme at Los Alamos. Specifically, he worked on the trigger for the Nagasaki bomb. 'My small but helpful part in the deaths of a hundred thousand people' (p. 91).

Bohr sailed, skied (slowly) and was highly competitive. Frayn shows his diplomatic manner ('Not to disagree, but', p. 25). But Bohr can also appear aggressive, as he prowls up and down demanding answers to questions. His sheer persistence had – at separate times – reduced Heisenberg and Bohr's wife, Margrethe, to tears. When the physicist Erwin Schrödinger came to stay Schrödinger had to retire to bed saying that he was ill. Bohr loved paradoxes and contradictions. He believed that science has to be expressed in plain language. Thomas Powers describes Bohr as 'searching, one painful word at a time, for some way to describe the essential strangeness of the subatomic world'.[69] Bohr defined an expert as someone who has made every conceivable mistake within a very narrow field. In *Celia's Secret* Frayn praised David Burke, the actor who originated the role of Bohr, for his incarnation of 'percipience and innocence, of toughness and lovability'.[70]

Margrethe Bohr (1890–1984)
Danish wife of Niels Bohr and his intimate companion. Margrethe never entirely liked Heisenberg. ('We had sons of our own' p.6.) Two of her six children died young. Christian, the firstborn, died in 1934 when he was out sailing with his father. The youngest, Harald, was incapacitated by a disease (thought by Bohr's biographer Abraham Pais to be meningitis), spent his life in institutions, and died aged about ten. Margrethe had no scientific training. Her knowledge, for instance, of complementarity came from typing out her husband's work again and again. In the play Margrethe thinks of herself as unfailingly courteous, unchangingly guarded. But she has a tendency to make everything personal. She is the audience's representative. Without her, the conversation would quickly become an exchange conducted in scientific shorthand between two experts. Margrethe also represents the many people who took a hostile view towards Heisenberg. In *Copenhagen* Margrethe is a severe, sceptical antagonist. She is outspoken in her criticisms. In real life, it must be said, she has been remembered as 'the perfect hostess'.[71]

The play in production

When *Copenhagen* opened in 1998, it felt thoroughly modern in its concerns and presentation. The hackneyed images of World War Two dramas were absent. There were no Nazi uniforms, clicking heels, goosesteps, cod German accents or *Heil Hitlers*. Nor were there the clichés of wild-eyed scientists chalking up diagrams on blackboards. The designer, Peter J. Davison, had constructed a stage that was circular, white and clinical. Some members of the audience sat at the back of the stage. It suggested a laboratory or courtroom or – to those who were less admiring – a lecture hall. 'When the audience comes in,' said the director, Michael Blakemore, 'they see what is in front of them, and it's obvious that is what they [are going to] get: three actors, three chairs and a very good text. It makes them sit up and listen hard because there's nothing else.'[72]

The diagnostic atmosphere, free from any period trappings, was possible because the play is set in the future. Bohr died in 1962, Heisenberg died in 1976 and Margrethe died in 1984. *Copenhagen* brings them together in a kind of present day. The shifts in time between the 1920s, 1940s and this 'afterlife' might sound hard to follow on the printed page. Onstage it feels perfectly natural. Certainly Frayn didn't think he was devising a complicated or artificial convention: 'We do, all of us, live in different time zones. In the most ordinary way we are remembering things that happened yesterday and things that happened twenty years ago. We are worrying about things that might or might not happen tomorrow, or next year, and we switch back and forth from one to the other quite informally and effortlessly.'[73]

It was a liberating device. When theatre is stripped down, it can move as fast as the imagination. 'In order for theatre to maintain its vitality and its interest,' said Blakemore, 'it has to do something that the other, better-equipped mediums, can't do.'[74] The script of *Copenhagen* doesn't have a single stage direction. Blakemore's powerful production turned that into a strength. It was stark and focused. Only three metal chairs stood on a white circular floor on which the cast circled round and round. The easiest job on the production team had belonged to the props buyer. All that was required was Bohr's pipe. Even that wasn't essential. 'You could do without the pipe if you wanted,'[75] said Blakemore. There were a few sound effects: a train, a seagull, a doorbell, the rumble of the atomic bomb. Otherwise switches in lighting denoted shifts in time, place and points of view. There was none of the usual naturalistic clutter. The cast did not shuffle scientific papers, pour out drinks for one another or lay the table for dinner.

The changes in atmosphere came down to the expert nuances of the actors.

The three actors in the original production gave performances of transparent integrity. There was no showiness. The cast chased the ideas with an unrelenting vigour. David Burke's Bohr had a clubbable charm and a dose of irony. Matthew Marsh played Heisenberg with a furrowed earnestness and a rapid deadpan delivery. As Margrethe, Sara Kestelman had a caustic intelligence that saw events in refreshingly personal terms.

In its own elegant and elaborate way *Copenhagen* follows the traditional three-act structure. 'They go notionally through the meeting in Copenhagen three times,' Frayn said. 'First they say remembering something is like being there again, and they actually go through the meeting. Then at the end of the Act, Bohr says, "Let's try it again," and he arrives at the house a second time, and we then switch back to what it was like in the 1920s when they were doing theoretical research together. At the end of the play he agrees that they still haven't hit upon an explanation as to why he went to Copenhagen, and Bohr says, "Let's do one final draft." He arrives at the house and this time you just hear odd lines of that scene, while we hear the thoughts of the characters as they look at each other, and try to work out what the other is doing.'[76]

There was one aspect of *Copenhagen* that Blakemore thought that neither he nor Frayn had fully appreciated before the play opened. It was a very obvious point and it worked strongly in the play's favour. *Copenhagen* deals with 'an *extremely* important subject, namely atomic annihilation. The moment someone says "plutonium" in the play, everybody in the audience sits up and starts paying close attention.'[77]

Copenhagen and the critics

Copenhagen opened at the Cottesloe Theatre, Royal National Theatre on 28 May 1998. When the reviews came out over the next few days it was clear that the critics were agreed on one point. None of them knew very much about physics. The *Financial Times* admitted: 'My physics ended way before O-level.' *The Times* admitted: 'Those of us whose physics stops short of changing lightbulbs . . .' The *Evening Standard* admitted: 'Those like me, without a shred of scientific knowledge . . .' The *Daily Mail* admitted: 'I absolutely switch off at any mention of matrix calculus or electrons passing through the cloud chamber.' The *Daily Telegraph* admitted: 'I got the lowest possible grade in chemistry-with-physics O-level.' The *Daily Express* admitted: 'Frankly, my brain started shorting out when we got on to nuclear fission.' The *Mail on Sunday*'s critic recorded the scene in the aisles before the play opened: 'The chatter in the audience before *Copenhagen* was whether physics O-level would be adequate for a two-and-a-half-hour discussion of quantum mechanics, uncertainty theory and the development of the atomic bomb. As it turned out, a degree in philosophy would have been more useful.'

Many of those who knew little about physics went on to admire the play. The *Financial Times* said it was 'a virtuoso exercise in dramatic irony'. *The Times* said 'it brims with intellectual excitement'. The *Daily Telegraph* said, 'Frayn makes ideas sing and zing.' The *Mail on Sunday* said it was 'brilliant, brave and demanding'. The *Guardian* said that *Copenhagen* is 'a logical extension of everything that he has done before'. 'It is unquestionably a play for non-scientists too,' said the *Independent on Sunday*. 'It deals with politics on the largest scale imaginable, and personal relationships at their most private and unspoken.' For the *Independent on Sunday* it was the best play of the year. *Copenhagen* went on to win the *Evening Standard* award for best new play.

The press reviews in the first week dealt with the play's success (or some thought, lack of it) as an evening in the theatre. Some regretted that there weren't more jokes. Some felt that the pared-down staging meant that it could have been a radio play. Some felt there was too much physics and it could have been a lecture. Except for an outburst by the poet and critic Tom Paulin on *Late*

Review, the reactions to the play, in terms of how accurately it represented the period, or the way it treated the scientific issues, took longer to emerge. As enthusiasm for the play grew so did the controversy about its portrayal of Heisenberg. This debate increased significantly when *Copenhagen* opened on Broadway. (In his Postscript Frayn deals with a number of the specific criticisms that have been made.)

Copenhagen received enough strong positive reviews to ensure a good audience. It soon became clear to the theatre-going public that here was an excellent production of an extremely intelligent play that dealt with one of the most important subjects of our time. There was always going to be an audience for that. Eight months after its opening *Copenhagen* transferred to the West End. Two years after its London première *Copenhagen* opened on Broadway. It won the 2000 Tony award for best play. Frayn had once written that plays could be classified in many ways, but the two most fundamental categories were 'hits' and 'flops'. *Copenhagen* was a hit.

[1] John Lanchester, *New York Review of Books*, 27 June 2002

[2] Claire Armistead, *Guardian*, 31 January 2002

[3] Duncan Wu (ed.), *Making Plays* (Macmillan, 2000), p.248

[4] www.bombsite.com/frayn

[5] P.M.S. Hacker, *Wittgenstein* (Phoenix, 2002), p.25

[6] Ibid., p.4

[7] 'The Battle of the Books' in *The Original Michael Frayn* (Methuen, 1990), p.130

[8] 'Creating Copenhagen', Dramatists Guild Website

[9] www.guardian.co.uk/saturday_review (14 August 1999)

[10] *The Two of Us* (Samuel French, 1970), p.33

[11] *The Russian Interpreter* (Penguin, 1967), p.51

[12] *Constructions* (Wildwood House, 1974), 160

[13] *Towards the End of the Morning* (Faber, 2000), pp.76–89

[14] *Constructions*, 185

[15] *Clouds* in *Frayn Plays: One* (Methuen, 1985), p.179

[16] Thomas Powers, *Heisenberg's War* (Cape, 1993), p.1

[17] www.bombsite.com/frayn

[18] *The Original Michael Frayn*, pp.213–16

[19] Ibid., p.197

[20] *Headlong* (Faber, 1999), p.25

[21] *The Original Michael Frayn*, p.196

[22] www.argument.independent.co.uk (17 May 2001)

[23] *Alphabetical Order* in *Frayn Plays: One*, p.39

[24] Ibid., p.8

[25] *Donkeys' Years* in *Frayn Plays: One*, p.52

[26] *Clouds* in *Frayn Plays: One*, p.239

[27] *Benefactors* in *Frayn Plays: Two*, p.14

[28] Ibid., p.58

[29] www.telegraph.co.uk (30 May 1998)

[30] *Headlong*, p.122

[31] Mark Arnold-Foster, *The World at War* (Pimlico, 2001), p.185

[32] Edward Davidson and Dale Manning, *Chronology of World War Two* (Cassell & Co., 1999), p.252

[33] David Halberstam, *The Fifties* (Fawcett Columbine, 1993), p.31

[34] Jeremy Bernstein (ed.), *Hitler's Uranium Club* (Copernicus Books, 2001), p.20

[35] R.A.C. Parker, *The Second World War: A Short History* (OUP, 2001), p.1

[36] *The Fifties*, pp.29 and 34

[37] *Off the Record: The Private Papers of Harry S. Truman*, 25 July 1945 (Harper & Row, 1986)

[38] *The Fifties*, p.24

[39] *Hitler's Uranium Club*, p.357

[40] *Heisenberg's War*, p.vii

[41] web.gc.cuny.edu/ashp/nml/Copenhagen/Cassidy.htm

[42] *Heisenberg's War*, p.122

[43] *Making Plays*, p.216

[44] *Heisenberg's War*, p.118

[45] *Making Plays*, p.217

[46] www.broadwayinboston.com

[47] *Making Plays*, p.217

[48] Anthony Gardner, *Independent*, 7 May 2001

[49] Alistair Owen (ed.), *Smoking in Bed* (Bloomsbury, 2001), p.68

[50] Ibid., p.81

[51] www.bombsite.com/frayn

[52] *Constructions*, 298

[53] www.pbs.org/hollywoodpresents/copenhagen

[54] Robert Butler, *Independent on Sunday*, 20 September 1998

[55] Ibid.

[56] web.gc.cuny.educ/ashp/nml/Copenhagen/Cassidy.htm

[57] Ian Kershaw, *Hitler: Hubris* (Penguin, 2001), p.480

[58] Michael Burleigh, *The Third Reich* (Macmillan, 2000), p.11

[59] David Edgar, 'Afterword', *Albert Speer* (Nick Hern Books, 2000), p.151

[60] C.P. Taylor, 'Author's Note', *Good* (Methuen, 1982)

[61] *Albert Speer*, p.134

[62] Ibid., p.147

[63] Ronald Harwood, *Taking Sides* (Faber, 2002), p.152

[64] *Making Plays*, p.224

[65] Ibid.

[66] www.bombsite.com/frayn

[67] *Constructions*, 62

[68] Michael Frayn and David Burke, *Celia's Secret: An Investigation* (Faber, 2000), p.54

[69] *Heisenberg's War*, p.46

[70] *Celia's Secret*, p.vi

[71] web.gc.cuny.educ/ashp/nml/Copenhagen/Lustig_Schwartz.htm

[72] www.broadwayinboston.com

[73] *Making Plays*, p.229

[74] Ibid., p.238

[75] Ibid., p.249

[76] Ibid., p.229

[77] Ibid., p.239

Further Reading

Works by Michael Frayn

Plays

Frayn Plays: One (Methuen, 1985) contains *Alphabetical Order, Donkeys' Years, Clouds, Make and Break, Noises Off*

Frayn Plays: Two (Methuen, 1991) contains *Benefactors, Balmoral, Wild Honey*

Frayn Plays: Three (Methuen, 2000) contains *Here, Now You Know, La Belle Vivette*

The subject matter in the plays differs widely but similar themes to *Copenhagen* can be found in, for instance, *Clouds, Alphabetical Order, Benefactors, Here* and *Noises Off. Democracy* (Methuen, 2003) deals with politics and espionage in post-war Germany.

Non-fiction

Michael Frayn and David Burke, *Celia's Secret: An Investigation* (Faber, 2000). The story of how one of the actors in the original production hoaxed Frayn with papers purporting to relate to historical events described in the play. It shows the playwright confronting a central theme of his writing (how we know what we know)

The Original Michael Frayn (Methuen, 1990), a collection of Frayn's early journalism

The Additional Michael Frayn (Methuen, 2000), Frayn's later journalism

Constructions (Wildwood House Ltd, 1974), his one work of philosophy

Works about Michael Frayn

Malcolm Page, *File on Frayn* (Methuen, 1994)

Duncan Wu (ed.), *Making Plays* (Macmillan, 2000) contains
    penetrating interviews with Frayn and Michael
    Blakemore about *Copenhagen*

Background

Frayn provides a reading list on pp.130–2 that directly
relates to Bohr, Heisenberg and the Copenhagen
Interpretation. On a more general level, Michael Burleigh's
The Third Reich is an excellent introduction to Germany in
the thirties and the theoretical physicist Richard Feynman's
Six Easy Pieces (Penguin, 1998) is a lively and concise
introduction to atomic physics and quantum behaviour.

Film

Howard Davies directed Francesca Annis as Margrethe,
Stephen Rea as Bohr and Daniel Craig as Heisenberg in a
film adaptation of *Copenhagen*. The website that accompanies
the film provides a detailed timeline and glossary of terms
(www.pbs.org/hollywoodpresents/copenhagen).

Websites

Other online resources include Dr Tom Kerns' introduction
to epistemology and quantum physics,
www.students.washington.educ/tkerns, and Harry Lustig's
biographies of the persons referred to in *Copenhagen*,
www.northonline.sccd.ctc.edu/wokcs/Copenhagen.

Copenhagen

Copenhagen was first previewed at the Cottesloe Theatre, Royal National Theatre, London, on 21 May 1998, and opened on 28 May 1998, with the following cast:

Margrethe	Sara Kestelman
Bohr	David Burke
Heisenberg	Matthew Marsh

Directed by Michael Blakemore
Designed by Peter J. Davison
Lighting by Mark Henderson
Sound by Simon Baker

This production moved to the Duchess Theatre, London, where it was presented by Michael Codron and Lee Dean, and opened on 5 February 1999.

It previewed at the Royale Theatre, New York, on 23 March 2000, and opened on 11 April 2000, with the following cast:

Margrethe	Blair Brown
Bohr	Philip Bosco
Heisenberg	Michael Cumpsty

Directed by Michael Blakemore
Designed by Peter J. Davison
Lighting by Mark Henderson and Michael Lincoln
Sound by Tony Meola

This revised edition of the text, including an extended version of the Postscript and a diagrammatic outline of the play's scientific and historical background, is published to coincide with the production in New York.

Act One

Margrethe But why?

Bohr You're still thinking about it?

Margrethe Why did he come to Copenhagen?

Bohr Does it matter, my love, now we're all three of us dead and gone?

Margrethe Some questions remain long after their owners have died. Lingering like ghosts. Looking for the answers they never found in life.

Bohr Some questions have no answers to find.

Margrethe Why did he come? What was he trying to tell you?

Bohr He did explain later.

Margrethe He explained over and over again. Each time he explained it became more obscure.

Bohr It was probably very simple, when you come right down to it: he wanted to have a talk.

Margrethe A talk? To the enemy? In the middle of a war?

Bohr Margrethe, my love, we were scarcely the enemy.

Margrethe It was 1941!

Bohr Heisenberg was one of our oldest friends.

Margrethe Heisenberg was German. We were Danes. We were under German occupation.

Bohr It put us in a difficult position, certainly.

Margrethe I've never seen you as angry with anyone as you were with Heisenberg that night.

Bohr Not to disagree, but I believe I remained

remarkably calm.

Margrethe   I know when you're angry.

Bohr   It was as difficult for him as it was for us.

Margrethe   So why did he do it? Now no one can be hurt, now no one can be betrayed.

Bohr   I doubt if he ever really knew himself.

Margrethe   And he wasn't a friend. Not after that visit. That was the end of the famous friendship between Niels Bohr and Werner Heisenberg.

Heisenberg   Now we're all dead and gone, yes, and there are only two things the world remembers about me. One is the uncertainty principle, and the other is my mysterious visit to Niels Bohr in Copenhagen in 1941. Everyone understands uncertainty. Or thinks he does. No one understands my trip to Copenhagen. Time and time again I've explained it. To Bohr himself, and Margrethe. To interrogators and intelligence officers, to journalists and historians. The more I've explained, the deeper the uncertainty has become. Well, I shall be happy to make one more attempt. Now we're all dead and gone. Now no one can be hurt, now no one can be betrayed.

Margrethe   I never entirely liked him, you know. Perhaps I can say that to you now.

Bohr   Yes, you did. When he was first here in the twenties? Of course you did. On the beach at Tisvilde with us and the boys? He was one of the family.

Margrethe   Something alien about him, even then.

Bohr   So quick and eager.

Margrethe   Too quick. Too eager.

Bohr   Those bright watchful eyes.

Margrethe   Too bright. Too watchful.

Bohr   Well, he was a very great physicist. I never

changed my mind about that.

Margrethe   They were all good, all the people who came
to Copenhagen to work with you. You had most of the
great pioneers in atomic theory here at one time or
another.

Bohr   And the more I look back on it, the more I think
Heisenberg was the greatest of them all.

Heisenberg   So what was Bohr? He was the first of us
all, the father of us all. Modern atomic physics began when
Bohr realised that quantum theory applied to matter as well
as to energy. 1913. Everything we did was based on that
great insight of his.

Bohr   When you think that he first came here to work
with me in 1924 . . .

Heisenberg   I'd only just finished my doctorate, and
Bohr was the most famous atomic physicist in the world.

Bohr   . . . and in just over a year he'd invented quantum
mechanics.

Margrethe   It came out of his work with you.

Bohr   Mostly out of what he'd been doing with Max Born
and Pascual Jordan at Göttingen. Another year or so and
he'd got uncertainty.

Margrethe   And you'd done complementarity.

Bohr   We argued them both out together.

Heisenberg   We did most of our best work together.

Bohr   Heisenberg usually led the way.

Heisenberg   Bohr made sense of it all.

Bohr   We operated like a business.

Heisenberg   Chairman and managing director.

Margrethe   Father and son.

Heisenberg   A family business.

Margrethe   Even though we had sons of our own.

Bohr   And we went on working together long after he ceased to be my assistant.

Heisenberg   Long after I'd left Copenhagen in 1927 and gone back to Germany. Long after I had a chair and a family of my own.

Margrethe   Then the Nazis came to power. . . .

Bohr   And it got more and more difficult. When the war broke out – impossible. Until that day in 1941.

Margrethe   When it finished forever.

Bohr   Yes, why did he do it?

Heisenberg   September, 1941. For years I had it down in my memory as October.

Margrethe   September. The end of September.

Bohr   A curious sort of diary memory is.

Heisenberg   You open the pages, and all the neat headings and tidy jottings dissolve around you.

Bohr   You step through the pages into the months and days themselves.

Margrethe   The past becomes the present inside your head.

Heisenberg   September, 1941, Copenhagen. . . . And at once – here I am, getting off the night train from Berlin with my colleague Carl von Weizsäcker. Two plain civilian suits and raincoats among all the field-grey Wehrmacht uniforms arriving with us, all the naval gold braid, all the well-tailored black of the SS. In my bag I have the text of the lecture I'm giving. In my head is another communication that has to be delivered. The lecture is on astrophysics. The text inside my head is a more difficult one.

Bohr   We obviously can't go to the lecture.

Margrethe   Not if he's giving it at the German Cultural Institute – it's a Nazi propaganda organisation.

Bohr   He must know what we feel about that.

Heisenberg   Weizsäcker has been my John the Baptist, and written to warn Bohr of my arrival.

Margrethe   He wants to see you?

Bohr   I assume that's why he's come.

Heisenberg   But how can the actual meeting with Bohr be arranged?

Margrethe   He must have something remarkably important to say.

Heisenberg   It has to seem natural. It has to be private.

Margrethe   You're not really thinking of inviting him to the house?

Bohr   That's obviously what he's hoping.

Margrethe   Niels! They've occupied our country!

Bohr   He is not they.

Margrethe   He's one of them.

Heisenberg   First of all there's an official visit to Bohr's workplace, the Institute for Theoretical Physics, with an awkward lunch in the old familiar canteen. No chance to talk to Bohr, of course. Is he even present? There's Rozental . . . Petersen, I think . . . Christian Møller, almost certainly. . . . It's like being in a dream. You can never quite focus the precise details of the scene around you. At the head of the table – is that Bohr? I turn to look, and it's Bohr, it's Rozental, it's Møller, it's whoever I appoint to be there. . . . A difficult occasion, though – I remember that clearly enough.

Bohr   It was a disaster. He made a very bad impression. Occupation of Denmark unfortunate. Occupation of Poland, however, perfectly acceptable. Germany now certain to win the war.

Heisenberg   Our tanks are almost at Moscow. What can stop us? Well, one thing, perhaps. One thing.

Bohr   He knows he's being watched, of course. One must remember that. He has to be careful about what he says.

Margrethe   Or he won't be allowed to travel abroad again.

Bohr   My love, the Gestapo planted microphones in his house. He told Goudsmit when he was in America. The SS brought him in for interrogation in the basement at the Prinz-Albrecht-Strasse.

Margrethe   And then they let him go again.

Heisenberg   I wonder if they suspect for one moment how painful it was to get permission for this trip. The humiliating appeals to the Party, the demeaning efforts to have strings pulled by our friends in the Foreign Office.

Margrethe   How did he seem? Is he greatly changed?

Bohr   A little older.

Margrethe   I still think of him as a boy.

Bohr   He's nearly forty. A middle-aged professor, fast catching up with the rest of us.

Margrethe   You still want to invite him here?

Bohr   Let's add up the arguments on either side in a reasonably scientific way. Firstly, Heisenberg is a friend. . . .

Margrethe   Firstly, Heisenberg is a German.

Bohr   A White Jew. That's what the Nazis called him. He taught relativity, and they said it was Jewish physics. He couldn't mention Einstein by name, but he stuck with relativity, in spite of the most terrible attacks.

Margrethe   All the real Jews have lost their jobs. He's still teaching.

Bohr   He's still teaching relativity.

Margrethe   Still a professor at Leipzig.

Bohr   At Leipzig, yes. Not at Munich. They kept him out of the chair at Munich.

Margrethe   He could have been at Columbia.

Bohr   Or Chicago. He had offers from both.

Margrethe   He wouldn't leave Germany.

Bohr   He wants to be there to rebuild German science when Hitler goes. He told Goudsmit.

Margrethe   And if he's being watched it will all be reported upon. Who he sees. What he says to them. What they say to him.

Heisenberg   I carry my surveillance around like an infectious disease. But then I happen to know that Bohr is also under surveillance.

Margrethe   And you know you're being watched yourself.

Bohr   By the Gestapo?

Heisenberg   Does he realise?

Bohr   I've nothing to hide.

Margrethe   By our fellow-Danes. It would be a terrible betrayal of all their trust in you if they thought you were collaborating.

Bohr   Inviting an old friend to dinner is hardly collaborating.

Margrethe   It might appear to be collaborating.

Bohr   Yes. He's put us in a difficult position.

Margrethe   I shall never forgive him.

Bohr   He must have good reason. He must have very good reason.

Heisenberg   This is going to be a deeply awkward occasion.

Margrethe   You won't talk about politics?

Bohr   We'll stick to physics. I assume it's physics he wants to talk to me about.

Margrethe   I think you must also assume that you and I aren't the only people who hear what's said in this house. If you want to speak privately you'd better go out in the open air.

Bohr   I shan't want to speak privately.

Margrethe   You could go for another of your walks together.

Heisenberg   Shall I be able to suggest a walk?

Bohr   I don't think we shall be going for any walks. Whatever he has to say he can say where everyone can hear it.

Margrethe   Some new idea he wants to try out on you, perhaps.

Bohr   What can it be, though? Where are we off to next?

Margrethe   So now of course your curiosity's aroused, in spite of everything.

Heisenberg   So now here I am, walking out through the autumn twilight to the Bohrs' house at Ny-Carlsberg. Followed, presumably, by my invisible shadow. What am I feeling? Fear, certainly – the touch of fear that one always feels for a teacher, for an employer, for a parent. Much worse fear about what I have to say. About how to express it. How to broach it in the first place. Worse fear still about what happens if I fail.

Margrethe   It's not something to do with the war?

Bohr   Heisenberg is a theoretical physicist. I don't think anyone has yet discovered a way you can use theoretical physics to kill people.

Margrethe   It couldn't be something about fission?

Bohr   Fission? Why would he want to talk to me about fission?

Margrethe   Because you're working on it.

Bohr   Heisenberg isn't.

Margrethe   Isn't he? Everybody else in the world seems to be. And you're the acknowledged authority.

Bohr   He hasn't published on fission.

Margrethe   It was Heisenberg who did all the original work on the physics of the nucleus. And he consulted you then, he consulted you at every step.

Bohr   That was back in 1932. Fission's only been around for the last three years.

Margrethe   But if the Germans were developing some kind of weapon based on nuclear fission . . .

Bohr   My love, no one is going to develop a weapon based on nuclear fission.

Margrethe   But if the Germans were trying to, Heisenberg would be involved.

Bohr   There's no shortage of good German physicists.

Margrethe   There's no shortage of good German physicists in America or Britain.

Bohr   The Jews have gone, obviously.

Heisenberg   Einstein, Wolfgang Pauli, Max Born . . . Otto Frisch, Lise Meitner. . . . We led the world in theoretical physics! Once.

Margrethe   So who is there still working in Germany?

Bohr   Sommerfeld, of course. Von Laue.

Margrethe   Old men.

Bohr   Wirtz. Harteck.

Margrethe   Heisenberg is head and shoulders above all of them.

Bohr   Otto Hahn – he's still there. He discovered fission, after all.

Margrethe   Hahn's a chemist. I thought that what Hahn discovered . . .

Bohr   . . . was that Enrico Fermi had discovered it in Rome four years earlier. Yes – he just didn't realise it was fission. It didn't occur to anyone that the uranium atom might have split, and turned into an atom of barium and an atom of krypton. Not until Hahn and Strassmann did the analysis, and detected the barium.

Margrethe   Fermi's in Chicago.

Bohr   His wife's Jewish.

Margrethe   So Heisenberg would be in charge of the work?

Bohr   Margrethe, there is no work! John Wheeler and I did it all in 1939. One of the implications of our paper is that there's no way in the foreseeable future in which fission can be used to produce any kind of weapon.

Margrethe   Then why is everyone still working on it?

Bohr   Because there's an element of magic in it. You fire a neutron at the nucleus of a uranium atom and it splits into two other elements. It's what the alchemists were trying to do – to turn one element into another.

Margrethe   So why is he coming?

Bohr   Now your curiosity's aroused.

Margrethe   My forebodings.

Heisenberg   I crunch over the familiar gravel to the Bohrs' front door, and tug at the familiar bell-pull. Fear, yes. And another sensation, that's become painfully familiar over the past year. A mixture of self-importance and sheer helpless absurdity – that of all the 2,000 million people in this world, I'm the one who's been charged with this impossible responsibility. . . . The heavy door swings open.

Bohr   My dear Heisenberg!

Heisenberg   My dear Bohr!

Bohr   Come in, come in . . .

Margrethe   And of course as soon as they catch sight of each other all their caution disappears. The old flames leap up from the ashes. If we can just negotiate all the treacherous little opening civilities . . .

Heisenberg   I'm so touched you felt able to ask me.

Bohr   We must try to go on behaving like human beings.

Heisenberg   I realise how awkward it is.

Bohr   We scarcely had a chance to do more than shake hands at lunch the other day.

Heisenberg   And Margrethe I haven't seen . . .

Bohr   Since you were here four years ago.

Margrethe   Niels is right. You look older.

Heisenberg   I had been hoping to see you both in 1938, at the congress in Warsaw . . .

Bohr   I believe you had some personal trouble.

Heisenberg   A little business in Berlin.

Margrethe   In the Prinz-Albrecht-Strasse?

Heisenberg   A slight misunderstanding.

Bohr   We heard, yes. I'm so sorry.

Heisenberg   These things happen. The question is now resolved. Happily resolved. We should all have met in Zürich . . .

Bohr   In September 1939.

Heisenberg   Only of course . . .

Margrethe   There was an unfortunate clash with the outbreak of war.

Heisenberg   Sadly.

Bohr   Sadly for us, certainly.

Margrethe   A lot more sadly still for many people.

Heisenberg   Yes. Indeed.

Bohr   Well, there it is.

Heisenberg   What can I say?

Margrethe   What can any of us say, in the present circumstances?

Heisenberg   No. And your sons?

Margrethe   Are well, thank you. Elisabeth? The children?

Heisenberg   Very well. They send their love, of course.

Margrethe   They so much wanted to see each other, in spite of everything! But now the moment has come they're so busy avoiding each other's eye that they can scarcely see each other at all.

Heisenberg   I wonder if you realise how much it means to me to be back here in Copenhagen. In this house. I have become rather isolated in these last few years.

Bohr   I can imagine.

Margrethe   Me he scarcely notices. I watch him discreetly from behind my expression of polite interest as he struggles on.

Heisenberg   Have things here been difficult?

Bohr   Difficult?

Margrethe   Of course. He has to ask. He has to get it out of the way.

Bohr   Difficult. . . . What can I say? We've not so far been treated to the gross abuses that have occurred elsewhere. The race laws have not been enforced.

Margrethe   Yet.

Bohr   A few months ago they started deporting Communists and other anti-German elements.

Heisenberg   But you personally . . . ?

Bohr   Have been left strictly alone.

Heisenberg   I've been anxious about you.

Bohr   Kind of you. No call for sleepless nights in Leipzig so far, though.

Margrethe   Another silence. He's done his duty. Now he can begin to steer the conversation round to pleasanter subjects.

Heisenberg   Are you still sailing?

Bohr   Sailing?

Margrethe   Not a good start.

Bohr   No, no sailing.

Heisenberg   The Sound is . . . ?

Bohr   Mined.

Heisenberg   Of course.

Margrethe   I assume he won't ask if Niels has been ski-ing.

Heisenberg   You've managed to get some ski-ing?

Bohr   Ski-ing? In Denmark?

Heisenberg   In Norway. You used to go to Norway.

Bohr   I did, yes.

Heisenberg   But since Norway is also . . . well . . .

Bohr   Also occupied? Yes, that might make it easier. In fact I suppose we could now holiday almost anywhere in Europe.

Heisenberg   I'm sorry. I hadn't thought of it quite in those terms.

Bohr   Perhaps I'm being a little oversensitive.

Heisenberg   Of course not. I should have thought.

Margrethe   He must almost be starting to wish he was back in the Prinz-Albrecht-Strasse.

Heisenberg   I don't suppose you feel you could ever come to Germany . . .

Margrethe   The boy's an idiot.

Bohr   My dear Heisenberg, it would be an easy mistake to make, to think that the citizens of a small nation, of a small nation overrun, wantonly and cruelly overrun, by its more powerful neighbour, don't have exactly the same feelings of national pride as their conquerors, exactly the same love of their country.

Margrethe   Niels, we agreed.

Bohr   To talk about physics, yes.

Margrethe   Not about politics.

Bohr   I'm sorry.

Heisenberg   No, no – I was simply going to say that I still have my old ski-hut at Bayrischzell. So if by any chance . . . at any time . . . for any reason . . .

Bohr   Perhaps Margrethe would be kind enough to sew a yellow star on my ski-jacket.

Heisenberg   Yes. Yes. Stupid of me.

Margrethe   Silence again. Those first brief sparks have disappeared, and the ashes have become very cold indeed. So now of course I'm starting to feel almost sorry for him. Sitting here all on his own in the midst of people who hate him, all on his own against the two of us. He looks younger again, like the boy who first came here in 1924. Younger than Christian would have been now. Shy and arrogant and anxious to be loved. Homesick and pleased to be away from home at last. And, yes, it's sad, because Niels loved him, he was a father to him.

Heisenberg   So . . . what are you working on?

Margrethe   And all he can do is press forward.

Bohr   Fission, mostly.

Heisenberg   I saw a couple of papers in the *Physical Review*. The velocity-range relations of fission fragments . . . ?

Bohr   And something about the interactions of nuclei with deuterons. And you?

Heisenberg   Various things.

Margrethe   Fission?

Heisenberg   I sometimes feel very envious of your cyclotron.

Margrethe   Why? Are you working on fission yourself?

Heisenberg   There are over thirty in the United States. Whereas in the whole of Germany . . . Well. . . . You still get to your country place, at any rate?

Bohr   We still go to Tisvilde, yes.

Margrethe   In the whole of Germany, you were going to say . . .

Bohr   . . . there is not one single cyclotron.

Heisenberg   So beautiful at this time of year. Tisvilde.

Bohr   You haven't come to borrow the cyclotron, have you? That's not why you've come to Copenhagen?

Heisenberg   That's not why I've come to Copenhagen.

Bohr   I'm sorry. We mustn't jump to conclusions.

Heisenberg   No, we must none of us jump to conclusions of any sort.

Margrethe   We must wait patiently to be told.

Heisenberg   It's not always easy to explain things to the world at large.

Bohr   I realise that we must always be conscious of the wider audience our words may have. But the lack of cyclotrons in Germany is surely not a military secret.

Heisenberg I've no idea what's a secret and what isn't.

Bohr No secret, either, about why there aren't any. You can't say it but I can. It's because the Nazis have systematically undermined theoretical physics. Why? Because so many people working in the field were Jews. And why were so many of them Jews? Because theoretical physics, the sort of physics done by Einstein, by Schrödinger and Pauli, by Born and Sommerfeld, by you and me, was always regarded in Germany as inferior to experimental physics, and the theoretical chairs and lectureships were the only ones that Jews could get.

Margrethe Physics, yes? Physics.

Bohr This is physics.

Margrethe It's also politics.

Heisenberg The two are sometimes painfully difficult to keep apart.

Bohr So, you saw those two papers. I haven't seen anything by you recently.

Heisenberg No.

Bohr Not like you. Too much teaching?

Heisenberg I'm not teaching. Not at the moment.

Bohr My dear Heisenberg – they haven't pushed you out of your chair at Leipzig? That's not what you've come to tell us?

Heisenberg No, I'm still at Leipzig. For part of each week.

Bohr And for the rest of the week?

Heisenberg Elsewhere. The problem is more work, not less.

Bohr I see. Do I?

Heisenberg Are you in touch with any of our friends in England? Born? Chadwick?

Bohr Heisenberg, we're under German occupation. Germany's at war with Britain.

Heisenberg I thought you might still have contacts of some sort. Or people in America? We're not at war with America.

Margrethe Yet.

Heisenberg You've heard nothing from Pauli, in Princeton? Goudsmit? Fermi?

Bohr What do you want to know?

Heisenberg I was simply curious ... I was thinking about Robert Oppenheimer the other day. I had a great set-to with him in Chicago in 1939.

Bohr About mesons.

Heisenberg Is he still working on mesons?

Bohr I'm quite out of touch.

Margrethe The only foreign visitor we've had was from Germany. Your friend Weizsäcker was here in March.

Heisenberg *My* friend? *Your* friend, too. I hope. You know he's come back to Copenhagen with me? He's very much hoping to see you again.

Margrethe When he came here in March he brought the head of the German Cultural Institute with him.

Heisenberg I'm sorry about that. He did it with the best of intentions. He may not have explained to you that the Institute is run by the Cultural Division of the Foreign Office. We have good friends in the foreign service. Particularly at the Embassy here.

Bohr Of course. I knew his father when he was Ambassador in Copenhagen in the twenties.

Heisenberg It hasn't changed so much since then, you

know, the German foreign service.

Bohr   It's a department of the Nazi government.

Heisenberg   Germany is more complex than it may perhaps appear from the outside. The different organs of state have quite different traditions, in spite of all attempts at reform. Particularly the foreign service. Our people in the Embassy here are quite old-fashioned in the way they use their influence. They would certainly be trying to see that distinguished local citizens were able to work undisturbed.

Bohr   Are you telling me that I'm being protected by your friends in the Embassy?

Heisenberg   What I'm saying, in case Weizsäcker failed to make it clear, is that you would find congenial company there. I know people would be very honoured if you felt able to accept an occasional invitation.

Bohr   To cocktail parties at the Germany Embassy? To coffee and cakes with the Nazi plenipotentiary?

Heisenberg   To lectures, perhaps. To discussion groups. Social contacts of any sort could be helpful.

Bohr   I'm sure they could.

Heisenberg   Essential, perhaps, in certain circumstances.

Bohr   In what circumstances?

Heisenberg   I think we both know.

Bohr   Because I'm half-Jewish?

Heisenberg   We all at one time or another may need the help of our friends.

Bohr   Is this why you've come to Copenhagen? To invite me to watch the deportation of my fellow-Danes from a grandstand seat in the windows of the German Embassy?

Heisenberg   Bohr, please! Please! What else can I do? How else can I help? It's an impossibly difficult situation for you, I understand that. It's also an impossibly difficult one for me.

Bohr   Yes. I'm sorry. I'm sure you also have the best of intentions.

Heisenberg   Forget what I said. Unless . . .

Bohr   Unless I need to remember it.

Heisenberg   In any case it's not why I've come.

Margrethe   Perhaps you should simply say what it is you want to say.

Heisenberg   What you and I often used to do in the old days was to take an evening stroll.

Bohr   Often. Yes. In the old days.

Heisenberg   You don't feel like a stroll this evening, for old times' sake?

Bohr   A little chilly tonight, perhaps, for strolling.

Heisenberg   This is so difficult. You remember where we first met?

Bohr   Of course. At Göttingen in 1922.

Heisenberg   At a lecture festival held in your honour.

Bohr   It was a high honour. I was very conscious of it.

Heisenberg   You were being honoured for two reasons. Firstly because you were a great physicist . . .

Bohr   Yes, yes.

Heisenberg   . . . and secondly because you were one of the very few people in Europe who were prepared to have dealings with Germany. The war had been over for four years, and we were still lepers. You held out your hand to us. You've always inspired love, you know that. Wherever you've been, wherever you've worked. Here in Denmark. In England, in America. But in Germany we worshipped you. Because you held out your hand to us.

Bohr   Germany's changed.

Heisenberg   Yes. Then we were down. And you could be generous.

Margrethe   And now you're up.

Heisenberg   And generosity's harder. But you held out your hand to us then, and we took it.

Bohr   Yes. . . . No! Not you. As a matter of fact. You bit it.

Heisenberg   Bit it?

Bohr   Bit my hand! You did! I held it out, in my most statesmanlike and reconciliatory way, and you gave it a very nasty nip.

Heisenberg   *I* did?

Bohr   The first time I ever set eyes on you. At one of those lectures I was giving in Göttingen.

Heisenberg   What are you talking about?

Bohr   You stood up and laid into me.

Heisenberg   Oh . . . I offered a few comments.

Bohr   Beautiful summer's day. The scent of roses drifting in from the gardens. Rows of eminent physicists and mathematicians, all nodding approval of my benevolence and wisdom. Suddenly, up jumps a cheeky young pup and tells me that my mathematics are wrong.

Heisenberg   They were wrong.

Bohr   How old were you?

Heisenberg   Twenty.

Bohr   Two years younger than the century.

Heisenberg   Not quite.

Bohr   December 5th, yes?

Heisenberg   1.93 years younger than the century.

Bohr   To be precise.

Heisenberg   No – to two places of decimals. To be *precise*, 1.928 . . . 7 . . . 6 . . . 7 . . . 1 . . .

Bohr   I can always keep track of you, all the same. And the century.

Margrethe   And Niels has suddenly decided to love him again, in spite of everything. Why? What happened? Was it the recollection of that summer's day in Göttingen? Or everything? Or nothing at all? Whatever it was, by the time we've sat down to dinner the cold ashes have started into flame once again.

Bohr   You were always so combative! It was the same when we played table-tennis at Tisvilde. You looked as if you were trying to kill me.

Heisenberg   I wanted to win. Of course I wanted to win. *You* wanted to win.

Bohr   I wanted an agreeable game of table-tennis.

Heisenberg   You couldn't see the expression on your face.

Bohr   I could see the expression on yours.

Heisenberg   What about those games of poker in the ski-hut at Bayrischzell, then? You once cleaned us all out! You remember that? With a non-existent straight! We're all mathematicians – we're all counting the cards – we're 90 per cent certain he hasn't got anything. But on he goes, raising us, raising us. This insane confidence. Until our faith in mathematical probability begins to waver, and one by one we all throw in.

Bohr   I thought I *had* a straight! I misread the cards! I bluffed myself!

Margrethe   Poor Niels.

Heisenberg   Poor Niels? He won! He bankrupted us! You were insanely competitive! He got us all playing poker once with imaginary cards!

Bohr   You played chess with Weizsäcker on an imaginary board!

Margrethe   Who won?

Bohr   Need you ask? At Bayrischzell we'd ski down from the hut to get provisions, and he'd make even that into some kind of race! You remember? When we were there with Weizsäcker and someone? You got out a stop-watch.

Heisenberg   It took poor Weizsäcker eighteen minutes.

Bohr   You were down there in ten, of course.

Heisenberg   Eight.

Bohr   I don't recall how long I took.

Heisenberg   Forty-five minutes.

Bohr   Thank you.

Margrethe   Some rather swift ski-ing going on here, I think.

Heisenberg   Your ski-ing was like your science. What were you waiting for? Me and Weizsäcker to come back and suggest some slight change of emphasis?

Bohr   Probably.

Heisenberg   You were doing seventeen drafts of each slalom?

Margrethe   And without me there to type them out.

Bohr   At least I knew where I was. At the speed you were going you were up against the uncertainty relationship. If you knew where you were when you were down you didn't know how fast you'd got there. If you knew how fast you'd been going you didn't know you were down.

Heisenberg   I certainly didn't stop to think about it.

Bohr   Not to criticise, but that's what might be criticised with some of your science.

Heisenberg I usually got there, all the same.

Bohr You never cared what got destroyed on the way, though. As long as the mathematics worked out you were satisfied.

Heisenberg If something works it works.

Bohr But the question is always, What does the mathematics mean, in plain language? What are the philosophical implications?

Heisenberg I always knew you'd be picking your way step by step down the slope behind me, digging all the capsized meanings and implications out of the snow.

Margrethe The faster you ski the sooner you're across the cracks and crevasses.

Heisenberg The faster you ski the better you think.

Bohr Not to disagree, but that is most . . . most interesting.

Heisenberg By which you mean it's nonsense. But it's not nonsense. Decisions make themselves when you're coming downhill at seventy kilometres an hour. Suddenly there's the edge of nothingness in front of you. Swerve left? Swerve right? Or think about it and die? In your head you swerve both ways . . .

Margrethe Like that particle.

Heisenberg What particle?

Margrethe The one that you said goes through two different slits at the same time.

Heisenberg Oh, in our old thought-experiment. Yes. Yes!

Margrethe Or Schrödinger's wretched cat.

Heisenberg That's alive and dead at the same time.

Margrethe   Poor beast.

Bohr   My love, it was an imaginary cat.

Margrethe   I know.

Bohr   Locked away with an imaginary phial of cyanide.

Margrethe   I know, I know.

Heisenberg   So the particle's here, the particle's there . . .

Bohr   The cat's alive, the cat's dead . . .

Margrethe   You've swerved left, you've swerved right . . .

Heisenberg   Until the experiment is over, this is the point, until the sealed chamber is opened, the abyss detoured; and it turns out that the particle has met itself again, the cat's dead . . .

Margrethe   And you're alive.

Bohr   Not so fast, Heisenberg . . .

Heisenberg   The swerve itself was the decision.

Bohr   Not so fast, not so fast!

Heisenberg   Isn't that how you shot Hendrik Casimir dead?

Bohr   Hendrik Casimir?

Heisenberg   When he was working here at the Institute.

Bohr   I never shot Hendrik Casimir.

Heisenberg   You told me you did.

Bohr   It was George Gamow. I shot George Gamow. *You* don't know – it was long after your time.

Heisenberg   Bohr, you shot Hendrik Casimir.

Bohr   Gamow, Gamow. Because he insisted that it was always quicker to act than to react. To make a decision to do something rather than respond to someone else's doing it.

Heisenberg And for that you shot him?

Bohr It was him! He went out and bought a pair of pistols! He puts one in his pocket, I put one in mine, and we get on with the day's work. Hours go by, and we're arguing ferociously about – I can't remember – our problems with the nitrogen nucleus, I expect – when suddenly Gamow reaches into his pocket . . .

Heisenberg Cap-pistols.

Bohr Cap-pistols, yes. Of course.

Heisenberg Margrethe was looking a little worried.

Margrethe No – a little surprised. At the turn of events.

Bohr Now you remember how quick he was.

Heisenberg Casimir?

Bohr Gamow.

Heisenberg Not as quick as me.

Bohr Of course not. But compared with me.

Heisenberg A fast neutron. However, or so you're going to tell me . . .

Bohr However, yes, before his gun is even out of his pocket . . .

Heisenberg You've drafted your reply.

Margrethe I've typed it out.

Heisenberg You've checked it with Klein.

Margrethe I've retyped it.

Heisenberg You've submitted it to Pauli in Hamburg.

Margrethe I've retyped it again.

Bohr Before his gun is even out of his pocket, mine is in my hand.

Heisenberg And poor Casimir has been blasted out of existence.

Bohr   Except that it was Gamow.

Heisenberg   It was Casimir! He told me!

Bohr   Yes, well, one of the two.

Heisenberg   Both of them simultaneously alive and dead in our memories.

Bohr   Like a pair of Schrödinger cats. Where were we?

Heisenberg   Ski-ing. Or music. That's another thing that decides everything for you. I play the piano and the way seems to open in front of me – all I have to do is follow. That's how I had my one success with women. At a musical evening at the Bückings in Leipzig – we've assembled a piano trio. 1937, just when all my troubles with the . . . when my troubles are coming to a head. We're playing the Beethoven G major. We finish the scherzo, and I look up from the piano to see if the others are ready to start the final presto. And in that instant I catch a glimpse of a young woman sitting at the side of the room. Just the briefest glimpse, but of course at once I've carried her off to Bayrischzell, we're engaged, we're married, etc. – the usual hopeless romantic fantasies. Then off we go into the presto, and it's terrifyingly fast – so fast there's no time to be afraid. And suddenly everything in the world seems easy. We reach the end and I just carry on ski-ing. Get myself introduced to the young woman – see her home – and, yes, a week later I've carried her off to Bayrischzell – another week and we're engaged – three months and we're married. All on the sheer momentum of that presto!

Bohr   You were saying you felt isolated. But you do have a companion, after all.

Heisenberg   Music?

Bohr   Elisabeth!

Heisenberg   Oh. Yes. Though, what with the children,

and so on . . . I've always envied the way you and Margrethe manage to talk about everything. Your work. Your problems. Me, no doubt.

Bohr I was formed by nature to be a mathematically curious entity: not one but half of two.

Heisenberg Mathematics becomes very odd when you apply it to people. One plus one can add up to so many different sums . . .

Margrethe Silence. What's he thinking about now? His life? Or ours?

Bohr So many things we think about at the same time. Our lives and our physics.

Margrethe All the things that come into our heads out of nowhere.

Bohr Our private consolations. Our private agonies.

Heisenberg Silence. And of course they're thinking about their children again.

Margrethe The same bright things. The same dark things. Back and back they come.

Heisenberg Their four children living, and their two children dead.

Margrethe Harald. Lying alone in that ward.

Bohr She's thinking about Christian and Harald.

Heisenberg The two lost boys. Harald . . .

Bohr All those years alone in that terrible ward.

Heisenberg And Christian. The firstborn. The eldest son.

Bohr And once again I see those same few moments that I see every day.

Heisenberg Those short moments on the boat, when the tiller slams over in the heavy sea, and Christian is falling.

Bohr   If I hadn't let him take the helm . . .

Heisenberg   Those long moments in the water.

Bohr   Those endless moments in the water.

Heisenberg   When he's struggling towards the lifebuoy.

Bohr   So near to touching it.

Margrethe   I'm at Tisvilde. I look up from my work. There's Niels in the doorway, silently watching me. He turns his head away, and I know at once what's happened.

Bohr   So near, so near! So slight a thing!

Heisenberg   Again and again the tiller slams over. Again and again . . .

Margrethe   Niels turns his head away . . .

Bohr   Christian reaches for the lifebuoy . . .

Heisenberg   But about some things even they never speak.

Bohr   About some things even we only think.

Margrethe   Because there's nothing to be said.

Bohr   Well . . . perhaps we *should* be warm enough. You suggested a stroll.

Heisenberg   In fact the weather is remarkably warm.

Bohr   We shan't be long.

Heisenberg   A week at most.

Bohr   What – our great hike through Zealand?

Heisenberg   We went to Elsinore. I often think about what you said there.

Bohr   You don't mind, my love? Half-an-hour?

Heisenberg   An hour, perhaps. No, the whole appearance of Elsinore, you said, was changed by our knowing that Hamlet had lived there. Every dark corner there reminds us of the darkness inside the human soul . . .

Margrethe   So, they're walking again. He's done it. And
if they're walking they're talking. Talking in a rather
different way, no doubt – I've typed out so much in my
time about how differently particles behave when they're
unobserved . . . I knew Niels would never hold out if they
could just get through the first few minutes. If only out of
curiosity. . . . Now they're started an hour will mean two, of
course, perhaps three. . . . The first thing they ever did was
to go for a walk together. At Göttingen, after that lecture.
Niels immediately went to look for the presumptuous young
man who'd queried his mathematics, and swept him off for
a tramp in the country. Walk – talk – make his
acquaintance. And when Heisenberg arrived here to work
for him, off they go again, on their great tour of Zealand.
A lot of this century's physics they did in the open air.
Strolling around the forest paths at Tisvilde. Going down to
the beach with the children. Heisenberg holding Christian's
hand. Yes, and every evening in Copenhagen, after dinner,
they'd walk round Faelled Park behind the Institute, or out
along Langelinie into the harbour. Walk, and talk. Long,
long before walls had ears . . . But this time, in 1941, their
walk takes a different course. Ten minutes after they set out
. . . they're back! I've scarcely had the table cleared when
there's Niels in the doorway. I see at once how upset he is
– he can't look me in the eye.

Bohr   Heisenberg wants to say goodbye. He's leaving.

Margrethe   *He* won't look at me, either.

Heisenberg   Thank you. A delightful evening. Almost
like old times. So kind of you.

Margrethe   You'll have some coffee? A glass of
something?

Heisenberg   I have to get back and prepare for my
lecture.

Margrethe   But you'll come and see us again before you
leave?

Bohr   He has a great deal to do.

Margrethe   It's like the worst moments of 1927 all over again, when Niels came back from Norway and first read Heisenberg's uncertainty paper. Something they both seemed to have forgotten about earlier in the evening, though I hadn't. Perhaps they've both suddenly remembered that time. Only from the look on their faces something even worse has happened.

Heisenberg   Forgive me if I've done or said anything that . . .

Bohr   Yes, yes.

Heisenberg   It meant a great deal to me, being here with you both again. More perhaps than you realise.

Margrethe   It was a pleasure for us. Our love to Elisabeth.

Bohr   Of course.

Margrethe   And the children.

Heisenberg   Perhaps, when this war is over. . . . If we're all spared. . . . Goodbye.

Margrethe   Politics?

Bohr   Physics. He's not right, though. How can he be right? John Wheeler and I . . .

Margrethe   A breath of air as we talk, why not?

Bohr   A breath of air?

Margrethe   A turn around the garden. Healthier than staying indoors, perhaps.

Bohr   Oh. Yes.

Margrethe   For everyone concerned.

Bohr   Yes. Thank you. . . . How can he possibly be right? Wheeler and I went through the whole thing in 1939.

Margrethe   What did he say?

Bohr   Nothing. I don't know. I was too angry to take it in.

Margrethe   Something about fission?

Bohr   What happens in fission? You fire a neutron at a uranium nucleus, it splits, and it releases energy.

Margrethe   A huge amount of energy. Yes?

Bohr   About enough to move a speck of dust. But it also releases two or three more neutrons. Each of which has the chance of splitting another nucleus.

Margrethe   So then those two or three split nuclei each release energy in their turn?

Bohr   And two or three more neutrons.

Heisenberg   You start a trickle of snow sliding as you ski. The trickle becomes a snowball . . .

Bohr   An ever-widening chain of split nuclei forks through the uranium, doubling and quadrupling in millionths of a second from one generation to the next. First two splits, let's say for simplicity. Then two squared, two cubed, two to the fourth, two to the fifth, two to the sixth . . .

Heisenberg   The thunder of the gathering avalanche echoes from all the surrounding mountains . . .

Bohr   Until eventually, after, let's say, eighty generations, 2^{80} specks of dust have been moved. 2^{80} is a number with 24 noughts. Enough specks of dust to constitute a city, and all who live in it.

Heisenberg   But there is a catch.

Bohr   There is a catch, thank God. Natural uranium consists of two different isotopes. Most of it's U-238, which you can only fission with fast neutrons. Most neutrons, though, will only fission the other isotope, U-235 – and less than one per cent of natural uranium is U-235.

Heisenberg   This was Bohr's great insight. Another of his amazing intuitions. It came to him when he was at Princeton in 1939, walking across the campus with Wheeler. A characteristic Bohr moment – I wish I'd been there to enjoy it. Five minutes deep silence as they walked, then: 'Now hear this – I have understood everything.'

Bohr   In fact it's a double catch, because the 238 also slows neutrons down and absorbs them. So an explosive chain reaction will never occur in natural uranium. To make an explosion you will have to separate out pure 235. And to make the chain long enough for a large explosion . . .

Heisenberg   Eighty generations, let's say . . .

Bohr   . . . you would need many tons of it. And it's extremely difficult to separate.

Heisenberg   Tantalisingly difficult.

Bohr   Mercifully difficult. The best estimates, when I was in America in 1939, were that to produce even one gram of U-235 would take 26,000 years. By which time, surely, this war will be over. So he's wrong, you see, he's wrong! Or could *I* be wrong? Could I have miscalculated? Let me see. . . . What are the absorption rates for fast neutrons in 238? What's the mean free path of slow neutrons in 235 . . . ?

Margrethe   But what exactly had Heisenberg said? That's what everyone wanted to know, then and forever after.

Bohr   It's what the British wanted to know, as soon as Chadwick managed to get in touch with me. What exactly did Heisenberg say?

Heisenberg   And what exactly did Bohr reply? That was of course the first thing my colleagues asked me when I got back to Germany.

Margrethe   What did Heisenberg tell Niels – what did

Niels reply? The person who wanted to know most of all
was Heisenberg himself.

Bohr   You mean when he came back to Copenhagen
after the war, in 1947?

Margrethe   Escorted this time not by unseen agents of
the Gestapo, but by a very conspicuous minder from British
intelligence.

Bohr   I think he wanted various things.

Margrethe   Two things. Food-parcels . . .

Bohr   For his family in Germany. They were on the
verge of starvation.

Margrethe   And for you to agree what you'd said to
each other in 1941.

Bohr   The conversation went wrong almost as fast as it
did before.

Margrethe   You couldn't even agree where you'd walked
that night.

Heisenberg   Where we walked? Faelled Park, of course.
Where we went so often in the old days.

Margrethe   But Faelled Park is behind the Institute, four
kilometres away from where we live!

Heisenberg   I can see the drift of autumn leaves under
the street-lamps next to the bandstand.

Bohr   Yes, because you remember it as October!

Margrethe   And it was September.

Bohr   No fallen leaves!

Margrethe   And it was 1941. No street-lamps!

Bohr   I thought we hadn't got any further than my study.

What I can see is the drift of papers under the reading-lamp on my desk.

Heisenberg   We must have been outside! What I was going to say was treasonable. If I'd been overheard I'd have been executed.

Margrethe   So what was this mysterious thing you said?

Heisenberg   There's no mystery about it. There never was any mystery. I remember it absolutely clearly, because my life was at stake, and I chose my words very carefully. I simply asked you if as a physicist one had the moral right to work on the practical exploitation of atomic energy. Yes?

Bohr   I don't recall.

Heisenberg   You don't recall, no, because you immediately became alarmed. You stopped dead in your tracks.

Bohr   I was horrified.

Heisenberg   Horrified. Good, you remember that. You stood there gazing at me, horrified.

Bohr   Because the implication was obvious. That you *were* working on it.

Heisenberg   And you jumped to the conclusion that I was trying to provide Hitler with nuclear weapons.

Bohr   And you were!

Heisenberg   No! A reactor! That's what we were trying to build! A machine to produce power! To generate electricity, to drive ships!

Bohr   You didn't say anything about a reactor.

Heisenberg   I didn't say anything about anything! Not in so many words. I couldn't! I'd no idea how much could be overheard. How much you'd repeat to others.

Bohr   But then I asked you if you actually thought that uranium fission could be used for the construction of weapons.

Heisenberg   Ah! It's coming back!

Bohr   And I clearly remember what you replied.

Heisenberg   I said I now knew that it could be.

Bohr   This is what really horrified me.

Heisenberg   Because you'd always been confident that weapons would need 235, and that we could never separate enough of it.

Bohr   A reactor – yes, maybe, because you can keep a slow chain reaction going in natural uranium.

Heisenberg   What we'd realised, though, was that if we could once get the reactor going . . .

Bohr   The 238 in the natural uranium would absorb the fast neutrons . . .

Heisenberg   Exactly as you predicted in 1939 – everything we were doing was based on that fundamental insight of yours. The 238 would absorb the fast neutrons. And would be transformed by them into a new element altogether.

Bohr   Neptunium. Which would decay in its turn into another new element . . .

Heisenberg   At least as fissile as the 235 that we couldn't separate . . .

Margrethe   Plutonium.

Heisenberg   Plutonium.

Bohr   I should have worked it out for myself.

Heisenberg   If we could build a reactor we could build bombs. That's what had brought me to Copenhagen. But none of this could I say. And at this point you stopped listening. The bomb had already gone off inside your head. I realised we were heading back towards the house. Our walk was over. Our one chance to talk had gone forever.

Bohr   Because I'd grasped the central point already. That one way or another you saw the possibility of supplying Hitler with nuclear weapons.

Heisenberg   You grasped at least four different central points, all of them wrong. You told Rozental that I'd tried to pick your brains about fission. You told Weisskopf that I'd asked you what you knew about the Allied nuclear programme. Chadwick thought I was hoping to persuade you that there was no German programme. But then you seem to have told some people that I'd tried to recruit you to work on it!

Bohr   Very well. Let's start all over again from the beginning. No Gestapo in the shadows this time. No British intelligence officer. No one watching us at all.

Margrethe   Only me.

Bohr   Only Margrethe. We're going to make the whole thing clear to Margrethe. You know how strongly I believe that we don't do science for ourselves, that we do it so we can explain to others . . .

Heisenberg   In plain language.

Bohr   In plain language. Not your view, I know – you'd be happy to describe what you were up to purely in differential equations if you could – but for Margrethe's sake . . .

Heisenberg   Plain language.

Bohr   Plain language. All right, so here we are, walking along the street once more. And this time I'm absolutely calm, I'm listening intently. What is it you want to say?

Heisenberg   It's not just what *I* want to say! The whole German nuclear team in Berlin! Not Diebner, of course, not the Nazis – but Weizsäcker, Hahn, Wirtz, Jensen, Houtermanns – they all wanted me to come and discuss it with you. We all see you as a kind of spiritual father.

Margrethe   The Pope. That's what you used to call Niels behind his back. And now you want him to give you absolution.

Heisenberg   Absolution? No!

Margrethe   According to your colleague Jensen.

Heisenberg   Absolution is the last thing I want!

Margrethe   You told one historian that Jensen had expressed it perfectly.

Heisenberg   Did I? Absolution. . . . Is that what I've come for? It's like trying to remember who was at that lunch you gave me at the Institute. Around the table sit all the different explanations for everything I did. I turn to look . . . Petersen, Rozental, and . . . yes . . . now the word absolution is taking its place among them all . . .

Margrethe   Though I thought absolution was granted for sins past and repented, not for sins intended and yet to be committed.

Heisenberg   Exactly! That's why I was so shocked!

Bohr   *You* were shocked?

Heisenberg   Because you *did* give me absolution! That's exactly what you did! As we were hurrying back to the house. You muttered something about everyone in wartime being obliged to do his best for his own country. Yes?

Bohr   Heaven knows what I said. But now here I am, profoundly calm and conscious, weighing my words. You don't want absolution. I understand. You want me to tell you *not* to do it? All right. I put my hand on your arm. I look you in the eye in my most papal way. Go back to Germany, Heisenberg. Gather your colleagues together in the laboratory. Get up on a table and tell them: 'Niels Bohr says that in his considered judgment supplying a homicidal maniac with an improved instrument of mass murder is . . .' What shall I say? '. . . an interesting idea.' No, not even an interesting idea. '. . . a really rather

seriously uninteresting idea.' What happens? You all fling
down your Geiger counters?

Heisenberg Obviously not.

Bohr Because they'll arrest you.

Heisenberg Whether they arrest us or not it won't make
any difference. In fact it will make things worse. I'm
running my programme for the Kaiser Wilhelm Institute.
But there's a rival one at Army Ordnance, run by Kurt
Diebner, and he's a party member. If I go they'll simply
get Diebner to take over my programme as well. He should
be running it anyway. Wirtz and the rest of them only
smuggled me in to keep Diebner and the Nazis out of it.
My one hope is to remain in control.

Bohr So you don't want me to say yes and you don't
want me to say no.

Heisenberg What I want is for you to listen carefully to
what I'm going on to say next, instead of running off down
the street like a madman.

Bohr Very well. Here I am, walking very slowly and
popishly. And I listen most carefully as you tell me . . .

Heisenberg That nuclear weapons will require an
enormous technical effort.

Bohr True.

Heisenberg That they will suck up huge resources.

Bohr Huge resources. Certainly.

Heisenberg That sooner or later governments will have
to turn to scientists and ask whether it's worth committing
those resources – whether there's any hope of producing
the weapons in time for them to be used.

Bohr Of course, but . . .

Heisenberg Wait. So they will have to come to you and
me. We are the ones who will have to advise them whether
to go ahead or not. In the end the decision will be in our

hands, whether we like it or not.

Bohr   And that's what you want to tell me?

Heisenberg   That's what I want to tell you.

Bohr   That's why you have come all this way, with so much difficulty? That's why you have thrown away nearly twenty years of friendship? Simply to tell me that?

Heisenberg   Simply to tell you that.

Bohr   But, Heisenberg, this is more mysterious than ever! What are you telling it me *for*? What am I supposed to do about it? The government of occupied Denmark isn't going to come to me and ask me whether we should produce nuclear weapons!

Heisenberg   No, but sooner or later, if I manage to remain in control of our programme, the German government is going to come to *me*! They will ask *me* whether to continue or not! *I* will have to decide what to tell them!

Bohr   Then you have an easy way out of your difficulties. You tell them the simple truth that you've just told me. You tell them how difficult it will be. And perhaps they'll be discouraged. Perhaps they'll lose interest.

Heisenberg   But, Bohr, where will that lead? What will be the consequences if we manage to fail?

Bohr   What can I possibly tell you that you can't tell yourself?

Heisenberg   There was a report in a Stockholm paper that the Americans are working on an atomic bomb.

Bohr   Ah. Now it comes, now it comes. Now I understand everything. You think I have contacts with the Americans?

Heisenberg   You may. It's just conceivable. If anyone in Occupied Europe does it will be you.

Bohr   So you *do* want to know about the Allied nuclear programme.

Heisenberg I simply want to know if there is one. Some hint. Some clue. I've just betrayed my country and risked my life to warn you of the German programme . . .

Bohr And now I'm to return the compliment?

Heisenberg Bohr, I have to know! I'm the one who has to decide! If the Allies are building a bomb, what am I choosing for my country? You said it would be easy to imagine that one might have less love for one's country if it's small and defenceless. Yes, and it would be another easy mistake to make, to think that one loved one's country less because it happened to be in the wrong. Germany is where I was born. Germany is where I became what I am. Germany is all the faces of my childhood, all the hands that picked me up when I fell, all the voices that encouraged me and set me on my way, all the hearts that speak to my heart. Germany is my widowed mother and my impossible brother. Germany is my wife. Germany is our children. I have to know what I'm deciding for them! Is it another defeat? Another nightmare like the nightmare I grew up with? Bohr, my childhood in Munich came to an end in anarchy and civil war. Are more children going to starve, as we did? Are they going to have to spend winter nights as I did when I was a schoolboy, crawling on my hands and knees through the enemy lines, creeping out into the country under cover of darkness in the snow to find food for my family? Are they going to sit up all night, as I did at the age of seventeen, guarding some terrified prisoner, talking to him and talking to him through the small hours, because he's going to be executed in the morning?

Bohr But, my dear Heisenberg, there's nothing I can tell you. I've no idea whether there's an Allied nuclear programme.

Heisenberg It's just getting under way even as you and I are talking. And maybe I'm choosing something worse even than defeat. Because the bomb they're building is to be used on us. On the evening of Hiroshima Oppenheimer said it was his one regret. That they hadn't produced the bomb in time to use on Germany.

Bohr   He tormented himself afterwards.

Heisenberg   Afterwards, yes. At least we tormented ourselves a little beforehand. Did a single one of them stop to think, even for one brief moment, about what they were doing? Did Oppenheimer? Did Fermi, or Teller, or Szilard? Did Einstein, when he wrote to Roosevelt in 1939 and urged him to finance research on the bomb? Did you, when you escaped from Copenhagen two years later, and went to Los Alamos?

Bohr   My dear, good Heisenberg, we weren't supplying the bomb to Hitler!

Heisenberg   You weren't dropping it on Hitler, either. You were dropping it on anyone who was in reach. On old men and women in the street, on mothers and their children. And if you'd produced it in time they would have been my fellow-countrymen. My wife. My children. That was the intention. Yes?

Bohr   That was the intention.

Heisenberg   You never had the slightest conception of what happens when bombs are dropped on cities. Even conventional bombs. None of you ever experienced it. Not a single one of you. I walked back from the centre of Berlin to the suburbs one night, after one of the big raids. No transport moving, of course. The whole city on fire. Even the puddles in the streets are burning. They're puddles of molten phosphorus. It gets on your shoes like some kind of incandescent dog-muck – I have to keep scraping it off – as if the streets have been fouled by the hounds of hell. It would have made you laugh – my shoes keep bursting into flame. All around me, I suppose, there are people trapped, people in various stages of burning to death. And all I can think is, How will I ever get hold of another pair of shoes in times like these?

Bohr   You know why Allied scientists worked on the bomb.

Heisenberg   Of course. Fear.

Bohr   The same fear that was consuming you. Because they were afraid that *you* were working on it.

Heisenberg   But, Bohr, you could have told them!

Bohr   Told them what?

Heisenberg   What I told you in 1941! That the choice is in our hands! In mine – in Oppenheimer's! That if I can tell them the simple truth when they ask me, the simple discouraging truth, so can he!

Bohr   This is what you want from me? Not to tell you what the Americans are doing but to stop them?

Heisenberg   To tell them that we can stop it together.

Bohr   I had no contact with the Americans!

Heisenberg   You did with the British.

Bohr   Only later.

Heisenberg   The Gestapo intercepted the message you sent them about our meeting.

Margrethe   And passed it to you?

Heisenberg   Why not? They'd begun to trust me. This is what gave me the possibility of remaining in control of events.

Bohr   Not to criticise, Heisenberg, but if this is your plan in coming to Copenhagen, it's ... what can I say? It's most interesting.

Heisenberg   It's not a plan. It's a hope. Not even a hope. A microscopically fine thread of possibility. A wild improbability. Worth trying, though, Bohr! Worth trying, surely! But already you're too angry to understand what I'm saying.

Margrethe   No – why he's angry is because he *is*
beginning to understand! The Germans drive out most of
their best physicists because they're Jews. America and
Britain give them sanctuary. Now it turns out that this
might offer the Allies a hope of salvation. And at once you
come howling to Niels begging him to persuade them to
give it up.

Bohr   Margrethe, my love, perhaps we should try to
express ourselves a little more temperately.

Margrethe   But the gall of it! The sheer, breathtaking
gall of it!

Bohr   Bold ski-ing, I have to say.

Heisenberg   But, Bohr, we're not ski-ing now! We're not
playing table-tennis! We're not juggling with cap-pistols and
non-existent cards! I refused to believe it, when I first heard
the news of Hiroshima. I thought that it was just one of
the strange dreams we were living in at the time. They'd
got stranger and stranger, God knows, as Germany fell into
ruins in those last months of the war. But by then we were
living in the strangest of them all. The ruins had suddenly
vanished – just the way things do in dreams – and all at
once we're in a stately home in the middle of the English
countryside. We've been rounded up by the British – the
whole team, everyone who worked on atomic research –
and we've been spirited away. To Farm Hall, in
Huntingdonshire, in the water-meadows of the River Ouse.
Our families in Germany are starving, and there are we
sitting down each evening to an excellent formal dinner
with our charming host, the British officer in charge of us.
It's like a pre-war house-party – one of those house-parties
in a play, that's cut off from any contact with the outside
world, where you know the guests have all been invited for
some secret sinister purpose. No one knows we're there –
no one in England, no one in Germany, not even our
families. But the war's over. What's happening? Perhaps, as
in a play, we're going to be quietly murdered, one by one.
In the meanwhile it's all delightfully civilised. I entertain the

party with Beethoven piano sonatas. Major Rittner, our
hospitable gaoler, reads Dickens to us, to improve our
English. . . . Did these things really happen to me . . . ? We
wait for the point of it all to be revealed to us. Then one
evening it is. And it's even more grotesque than the one we
were fearing. It's on the radio: you have actually done the
deed that we were tormenting ourselves about. That's why
we're there, dining with our gracious host, listening to our
Dickens. We've been kept locked up to stop us discussing
the subject with anyone until it's too late. When Major
Rittner tells us I simply refuse to believe it until I hear it
with my own ears on the nine o'clock news. We'd no idea
how far ahead you'd got. I can't describe the effect it has
on us. You play happily with your toy cap-pistol. Then
someone else picks it up and pulls the trigger . . . and all at
once there's blood everywhere and people screaming,
because it wasn't a toy at all. . . . We sit up half the night,
talking about it, trying to take it in. We're all literally in
shock.

Margrethe   Because it had been done? Or because it
wasn't you who'd done it?

Heisenberg   Both. Both. Otto Hahn wants to kill himself,
because it was he who discovered fission, and he can see
the blood on his hands. Gerlach, our old Government
administrator, also wants to die, because his hands are so
shamefully clean. You've done it, though. You've built the
bomb.

Bohr   Yes.

Heisenberg   And you've used it on a living target.

Bohr   On a living target.

Margrethe   You're not suggesting that Niels did anything
wrong in working at Los Alamos?

Heisenberg   Of course not. Bohr has never done
anything wrong.

Margrethe   The decision had been taken long before
Niels arrived. The bomb would have been built whether

Niels had gone or not.

Bohr   In any case, my part was very small.

Heisenberg   Oppenheimer described you as the team's father-confessor.

Bohr   It seems to be my role in life.

Heisenberg   He said you made a great contribution.

Bohr   Spiritual, possibly. Not practical.

Heisenberg   Fermi says it was you who worked out how to trigger the Nagasaki bomb.

Bohr   I put forward an idea.

Margrethe   You're not implying that there's anything that *Niels* needs to explain or defend?

Heisenberg   No one has ever expected him to explain or defend anything. He's a profoundly good man.

Bohr   It's not a question of goodness. I was spared the decision.

Heisenberg   Yes, and I was not. So explaining and defending myself was how I spent the last thirty years of my life. When I went to America in 1949 a lot of physicists wouldn't even shake my hand. Hands that had actually built the bomb wouldn't touch mine.

Margrethe   And let me tell you, if you think you're making it any clearer to me now, you're not.

Bohr   Margrethe, I understand his feelings . . .

Margrethe   I don't. I'm as angry as you were before! It's so easy to make you feel conscience-stricken. Why should he transfer his burden to you? Because what does he do after his great consultation with you? He goes back to Berlin and tells the Nazis that he can produce atomic bombs!

Heisenberg   But what I stress is the difficulty of separating 235.

Margrethe   You tell them about plutonium.

Heisenberg   I tell some of the minor officials. I have to keep people's hopes alive!

Margrethe   Otherwise they'll send for the other one.

Heisenberg   Diebner. Very possibly.

Margrethe   There's always a Diebner at hand ready to take over our crimes.

Heisenberg   Diebner might manage to get a little further than me.

Bohr   Diebner?

Heisenberg   Might. Just possibly might.

Bohr   He hasn't a quarter of your ability!

Heisenberg   Not a tenth of it. But he has ten times the eagerness to do it. It might be a very different story if it's Diebner who puts the case at our meeting with Albert Speer, instead of me.

Margrethe   The famous meeting with Speer.

Heisenberg   But this is when it counts. This is the real moment of decision. It's June 1942. Nine months after my trip to Copenhagen. All research cancelled by Hitler unless it produces immediate results – and Speer is the sole arbiter of what will qualify. Now, we've just got the first sign that our reactor's going to work. Our first increase in neutrons. Not much – thirteen per cent – but it's a start.

Bohr   June 1942? You're slightly ahead of Fermi in Chicago.

Heisenberg   Only we don't know that. But the RAF have begun terror-bombing. They've obliterated half of Lübeck, and the whole centre of Rostock and Cologne. We're desperate for new weapons to strike back with. If ever there's a moment to make our case, this is it.

Margrethe   You don't ask him for the funding to continue?

Heisenberg   To continue with the reactor? Of course I
do. But I ask for so little that he doesn't take the
programme seriously.

Margrethe   Do you tell him the reactor will produce
plutonium?

Heisenberg   I don't tell him the reactor will produce
plutonium. Not Speer, no. I don't tell him the reactor will
produce plutonium.

Bohr   A striking omission, I have to admit.

Heisenberg   And what happens? It works! He gives us
barely enough money to keep the reactor programme
ticking over. And that is the end of the German atomic
bomb. That is the end of it.

Margrethe   You go on with the reactor, though.

Heisenberg   We go on with the reactor. Of course.
Because now there's no risk of getting it running in time to
produce enough plutonium for a bomb. No, we go on with
the reactor all right. We work like madmen on the reactor.
We have to drag it all the way across Germany, from east
to west, from Berlin to Swabia, to get it away from the
bombing, to keep it out of the hands of the Russians.
Diebner tries to hijack it on the way. We get it away from
him, and we set it up in a little village in the Swabian
Jura.

Bohr   This is Haigerloch?

Heisenberg   There's a natural shelter there – the village
inn has a wine-cellar cut into the base of a cliff. We dig a
hole in the floor for the reactor, and I keep that
programme going, I keep it under my control, until the
bitter end.

Bohr   But, Heisenberg, with respect now, with the greatest
respect, you couldn't even keep the reactor under your
control. That reactor was going to kill you.

Heisenberg   It wasn't put to the test. It never went critical.

Bohr   Thank God. Hambro and Perrin examined it after the Allied troops took over. They said it had no cadmium control rods. There was nothing to absorb any excess of neutrons, to slow the reaction down when it overheated.

Heisenberg   No rods, no.

Bohr   You believed the reaction would be self-limiting.

Heisenberg   That's what I originally believed.

Bohr   Heisenberg, the reaction would not have been self-limiting.

Heisenberg   By 1945 I understood that.

Bohr   So if you ever had got it to go critical, it would have melted down, and vanished into the centre of the earth!

Heisenberg   Not at all. We had a lump of cadmium to hand.

Bohr   A *lump* of cadmium? What were you proposing to do with a *lump* of cadmium?

Heisenberg   Throw it into the water.

Bohr   What water?

Heisenberg   The heavy water. The moderator that the uranium was immersed in.

Bohr   My dear good Heisenberg, not to criticise, but you'd all gone mad!

Heisenberg   We were almost there! We had this fantastic neutron growth! We had 670 per cent growth!

Bohr   You'd lost all contact with reality down in that hole!

Heisenberg   Another week. Another fortnight. That's all we needed!

Bohr It was only the arrival of the Allies that saved you!

Heisenberg We'd almost reached the critical mass! A tiny bit bigger and the chain would sustain itself indefinitely. All we need is a little more uranium. I set off with Weizsäcker to try and get our hands on Diebner's. Another hair-raising journey all the way back across Germany. Constant air raids – no trains – we try bicycles – we never make it! We end up stuck in a little inn somewhere in the middle of nowhere, listening to the thump of bombs falling all round us. And on the radio someone playing the Beethoven G minor cello sonata . . .

Bohr And everything was still under your control?

Heisenberg Under my control – yes! That's the point! Under my control!

Bohr Nothing was under anyone's control by that time!

Heisenberg Yes, because at last we were free of all constraints! The nearer the end came the faster we could work!

Bohr You were no longer running that programme, Heisenberg. The programme was running you.

Heisenberg Two more weeks, two more blocks of uranium, and it would have been German physics that achieved the world's first self-sustaining chain reaction.

Bohr Except that Fermi had already done it in Chicago, two years earlier.

Heisenberg We didn't know that.

Bohr You didn't know anything down in that cave. You were as blind as moles in a hole. Perrin said that there wasn't even anything to protect you all from the radiation.

Heisenberg We didn't have time to think about it.

Bohr So if it *had* gone critical . . .

Margrethe You'd all have died of radiation sickness.

Bohr My dear Heisenberg! My dear boy!

Heisenberg Yes, but by then the reactor would have been running.

Bohr I should have been there to look after you.

Heisenberg That's all we could think of at the time. To get the reactor running, to get the reactor running.

Bohr You always needed me there to slow you down a little. Your own walking lump of cadmium.

Heisenberg If I had died then, what should I have missed? Thirty years of attempting to explain. Thirty years of reproach and hostility. Even you turned your back on me.

Margrethe You came to Copenhagen again. You came to Tisvilde.

Heisenberg It was never the same.

Bohr No. It was never the same.

Heisenberg I sometimes think that those final few weeks at Haigerloch were the last happy time in my life. In a strange way it was very peaceful. Suddenly we were out of all the politics of Berlin. Out of the bombing. The war was coming to an end. There was nothing to think about except the reactor. And we didn't go mad, in fact. We didn't work all the time. There was a monastery on top of the rock above our cave. I used to retire to the organ-loft in the church, and play Bach fugues.

Margrethe Look at him. He's lost. He's like a lost child. He's been out in the woods all day, running here, running there. He's shown off, he's been brave, he's been cowardly. He's done wrong, he's done right. And now the evening's come, and all he wants is to go home, and he's lost.

Heisenberg Silence.

Bohr Silence.

Margrethe Silence.

Heisenberg And once again the tiller slams over, and Christian is falling.

Bohr Once again he's struggling towards the lifebuoy.

Margrethe Once again I look up from my work, and there's Niels in the doorway, silently watching me . . .

Bohr So, Heisenberg, why did you come to Copenhagen in 1941? It was right that you told us about all the fears you had. But you didn't really think I'd tell you whether the Americans were working on a bomb.

Heisenberg No.

Bohr You didn't seriously hope that I'd stop them.

Heisenberg No.

Bohr You were going back to work on that reactor whatever I said.

Heisenberg Yes.

Bohr So, Heisenberg, why did you come?

Heisenberg Why did I come?

Bohr Tell us once again. Another draft of the paper. And this time we shall get it right. This time we shall understand.

Margrethe Maybe you'll even understand yourself.

Bohr After all, the workings of the atom were difficult to explain. We made many attempts. Each time we tried they became more obscure. We got there in the end, however. So – another draft, another draft.

Heisenberg Why did I come? And once again I go through that evening in 1941. I crunch over the familiar gravel, and tug at the familiar bell-pull. What's in my head? Fear, certainly, and the absurd and horrible importance of someone bearing bad news. But . . . yes . . . something else as well. Here it comes again. I can almost see its face. Something good. Something bright and eager and hopeful.

Bohr   I open the door . . .

Heisenberg   And there he is. I see his eyes light up at the sight of me.

Bohr   He's smiling his wary schoolboy smile.

Heisenberg   And I feel a moment of such consolation.

Bohr   A flash of such pure gladness.

Heisenberg   As if I'd come home after a long journey.

Bohr   As if a long-lost child had appeared on the doorstep.

Heisenberg   Suddenly I'm free of all the dark tangled currents in the water.

Bohr   Christian is alive, Harald still unborn.

Heisenberg   The world is at peace again.

Margrethe   Look at them. Father and son still. Just for a moment. Even now we're all dead.

Bohr   For a moment, yes, it's the twenties again.

Heisenberg   And we shall speak to each other and understand each other in the way we did before.

Margrethe   And from those two heads the future will emerge. Which cities will be destroyed, and which survive. Who will die, and who will live. Which world will go down to obliteration, and which will triumph.

Bohr   My dear Heisenberg!

Heisenberg   My dear Bohr!

Bohr   Come in, come in . . .

Act Two

Heisenberg   It was the very beginning of spring. The first time I came to Copenhagen, in 1924. March: raw, blustery northern weather. But every now and then the sun would come out and leave that first marvellous warmth of the year on your skin. That first breath of returning life.

Bohr   You were twenty-two. So I must have been . . .

Heisenberg   Thirty-eight.

Bohr   Almost the same age as you were when you came in 1941.

Heisenberg   So what do we do?

Bohr   Put on our boots and rucksacks . . .

Heisenberg   Take the tram to the end of the line . . .

Bohr   And start walking!

Heisenberg   Northwards to Elsinore.

Bohr   If you walk you talk.

Heisenberg   Then westwards to Tisvilde.

Bohr   And back by way of Hillerød.

Heisenberg   Walking, talking, for a hundred miles.

Bohr   After which we talked more or less non-stop for the next three years.

Heisenberg   We'd split a bottle of wine over dinner in your flat at the Institute.

Bohr   Then I'd come up to your room . . .

Heisenberg   That terrible little room in the servants' quarters in the attic.

Bohr   And we'd talk on into the small hours.

Heisenberg   How, though?

Bohr   How?

Heisenberg   How did we talk? In Danish?

Bohr   In German, surely.

Heisenberg   I lectured in Danish. I had to give my first colloquium when I'd only been here for ten weeks.

Bohr   I remember it. Your Danish was already excellent.

Heisenberg   No. You did a terrible thing to me. Half-an-hour before it started you said casually, Oh, I think we'll speak English today.

Bohr   But when you explained . . . ?

Heisenberg   Explain to the Pope? I didn't dare. That excellent Danish you heard was my first attempt at English.

Bohr   My dear Heisenberg! On our own together, though? My love, do you recall?

Margrethe   What language you spoke when I wasn't there? You think I had microphones hidden?

Bohr   No, no – but patience, my love, patience!

Margrethe   Patience?

Bohr   You sounded a little sharp.

Margrethe   Not at all.

Bohr   We have to follow the threads right back to the beginning of the maze.

Margrethe   I'm watching every step.

Bohr   You didn't mind? I hope.

Margrethe   Mind?

Bohr   Being left at home?

Margrethe   While you went off on your hike? Of course not. Why should I have minded? You had to get out of the house. Two new sons arriving on top of each other would be rather a lot for any man to put up with.

Bohr   Two new sons?

Margrethe   Heisenberg.

Bohr   Yes, yes.

Margrethe   And our own son.

Bohr   Aage?

Margrethe   Ernest!

Bohr   1924 – of course – Ernest.

Margrethe   Number five. Yes?

Bohr   Yes, yes, yes. And if it was March, you're right – he couldn't have been much more than . . .

Margrethe   One week.

Bohr   One week? One week, yes. And you really didn't mind?

Margrethe   Not at all. I was pleased you had an excuse to get away. And you always went off hiking with your new assistants. You went off with Kramers, when he arrived in 1916.

Bohr   Yes, when I suppose Christian was still only . . .

Margrethe   One week.

Bohr   Yes. . . . Yes. . . . I almost killed Kramers, you know.

Heisenberg   Not with a cap-pistol?

Bohr   With a mine. On our walk.

Heisenberg   Oh, the mine. Yes, you told me, on ours. Never mind Kramers – you almost killed yourself!

Bohr   A mine washed up in the shallows . . .

Heisenberg   And of course at once they compete to throw stones at it. What were you thinking of?

Bohr   I've no idea.

Heisenberg   A touch of Elsinore there, perhaps.

Bohr   Elsinore?

Heisenberg   The darkness inside the human soul.

Bohr   You did something just as idiotic.

Heisenberg   *I* did?

Bohr   With Dirac in Japan. You climbed a pagoda.

Heisenberg   Oh, the pagoda.

Bohr   Then balanced on the pinnacle. According to Dirac. On one foot. In a high wind. I'm glad I wasn't there.

Heisenberg   Elsinore, I confess.

Bohr   Elsinore, certainly.

Heisenberg   I was jealous of Kramers, you know.

Bohr   His Eminence. Isn't that what you called him?

Heisenberg   Because that's what he was. Your leading cardinal. Your favourite son. Till I arrived on the scene.

Margrethe   He was a wonderful cellist.

Bohr   He was a wonderful everything.

Heisenberg   Far too wonderful.

Margrethe   I liked him.

Heisenberg   I was terrified of him. When I first started at the Institute. I was terrified of all of them. All the boy wonders you had here – they were all so brilliant and accomplished. But Kramers was the heir apparent. All the rest of us had to work in the general study hall. Kramers had the private office next to yours, like the electron on the inmost orbit around the nucleus. And he didn't think much of my physics. He insisted you could explain everything about the atom by classical mechanics.

Bohr   Well, he was wrong.

Margrethe   And very soon the private office was vacant.

Bohr   And there was another electron on the inmost orbit.

Heisenberg   Yes, and for three years we lived inside the atom.

Bohr   With other electrons on the outer orbits around us all over Europe.

Heisenberg   Max Born and Pascual Jordan in Göttingen.

Bohr   Yes, but Schrödinger in Zürich, Fermi in Rome.

Heisenberg   Chadwick and Dirac in England.

Bohr   Joliot and de Broglie in Paris.

Heisenberg   Gamow and Landau in Russia.

Bohr   Everyone in and out of each other's departments.

Heisenberg   Papers and drafts of papers on every international mail-train.

Bohr   You remember when Goudsmit and Uhlenbeck did spin?

Heisenberg   There's this one last variable in the quantum state of the atom that no one can make sense of. The last hurdle . . .

Bohr   And these two crazy Dutchmen go back to a ridiculous idea that electrons can spin in different ways.

Heisenberg   And of course the first thing that everyone wants to know is, What line is Copenhagen going to take?

Bohr   I'm on my way to Leiden, as it happens.

Heisenberg   And it turns into a papal progress! The train stops on the way at Hamburg . . .

Bohr   Pauli and Stern are waiting on the platform to ask me what I think about spin.

Heisenberg   You tell them it's wrong.

Bohr   No, I tell them it's very . . .

Heisenberg   Interesting.

Bohr   I think that is precisely the word I choose.

Heisenberg   Then the train pulls into Leiden.

Bohr   And I'm met at the barrier by Einstein and Ehrenfest. And I change my mind because Einstein – Einstein, you see? – I'm the Pope – he's God – because Einstein has made a relativistic analysis, and it resolves all my doubts.

Heisenberg   Meanwhile I'm standing in for Max Born at Göttingen, so you make a detour there on your way home.

Bohr   And you and Jordan meet me at the station.

Heisenberg   Same question: what do you think of spin?

Bohr   And when the train stops at Berlin there's Pauli on the platform.

Heisenberg   Wolfgang Pauli, who never gets out of bed if he can possibly avoid it . . .

Bohr   And who's already met me once at Hamburg on the journey out . . .

Heisenberg   He's travelled all the way from Hamburg to Berlin purely in order to see you for the second time round . . .

Bohr   And find out how my ideas on spin have developed en route.

Heisenberg   Oh, those years! Those amazing years! Those three short years!

Bohr   From 1924 to 1927.

Heisenberg   From when I arrived in Copenhagen to work with you . . .

Bohr   To when you departed, to take up your chair at Leipzig.

Heisenberg   Three years of raw, bracing northern springtime.

Bohr   At the end of which we had quantum mechanics, we had uncertainty . . .

Heisenberg   We had complementarity . . .

Bohr   We had the whole Copenhagen Interpretation.

Heisenberg   Europe in all its glory again. A new Enlightenment, with Germany back in her rightful place at the heart of it. And who led the way for everyone else?

Margrethe   You and Niels.

Heisenberg   Well, we did.

Bohr   We did.

Margrethe   And that's what you were trying to get back to in 1941?

Heisenberg   To something we did in those three years. . . . Something we said, something we thought. . . . I keep almost seeing it out of the corner of my eye as we talk! Something about the way we worked. Something about the way we did all those things . . .

Bohr   Together.

Heisenberg   Together. Yes, together.

Margrethe   No.

Bohr   No? What do you mean, no?

Margrethe   Not together. You didn't do any of those things together.

Bohr   Yes, we did. Of course we did.

Margrethe   No, you didn't. Every single one of them you did when you were apart. *You* first worked out quantum mechanics on Heligoland.

Heisenberg   Well, it was summer by then. I had my hay fever.

Margrethe   And on Heligoland, on your own, on a rocky bare island in the middle of the North Sea, you said there was nothing to distract you . . .

Heisenberg   My head began to clear, and I had this very sharp picture of what atomic physics ought to be like. I suddenly realised that we had to limit it to the measurements we could actually make, to what we could actually observe. We can't see the electrons inside the atom . . .

Margrethe   Any more than Niels can see the thoughts in your head, or you the thoughts in Niels's.

Heisenberg   All we can see are the effects that the electrons produce, on the light that they reflect . . .

Bohr   But the difficulties you were trying to resolve were the ones we'd explored together, over dinner in the flat, on the beach at Tisvilde.

Heisenberg   Of course. But I remember the evening when the mathematics first began to chime with the principle.

Margrethe   On Heligoland.

Heisenberg   On Heligoland.

Margrethe   On your own.

Heisenberg   It was terribly laborious – I didn't understand matrix calculus then . . . I get so excited I keep making mistakes. But by three in the morning I've got it. I seem to be looking through the surface of atomic phenomena into a strangely beautiful interior world. A world of pure mathematical structures. I'm too excited to sleep. I go down to the southern end of the island. There's a rock jutting out into the sea that I've been longing to climb. I get up it in the half-light before the dawn, and lie on top, gazing out to sea.

Margrethe On your own.

Heisenberg On my own. And yes – I was happy.

Margrethe Happier than you were back here with us all in Copenhagen the following winter.

Heisenberg What, with all the Schrödinger nonsense?

Bohr Nonsense? Come, come. Schrödinger's wave formulation?

Margrethe Yes, suddenly everyone's turned their backs on your wonderful new matrix mechanics.

Heisenberg No one can understand it.

Margrethe And they *can* understand Schrödinger's wave mechanics.

Heisenberg Because they'd learnt it in school! We're going backwards to classical physics! And when I'm a little cautious about accepting it . . .

Bohr A little cautious? Not to criticise, but . . .

Margrethe . . . You described it as repulsive!

Heisenberg I said the physical implications were repulsive. Schrödinger said my mathematics were repulsive.

Bohr I seem to recall you used the word . . . well, I won't repeat it in mixed company.

Heisenberg In private. But by that time people had gone crazy.

Margrethe They thought you were simply jealous.

Heisenberg Someone even suggested some bizarre kind of intellectual snobbery. You got extremely excited.

Bohr On your behalf.

Heisenberg You invited Schrödinger here . . .

Bohr   To have a calm debate about our differences.

Heisenberg   And you fell on him like a madman. You meet him at the station – of course – and you pitch into him before he's even got his bags off the train. Then you go on at him from first thing in the morning until last thing at night.

Bohr   *I* go on? *He* goes on!

Heisenberg   Because you won't make the least concession!

Bohr   Nor will he!

Heisenberg   You made him ill! He had to retire to bed to get away from you!

Bohr   He had a slight feverish cold.

Heisenberg   Margrethe had to nurse him!

Margrethe   I dosed him with tea and cake to keep his strength up.

Heisenberg   Yes, while you pursued him even into the sickroom! Sat on his bed and hammered away at him!

Bohr   Perfectly politely.

Heisenberg   You were the Pope and the Holy Office and the Inquisition all rolled into one! And then, and then, after Schrödinger had fled back to Zürich – and this I will never forget, Bohr, this I will never let you forget – you started to take his side! You turned on me!

Bohr   Because *you'd* gone mad by this time! You'd become fanatical! You were refusing to allow wave theory any place in quantum mechanics at all!

Heisenberg   You'd completely turned your coat!

Bohr   I said wave mechanics and matrix mechanics were simply alternative tools.

Heisenberg   Something you're always accusing me of. 'If it works it works.' Never mind what it means.

Bohr   Of course I mind what it means.

Heisenberg   What it means in language.

Bohr   In plain language, yes.

Heisenberg   What something means is what it means in mathematics.

Bohr   You think that so long as the mathematics works out, the sense doesn't matter.

Heisenberg   Mathematics *is* sense! That's what sense is!

Bohr   But in the end, in the end, remember, we have to be able to explain it all to Margrethe!

Margrethe   Explain it to me? You couldn't even explain it to each other! You went on arguing into the small hours every night! You both got so angry!

Bohr   We also both got completely exhausted.

Margrethe   It was the cloud chamber that finished you.

Bohr   Yes, because if you detach an electron from an atom, and send it through a cloud chamber, you can see the track it leaves.

Heisenberg   And it's a scandal. There shouldn't be a track!

Margrethe   According to your quantum mechanics.

Heisenberg   There *isn't* a track! No orbits! No tracks or trajectories! Only external effects!

Margrethe   Only there the track is. I've seen it myself, as clear as the wake left by a passing ship.

Bohr   It was a fascinating paradox.

Heisenberg   You actually loved the paradoxes, that's your problem. You revelled in the contradictions.

Bohr   Yes, and you've never been able to understand the suggestiveness of paradox and contradiction. That's *your* problem. You live and breathe paradox and contradiction, but you can no more see the beauty of them than the fish can see the beauty of the water.

Heisenberg   I sometimes felt as if I was trapped in a kind of windowless hell. You don't realise how aggressive you are. Prowling up and down the room as if you're going to eat someone – and I can guess who it's going to be.

Bohr   That's the way we did the physics, though.

Margrethe   No. No! In the end you did it on your own again! Even you! You went off ski-ing in Norway.

Bohr   I had to get away from it all!

Margrethe   And you worked out complementarity in Norway, on your own.

Heisenberg   The speed he skis at he had to do *something* to keep the blood going round. It was either physics or frostbite.

Bohr   Yes, and you stayed behind in Copenhagen . . .

Heisenberg   And started to think at last.

Margrethe   You're a lot better off apart, you two.

Heisenberg   Having him out of town was as liberating as getting away from my hay fever on Heligoland.

Margrethe   I shouldn't let you sit anywhere near each other, if I were the teacher.

Heisenberg   And that's when I did uncertainty. Walking round Faelled Park on my own one horrible raw February night. It's very late, and as soon as I've turned off into the park I'm completely alone in the darkness. I start to think about what you'd see, if you could train a telescope on me from the mountains of Norway. You'd see me by the street-lamps on the Blegdamsvej, then nothing as I vanished into the darkness, then another glimpse of me as I passed the lamp-post in front of the bandstand. And that's what we see in the cloud chamber. Not a continuous track but a series of glimpses – a series of collisions between the

passing electron and various molecules of water vapour. . . .
Or think of you, on your great papal progress to Leiden in
1925. What did Margrethe see of that, at home here in
Copenhagen? A picture postcard from Hamburg, perhaps.
Then one from Leiden. One from Göttingen. One from
Berlin. Because what we see in the cloud chamber are not
even the collisions themselves, but the water-droplets that
condense around them, as big as cities around a traveller –
no, vastly bigger still, relatively – complete countries –
Germany . . . Holland . . . Germany again. There is no
track, there are no precise addresses; only a vague list of
countries visited. I don't know why we hadn't thought of it
before, except that we were too busy arguing to think at
all.

Bohr You seem to have given up on all forms of
discussion. By the time I get back from Norway I find
you've done a draft of your uncertainty paper and you've
already sent it for publication!

Margrethe And an even worse battle begins.

Bohr My dear good Heisenberg, it's not open behaviour
to rush a first draft into print before we've discussed it
together! It's not the way we work!

Heisenberg No, the way we work is that you hound me
from first thing in the morning till last thing at night! The
way we work is that you drive me mad!

Bohr Yes, because the paper contains a fundamental
error.

Margrethe And here we go again.

Heisenberg No, but I show him the strangest truth
about the universe that any of us has stumbled on since
relativity – that you can never know everything about the
whereabouts of a particle, or anything else, even Bohr now,
as he prowls up and down the room in that maddening
way of his, because we can't observe it without introducing
some new element into the situation, a molecule of water
vapour for it to hit, or a piece of light – things which have

an energy of their own, and which therefore have an effect on what they hit. A small one, admittedly, in the case of Bohr . . .

Bohr   Yes, if you know where I am with the kind of accuracy we're talking about when we're dealing with particles, you can still measure my velocity to within – what . . .?

Heisenberg   Something like a billionth of a billionth of a kilometre per second. The theoretical point remains, though, that you have no absolutely determinate situation in the world, which among other things lays waste to the idea of causality, the whole foundation of science – because if you don't know how things are today you certainly can't know how they're going to be tomorrow. I shatter the objective universe around you – and all you can say is that there's an error in the formulation!

Bohr   There is!

Margrethe   Tea, anyone? Cake?

Heisenberg   Listen, in my paper what we're trying to locate is not a free electron off on its travels through a cloud chamber, but an electron when it's at home, moving around inside an atom . . .

Bohr   And the uncertainty arises not, as you claim, through its indeterminate recoil when it's hit by an incoming photon . . .

Heisenberg   Plain language, plain language!

Bohr   This *is* plain language.

Heisenberg   Listen . . .

Bohr   The language of classical mechanics.

Heisenberg   Listen! Copenhagen is an atom. Margrethe is its nucleus. About right, the scale? Ten thousand to one?

Bohr   Yes, yes.

Heisenberg   Now, Bohr's an electron. He's wandering

about the city somewhere in the darkness, no one knows where. He's here, he's there, he's everywhere and nowhere. Up in Faelled Park, down at Carlsberg. Passing City Hall, out by the harbour. I'm a photon. A quantum of light. I'm despatched into the darkness to find Bohr. And I succeed, because I manage to collide with him. . . . But what's happened? Look – he's been slowed down, he's been deflected! He's no longer doing exactly what he was so maddeningly doing when I walked into him!

Bohr But, Heisenberg, Heisenberg! You also have been deflected! If people can see what's happened to you, to their piece of light, then they can work out what must have happened to me! The trouble is knowing what's happened to you! Because to understand how people see you we have to treat you not just as a particle, but as a wave. I have to use not only your particle mechanics, I have to use the Schrödinger wave function.

Heisenberg I know – I put it in a postscript to my paper.

Bohr Everyone remembers the paper – no one remembers the postscript. But the question is fundamental. Particles are things, complete in themselves. Waves are disturbances in something else.

Heisenberg I know. Complementarity. It's in the postscript.

Bohr They're either one thing or the other. They can't be both. We have to choose one way of seeing them or the other. But as soon as we do we can't know everything about them.

Heisenberg And off he goes into orbit again. Incidentally exemplifying another application of complementarity. Exactly where you go as you ramble around is of course completely determined by your genes and the various physical forces acting on you. But it's also completely determined by your own entirely inscrutable whims from one moment to the next. So we can't completely understand your behaviour without seeing it both ways at once, and that's impossible. Which means that your extraordinary peregrinations are not fully objective aspects of the universe. They exist only partially, through the efforts of me or Margrethe, as our minds shift endlessly back and forth between the two approaches.

Bohr   You've never absolutely and totally accepted complementarity, have you?

Heisenberg   Yes! Absolutely and totally! I defended it at the Como Conference in 1927! I have adhered to it ever afterwards with religious fervour! You convinced me. I humbly accepted your criticisms.

Bohr   Not before you'd said some deeply wounding things.

Heisenberg   Good God, at one point you literally reduced me to tears!

Bohr   Forgive me, but I diagnosed them as tears of frustration and rage.

Heisenberg   I was having a tantrum?

Bohr   I have brought up children of my own.

Heisenberg   And what about Margrethe? Was *she* having a tantrum? Klein told me you reduced *her* to tears after I'd gone, making her type out your endless redraftings of the complementarity paper.

Bohr   I don't recall that.

Margrethe   I do.

Heisenberg   We had to drag Pauli out of bed in Hamburg once again to come to Copenhagen and negotiate peace.

Bohr   He succeeded. We ended up with a treaty. Uncertainty and complementarity became the two central tenets of the Copenhagen Interpretation of Quantum Mechanics.

Heisenberg   A political compromise, of course, like most treaties.

Bohr   You see? Somewhere inside you there are still secret reservations.

Heisenberg   Not at all – it works. That's what matters. It works, it works, it works!

Bohr   It works, yes. But it's more important than that. Because you see what we did in those three years, Heisenberg? Not to exaggerate, but we turned the world inside out! Yes, listen, now it comes, now it comes. . . . We put man back at the centre of the universe. Throughout history we keep finding ourselves displaced. We keep exiling ourselves to the periphery of things. First we turn ourselves into a mere adjunct of God's unknowable purposes, tiny figures kneeling in the great cathedral of creation. And no sooner have we recovered ourselves in the Renaissance, no sooner has man become, as Protagoras proclaimed him, the measure of all things, than we're pushed aside again by the products of our own reasoning! We're dwarfed again as physicists build the great new cathedrals for us to wonder at – the laws of classical mechanics that pre-date us from the beginning of eternity, that will survive us to eternity's end, that exist whether we exist or not. Until we come to the beginning of the twentieth century, and we're suddenly forced to rise from our knees again.

Heisenberg   It starts with Einstein.

Bohr   It starts with Einstein. He shows that measurement – measurement, on which the whole possibility of science depends – measurement is not an impersonal event that occurs with impartial universality. It's a human act, carried out from a specific point of view in time and space, from the one particular viewpoint of a possible observer. Then, here in Copenhagen in those three years in the mid-twenties we discover that there is no precisely determinable objective universe. That the universe exists only as a series of approximations. Only within the limits determined by our relationship with it. Only through the understanding lodged inside the human head.

Margrethe   So this man you've put at the centre of the universe – is it you, or is it Heisenberg?

Bohr   Now, now, my love.

Margrethe   Yes, but it makes a difference.

Bohr   Either of us. Both of us. Yourself. All of us.

Margrethe   If it's Heisenberg at the centre of the universe, then the one bit of the universe that he can't see is Heisenberg.

Heisenberg   So . . .

Margrethe   So it's no good asking him why he came to Copenhagen in 1941. He doesn't know!

Heisenberg   I thought for a moment just then I caught a glimpse of it.

Margrethe   Then you turned to look.

Heisenberg   And away it went.

Margrethe   Complementarity again. Yes?

Bohr   Yes, yes.

Margrethe   I've typed it out often enough. If you're doing something you have to concentrate on you can't also be thinking about doing it, and if you're thinking about doing it then you can't actually be doing it. Yes?

Heisenberg   Swerve left, swerve right, or think about it and die.

Bohr   But *after* you've done it . . .

Margrethe   You look back and make a guess, just like the rest of us. Only a worse guess, because you didn't see yourself doing it, and we did. Forgive me, but you don't even know why you did uncertainty in the first place.

Bohr Whereas if *you're* the one at the centre of the universe . . .

Margrethe Then I can tell you that it was because you wanted to drop a bomb on Schrödinger.

Heisenberg I wanted to show he was wrong, certainly.

Margrethe And Schrödinger was winning the war. When the Leipzig chair first became vacant that autumn he was short-listed for it and you weren't. You needed a wonderful new weapon.

Bohr Not to criticise, Margrethe, but you have a tendency to make everything personal.

Margrethe Because everything *is* personal! You've just read us all a lecture about it! You know how much Heisenberg wanted a chair. You know the pressure he was under from his family. I'm sorry, but you want to make everything seem heroically abstract and logical. And when you tell the story, yes, it all falls into place, it all has a beginning and a middle and an end. But I was there, and when I remember what it was like I'm there still, and I look around me and what I see isn't a story! It's confusion and rage and jealousy and tears and no one knowing what things mean or which way they're going to go.

Heisenberg All the same, it works, it works.

Margrethe Yes, it works wonderfully. Within three months of publishing your uncertainty paper you're offered Leipzig.

Heisenberg I didn't mean that.

Margrethe Not to mention somewhere else and somewhere else.

Heisenberg Halle and Munich and Zürich.

Bohr And various American universities.

Heisenberg But I didn't mean that.

Margrethe   And when you take up your chair at Leipzig you're how old?

Heisenberg   Twenty-six.

Bohr   The youngest full professor in Germany.

Heisenberg   I mean the Copenhagen Interpretation. The Copenhagen Interpretation works. However we got there, by whatever combination of high principles and low calculation, of most painfully hard thought and most painfully childish tears, it works. It goes on working.

Margrethe   Yes, and why did you both accept the Interpretation in the end? Was it really because you wanted to re-establish humanism?

Bohr   Of course not. It was because it was the only way to explain what the experimenters had observed.

Margrethe   Or was it because now you were becoming a professor you wanted a solidly established doctrine to teach? Because you wanted to have your new ideas publicly endorsed by the head of the church in Copenhagen? And perhaps Niels agreed to endorse them in return for your accepting *his* doctrines. For recognising him as head of the church. And if you want to know why you came to Copenhagen in 1941 I'll tell you that as well. You're right – there's no great mystery about it. You came to show yourself off to us.

Bohr   Margrethe!

Margrethe   No! When he first came in 1924 he was a humble assistant lecturer from a humiliated nation, grateful to have a job. Now here you are, back in triumph – the leading scientist in a nation that's conquered most of Europe. You've come to show us how well you've done in life.

Bohr   This is so unlike you!

Margrethe   I'm sorry, but isn't that really why he's here? Because he's burning to let us know that he's in charge of some vital piece of secret research. And that even so he's preserved a lofty moral independence. Preserved it so famously that he's being watched by the Gestapo. Preserved it so successfully that he's now also got a wonderfully important moral dilemma to face.

Bohr Yes, well, now you're simply working yourself up.

Margrethe A chain reaction. You tell one painful truth and it leads to two more. And as you frankly admit, you're going to go back and continue doing precisely what you were doing before, whatever Niels tells you.

Heisenberg Yes.

Margrethe Because you wouldn't dream of giving up such a wonderful opportunity for research.

Heisenberg Not if I can possibly help it.

Margrethe Also you want to demonstrate to the Nazis how useful theoretical physics can be. You want to save the honour of German science. You want to be there to re-establish it in all its glory as soon as the war's over.

Heisenberg All the same, I don't tell Speer that the reactor . . .

Margrethe . . . will produce plutonium, no, because you're afraid of what will happen if the Nazis commit huge resources, and you fail to deliver the bombs. Please don't try to tell us that you're a hero of the resistance.

Heisenberg I've never claimed to be a hero.

Margrethe Your talent is for ski-ing too fast for anyone to see where you are. For always being in more than one position at a time, like one of your particles.

Heisenberg I can only say that it worked. Unlike most of the gestures made by heroes of the resistance. It worked! I know what you think. You think I should have joined the plot against Hitler, and got myself hanged like the others.

Bohr Of course not.

Heisenberg You don't say it, because there are some things that can't be said. But you think it.

Bohr No.

Heisenberg What would it have achieved? What would it have achieved if you'd dived in after Christian, and drowned as well? But that's another thing that can't be said.

Bohr Only thought.

Heisenberg Yes. I'm sorry.

Bohr And rethought. Every day.

Heisenberg You had to be held back, I know.

Margrethe Whereas you held yourself back.

Heisenberg Better to stay on the boat, though, and fetch it about. Better to remain alive, and throw the lifebuoy. Surely!

Bohr Perhaps. Perhaps not.

Heisenberg Better. Better.

Margrethe Really it is ridiculous. You reasoned your way, both of you, with such astonishing delicacy and precision into the tiny world of the atom. Now it turns out that everything depends upon these really rather large objects on our shoulders. And what's going on in there is . . .

Heisenberg Elsinore.

Margrethe Elsinore, yes.

Heisenberg And you may be right. I *was* afraid of what would happen. I *was* conscious of being on the winning side. . . So many explanations for everything I did! So many of them sitting round the lunch-table! Somewhere at the head of the table, I think, is the real reason I came

to Copenhagen. Again I turn to look. . . . And for a
moment I almost see its face. Then next time I look the
chair at the head of the table is completely empty. There's
no reason at all. I didn't tell Speer simply because I didn't
think of it. I came to Copenhagen simply because I did
think of it. A million things we might do or might not do
every day. A million decisions that make themselves. Why
didn't you kill me?

Bohr   Why didn't I . . . ?

Heisenberg   Kill me. Murder me. That evening in 1941.
Here we are, walking back towards the house, and you've
just leapt to the conclusion that I'm going to arm Hitler
with nuclear weapons. You'll surely take any reasonable
steps to prevent it happening.

Bohr   By murdering you?

Heisenberg   We're in the middle of a war. I'm an
enemy. There's nothing odd or immoral about killing
enemies.

Bohr   I should fetch out my cap-pistol?

Heisenberg   You won't need your cap-pistol. You won't
even need a mine. You can do it without any loud bangs,
without any blood, without any spectacle of suffering. As
cleanly as a bomb-aimer pressing his release three thousand
metres above the earth. You simply wait till I've gone.
Then you sit quietly down in your favourite armchair here
and repeat aloud to Margrethe, in front of our unseen
audience, what I've just told you. I shall be dead almost as
soon as poor Casimir. A lot sooner than Gamow.

Bohr   My dear Heisenberg, the suggestion is of course . . .

Heisenberg   Most interesting. So interesting that it never
even occurred to you. Complementarity, once again. I'm
your enemy; I'm also your friend. I'm a danger to
mankind; I'm also your guest. I'm a particle; I'm also a
wave. We have one set of obligations to the world in
general, and we have other sets, never to be reconciled, to

our fellow-countrymen, to our neighbours, to our friends, to our family, to our children. We have to go through not two slits at the same time but twenty-two. All we can do is to look afterwards, and see what happened.

Margrethe I'll tell you another reason why you did uncertainty: you have a natural affinity for it.

Heisenberg Well, I must cut a gratifyingly chastened figure when I return in 1947. Crawling on my hands and knees again. My nation back in ruins.

Margrethe Not really. You're demonstrating that once more you personally have come out on top.

Heisenberg Begging for food parcels?

Margrethe Established in Göttingen under British protection, in charge of post-war German science.

Heisenberg That first year in Göttingen I slept on straw.

Margrethe Elisabeth said you had a most charming house thereafter.

Heisenberg I was given it by the British.

Margrethe Your new foster-parents. Who'd confiscated it from someone else.

Bohr Enough, my love, enough.

Margrethe No, I've kept my thoughts to myself for all these years. But it's maddening to have this clever son forever dancing about in front of our eyes, forever demanding our approval, forever struggling to shock us, forever begging to be told what the limits to his freedom are, if only so that he can go out and transgress them! I'm sorry, but really. . . . On your hands and knees? It's my dear, good, kind husband who's on his hands and knees! Literally. Crawling down to the beach in the darkness in 1943, fleeing like a thief in the night from his own homeland to escape being murdered. The protection of the

German Embassy that you boasted about didn't last for long. We were incorporated into the Reich.

Heisenberg I warned you in 1941. You wouldn't listen. At least Bohr got across to Sweden.

Margrethe And even as the fishing-boat was taking him across the Sound two freighters were arriving in the harbour to ship the entire Jewish population of Denmark eastwards. That great darkness inside the human soul was flooding out to engulf us all.

Heisenberg I did try to warn you.

Margrethe Yes, and where are you? Shut away in a cave like a savage, trying to conjure an evil spirit out of a hole in the ground. That's what it came down to in the end, all that shining springtime in the 1920s, that's what it produced – a more efficient machine for killing people.

Bohr It breaks my heart every time I think of it.

Heisenberg It broke all our hearts.

Margrethe And this wonderful machine may yet kill every man, woman, and child in the world. And if we really are the centre of the universe, if we really are all that's keeping it in being, what will be left?

Bohr Darkness. Total and final darkness.

Margrethe Even the questions that haunt us will at last be extinguished. Even the ghosts will die.

Heisenberg I can only say that I didn't do it. I didn't build the bomb.

Margrethe No, and why didn't you? I'll tell you that, too. It's the simplest reason of all. Because you couldn't. You didn't understand the physics.

Heisenberg That's what Goudsmit said.

Margrethe And Goudsmit knew. He was one of your magic circle. He and Uhlenbeck were the ones who did spin.

Heisenberg All the same, he had no idea of what I did or didn't understand about a bomb.

Margrethe He tracked you down across Europe for Allied Intelligence. He interrogated you after you were captured.

Heisenberg He blamed me, of course. His parents died in Auschwitz. He thought I should have done something to save them. I don't know what. So many hands stretching up from the darkness for a lifeline, and no lifeline that could ever reach them . . .

Margrethe He said you didn't understand the crucial difference between a reactor and a bomb.

Heisenberg I understood very clearly. I simply didn't tell the others.

Margrethe Ah.

Heisenberg I understood, though.

Margrethe But secretly.

Heisenberg You can check if you don't believe me.

Margrethe There's evidence, for once?

Heisenberg It was all most carefully recorded.

Margrethe Witnesses, even?

Heisenberg Unimpeachable witnesses.

Margrethe Who wrote it down?

Heisenberg Who recorded it and transcribed it.

Margrethe Even though you didn't tell anyone?

Heisenberg I told one person. I told Otto Hahn. That terrible night at Farm Hall, after we'd heard the news. Somewhere in the small hours, after everyone had finally gone to bed, and we were alone together. I gave him a reasonably good account of how the bomb had worked.

Margrethe After the event.

Heisenberg   After the event. Yes. When it didn't matter any more. All the things Goudsmit said I didn't understand. Fast neutrons in 235. The plutonium option. A reflective shell to reduce neutron escape. Even the method of triggering it.

Bohr   The critical mass. That was the most important thing. The amount of material you needed to establish the chain-reaction. Did you tell him the critical mass?

Heisenberg   I gave him a figure, yes. You can look it up! Because that was the other secret of the house-party. Diebner asked me when we first arrived if I thought there were hidden microphones. I laughed. I told him the British were far too old-fashioned to know about Gestapo methods. I underestimated them. They had microphones everywhere – they were recording everything. Look it up! Everything we said. Everything we went through that terrible night. Everything I told Hahn alone in the small hours.

Bohr   But the critical mass. You gave him a figure. What was the figure you gave him?

Heisenberg   I forget.

Bohr   Heisenberg . . .

Heisenberg   It's all on the record. You can see for yourself.

Bohr   The figure for the Hiroshima bomb . . .

Heisenberg   Was fifty kilograms.

Bohr   So that was the figure you gave Hahn? Fifty kilograms?

Heisenberg   I said about a ton.

Bohr   About a ton? A thousand kilograms? Heisenberg, I believe I am at last beginning to understand something.

Heisenberg   The one thing I was wrong about.

Bohr   You were twenty times over.

Heisenberg   The one thing.

Bohr   But, Heisenberg, your mathematics, your mathematics! How could they have been so far out?

Heisenberg   They weren't. As soon as I calculated the diffusion I got it just about right.

Bohr   As soon as you calculated it?

Heisenberg   I gave everyone a seminar on it a week later. It's in the record! Look it up!

Bohr   You mean . . . you hadn't calculated it before? You hadn't done the diffusion equation?

Heisenberg   There was no need to.

Bohr   No need to?

Heisenberg   The calculation had already been done.

Bohr   Done by whom?

Heisenberg   By Perrin and Flügge in 1939.

Bohr   By Perrin and Flügge? But, my dear Heisenberg, that was for natural uranium. Wheeler and I showed that it was only the 235 that fissioned.

Heisenberg   Your great paper. The basis of everything we did.

Bohr   So you needed to calculate the figure for pure 235.

Heisenberg   Obviously.

Bohr   And you didn't?

Heisenberg   I didn't.

Bohr   And that's why you were so confident you couldn't do it until you had the plutonium. Because you spent the entire war believing that it would take not a few kilograms of 235, but a ton or more. And to make a ton of 235 in any plausible time . . .

Heisenberg   Would have needed something like two

hundred million separator units. It was plainly
unimaginable.

Bohr   If you'd realised you had to produce only a few
kilograms . . .

Heisenberg   Even to make a single kilogram would need
something like two hundred thousand units.

Bohr   But two hundred million is one thing; two hundred
thousand is another. You might just possibly have imagined
setting up two hundred thousand.

Heisenberg   Just possibly.

Bohr   The Americans did imagine it.

Heisenberg   Because Otto Frisch and Rudolf Peierls
actually did the calculation. They solved the diffusion
equation.

Bohr   Frisch was my old assistant.

Heisenberg   Peierls was my old pupil.

Bohr   An Austrian and a German.

Heisenberg   So they should have been making their
calculation for us, at the Kaiser Wilhelm Institute in Berlin.
But instead they made it at the University of Birmingham,
in England.

Margrethe   Because they were Jews.

Heisenberg   There's something almost mathematically
elegant about that.

Bohr   They also started with Perrin and Flügge.

Heisenberg   They also thought it would take tons. They
also thought it was unimaginable.

Bohr   Until one day . . .

Heisenberg   They did the calculation.

Bohr   They discovered just how fast the chain reaction
would go.

Heisenberg   And therefore how little material you'd need.

Bohr   They said slightly over half a kilogram.

Heisenberg   About the size of a tennis ball.

Bohr   They were wrong, of course.

Heisenberg   It was a hundredth of the correct figure.

Bohr   Which made it seem a hundred times more imaginable than it actually was.

Heisenberg   Whereas I left it seeming twenty times more unimaginable.

Bohr   So all your agonising in Copenhagen about plutonium was beside the point. You could have done it without ever building the reactor. You could have done it with 235 all the time.

Heisenberg   Almost certainly not.

Bohr   Just possibly, though.

Heisenberg   Just possibly.

Bohr   And *that* question you'd settled long before you arrived in Copenhagen. Simply by failing to try the diffusion equation.

Heisenberg   Such a tiny failure.

Bohr   But the consequences went branching out over the years, doubling and redoubling.

Heisenberg   Until they were large enough to save a city. Which city? Any of the cities that we never dropped our bomb on.

Bohr   London, presumably, if you'd had it in time. If the Americans had already entered the war, and the Allies had begun to liberate Europe, then . . .

Heisenberg   Who knows? Paris as well. Amsterdam. Perhaps Copenhagen.

Bohr   So, Heisenberg, tell us this one simple thing: why didn't you do the calculation?

Heisenberg   The question is why Frisch and Peierls *did* do it. It was a stupid waste of time. However much 235 it turned out to be, it was obviously going to be more than anyone could imagine producing.

Bohr   Except that it wasn't!

Heisenberg   Except that it wasn't.

Bohr   So why . . . ?

Heisenberg   I don't know! I don't know why I didn't do it! Because I never thought of it! Because it didn't occur to me! Because I assumed it wasn't worth doing!

Bohr   Assumed? Assumed? You never assumed things! That's how you got uncertainty, because you rejected our assumptions! You calculated, Heisenberg! You calculated everything! The first thing you did with a problem was the mathematics!

Heisenberg   You should have been there to slow me down.

Bohr   Yes, you wouldn't have got away with it if I'd been standing over you.

Heisenberg   Though in fact you made exactly the same assumption! You thought there was no danger for exactly the same reason as I did! Why didn't *you* calculate it?

Bohr   Why didn't *I* calculate it?

Heisenberg   Tell us why *you* didn't calculate it and we'll know why *I* didn't!

Bohr   It's obvious why *I* didn't!

Heisenberg   Go on.

Margrethe   Because he wasn't trying to build a bomb!

Heisenberg   Yes. Thank you. Because he wasn't trying to build a bomb. I imagine it was the same with me. Because

I wasn't trying to build a bomb. Thank you.

Bohr   So, you bluffed yourself, the way I did at poker with the straight I never had. But in that case ...

Heisenberg   Why did I come to Copenhagen? Yes, why did I come ... ?

Bohr   One more draft, yes? One final draft!

Heisenberg   And once again I crunch over the familiar gravel to the Bohrs' front door, and tug at the familiar bell-pull. Why have I come? I know perfectly well. Know so well that I've no need to ask myself. Until once again the heavy front door opens.

Bohr   He stands on the doorstep blinking in the sudden flood of light from the house. Until this instant his thoughts have been everywhere and nowhere, like unobserved particles, through all the slits in the diffraction grating simultaneously. Now they have to be observed and specified.

Heisenberg   And at once the clear purposes inside my head lose all definite shape. The light falls on them and they scatter.

Bohr   My dear Heisenberg!

Heisenberg   My dear Bohr!

Bohr   Come in, come in ...

Heisenberg   How difficult it is to see even what's in front of one's eyes. All we possess is the present, and the present endlessly dissolves into the past. Bohr has gone even as I turn to see Margrethe.

Margrethe   Niels is right. You look older.

Bohr   I believe you had some personal trouble.

Heisenberg   Margrethe slips into history even as I turn back to Bohr. And yet how much more difficult still it is to catch the slightest glimpse of what's behind one's eyes. Here I am at the centre of the universe, and yet all I can see are two smiles that don't belong to me.

Margrethe   How is Elisabeth? How are the children?

Heisenberg   Very well. They send their love, of course
... I can feel a third smile in the room, very close to me.
Could it be the one I suddenly see for a moment in the
mirror there? And is the awkward stranger wearing it in
any way connected with this presence that I can feel in the
room? This all-enveloping, unobserved presence?

Margrethe   I watch the two smiles in the room, one
awkward and ingratiating, the other rapidly fading from
incautious warmth to bare politeness. There's also a third
smile in the room, I know, unchangingly courteous, I hope,
and unchangingly guarded.

Heisenberg   You've managed to get some ski-ing?

Bohr   I glance at Margrethe, and for a moment I see
what she can see and I can't – myself, and the smile
vanishing from my face as poor Heisenberg blunders on.

Heisenberg   I look at the two of them looking at me,
and for a moment I see the third person in the room as
clearly as I see them. Their importunate guest, stumbling
from one crass and unwelcome thoughtfulness to the next.

Bohr   I look at him looking at me, anxiously, pleadingly,
urging me back to the old days, and I see what he sees.
And yes – now it comes, now it comes – there's someone
missing from the room. He sees me. He sees Margrethe.
He doesn't see himself.

Heisenberg   Two thousand million people in the world,
and the one who has to decide their fate is the only one
who's always hidden from me.

Bohr   You suggested a stroll.

Heisenberg   You remember Elsinore? The darkness
inside the human soul . . . ?

Bohr   And out we go. Out under the autumn trees.

Through the blacked-out streets.

Heisenberg Now there's no one in the world except Bohr and the invisible other. Who is he, this all-enveloping presence in the darkness?

Margrethe The flying particle wanders the darkness, no one knows where. It's here, it's there, it's everywhere and nowhere.

Bohr With careful casualness he begins to ask the question he's prepared.

Heisenberg Does one as a physicist have the moral right to work on the practical exploitation of atomic energy?

Margrethe The great collision.

Bohr I stop. He stops . . .

Margrethe This is how they work.

Heisenberg He gazes at me, horrified.

Margrethe Now at last he knows where he is and what he's doing.

Heisenberg He turns away.

Margrethe And even as the moment of collision begins it's over.

Bohr Already we're hurrying back towards the house.

Margrethe Already they're both flying away from each other into the darkness again.

Heisenberg Our conversation's over.

Bohr Our great partnership.

Heisenberg All our friendship.

Margrethe And everything about him becomes as uncertain as it was before.

Bohr Unless . . . yes . . . a thought-experiment. . . . Let's suppose for a moment that I don't go flying off into the night. Let's see what happens if instead I remember the paternal role I'm supposed to play. If I stop, and control my anger, and turn to him. And ask him why.

Heisenberg Why?

Bohr Why are you confident that it's going to be so reassuringly difficult to build a bomb with 235? Is it because you've done the calculation?

Heisenberg The calculation?

Bohr Of the diffusion in 235. No. It's because you haven't calculated it. You haven't considered calculating it. You hadn't consciously realised there was a calculation to be made.

Heisenberg And of course now I *have* realised. In fact it wouldn't be all that difficult. Let's see. . . . The scattering cross-section's about 6×10^{-24}, so the mean free path would be . . . Hold on . . .

Bohr And suddenly a very different and very terrible new world begins to take shape . . .

Margrethe That was the last and greatest demand that Heisenberg made on his friendship with you. To be understood when he couldn't understand himself. And that was the last and greatest act of friendship for Heisenberg that you performed in return. To leave him misunderstood.

Heisenberg Yes. Perhaps I should thank you.

Bohr Perhaps you should.

Margrethe Anyway, it was the end of the story.

Bohr Though perhaps there was also something I should thank *you* for. That summer night in 1943, when I escaped across the Sound in the fishing-boat, and the freighters arrived from Germany . . .

Margrethe What's that to do with Heisenberg?

Bohr When the ships arrived on the Wednesday there were eight thousand Jews in Denmark to be arrested and crammed into their holds. On the Friday evening, at the start of the Sabbath, when the SS began their round-up, there was scarcely a Jew to be found.

Margrethe They'd all been hidden in churches and hospitals, in people's homes and country cottages.

Bohr But how was that possible? – Because we'd been tipped off by someone in the German Embassy.

Heisenberg Georg Duckwitz, their shipping specialist.

Bohr Your man?

Heisenberg One of them.

Bohr He was a remarkable informant. He told us the day before the freighters arrived – the very day that Hitler issued the order. He gave us the exact time that the SS would move.

Margrethe It was the Resistance who got them out of their hiding-places and smuggled them across the Sound.

Bohr For a handful of us in one fishing smack to get past the German patrol-boats was remarkable enough. For a whole armada to get past, with the best part of eight thousand people on board, was like the Red Sea parting.

Margrethe I thought there *were* no German patrol-boats that night?

Bohr No – the whole squadron had suddenly been reported unseaworthy.

Heisenberg How they got away with it I can't imagine.

Bohr Duckwitz again?

Heisenberg He also went to Stockholm and asked the Swedish Government to accept everyone.

Bohr So perhaps I should thank you.

Heisenberg For what?

Bohr My life. All our lives.

Heisenberg   Nothing to do with me by that time. I regret to say.

Bohr   But after I'd gone you came back to Copenhagen.

Heisenberg   To make sure that our people didn't take over the Institute in your absence.

Bohr   I've never thanked you for that, either.

Heisenberg   You know they offered me your cyclotron?

Bohr   You could have separated a little 235 with it.

Heisenberg   Meanwhile you were going on from Sweden to Los Alamos.

Bohr   To play my small but helpful part in the deaths of a hundred thousand people.

Margrethe   Niels, you did nothing wrong!

Bohr   Didn't I?

Heisenberg   Of course not. You were a good man, from first to last, and no one could ever say otherwise. Whereas I . . .

Bohr   Whereas you, my dear Heisenberg, never managed to contribute to the death of one single solitary person in all your life.

Margrethe   Well, yes.

Heisenberg   Did I?

Margrethe   One. Or so you told us. The poor fellow you guarded overnight, when you were a boy in Munich, while he was waiting to be shot in the morning.

Bohr   All right then, one. One single soul on his conscience, to set against all the others.

Margrethe   But that one single soul was emperor of the universe, no less than each of us. Until the morning came.

Heisenberg   No, when the morning came I persuaded them to let him go.

Bohr   Heisenberg, I have to say – if people are to be measured strictly in terms of observable quantities . . .

Heisenberg   Then we should need a strange new quantum ethics. There'd be a place in heaven for me. And another one for the SS man I met on my way home from Haigerloch. That was the end of my war. The Allied troops were closing in; there was nothing more we could do. Elisabeth and the children had taken refuge in a village in Bavaria, so I went to see them before I was captured. I had to go by bicycle – there were no trains or road transport by that time – and I had to travel by night and sleep under a hedge by day, because all through the daylight hours the skies were full of Allied planes, scouring the roads for anything that moved. A man on a bicycle would have been the biggest target left in Germany. Three days and three nights I travelled. Out of Württemberg, down through the Swabian Jura and the first foothills of the Alps. Across my ruined homeland. Was this what I'd chosen for it? This endless rubble? This perpetual smoke in the sky? These hungry faces? Was this my doing? And all the desperate people on the roads. The most desperate of all were the SS. Bands of fanatics with nothing left to lose, roaming around shooting deserters out of hand, hanging them from roadside trees. The second night, and suddenly there it is – the terrible familiar black tunic emerging from the twilight in front of me. On his lips as I stop – the one terrible familiar word. 'Deserter,' he says. He sounds as exhausted as I am. I give him the travel order I've written for myself. But there's hardly enough light in the sky to read by, and he's too weary to bother. He begins to open his holster instead. He's going to shoot me because it's simply less labour. And suddenly I'm thinking very quickly and clearly – it's like ski-ing, or that night on Heligoland, or the one in Faelled Park. What comes into my mind this time is the pack of American cigarettes I've got in my pocket. And already it's in my hand – I'm holding it out to him. The most desperate solution to a problem yet. I wait while he stands there looking at it, trying to make it out, trying to think, his left hand holding my useless piece of paper, his right on the fastening of the holster. There are two simple words in large print on the pack: Lucky Strike. He closes the holster, and takes the cigarettes instead. . . . It had worked, it had worked! Like all the other solutions to all the other problems. For twenty cigarettes he let me live. And on I went. Three days and three nights. Past the weeping children, the lost and hungry children, drafted to fight, then abandoned by their commanders. Past the starving slave-labourers walking home to France, to Poland, to Estonia. Through Gammertingen and Biberach and Memmingen. Mindelheim, Kaufbeuren, and Schöngau. Across my beloved homeland. My ruined and dishonoured and beloved homeland.

Bohr   My dear Heisenberg! My dear friend!

Margrethe   Silence. The silence we always in the end return to.

Heisenberg   And of course I know what they're thinking about.

Margrethe   All those lost children on the road.

Bohr   Heisenberg wandering the world like a lost child himself.

Margrethe   Our own lost children.

Heisenberg   And over goes the tiller once again.

Bohr   So near, so near! So slight a thing!

Margrethe   He stands in the doorway, watching me, then he turns his head away . . .

Heisenberg   And once again away he goes, into the dark waters.

Bohr   Before we can lay our hands on anything, our life's over.

Heisenberg   Before we can glimpse who or what we are, we're gone and laid to dust.

Bohr   Settled among all the dust we raised.

Margrethe   And sooner or later there will come a time when all our children are laid to dust, and all our children's children.

Bohr   When no more decisions, great or small, are ever made again. When there's no more uncertainty, because there's no more knowledge.

Margrethe   And when all our eyes are closed, when even the ghosts have gone, what will be left of our beloved world? Our ruined and dishonoured and beloved world?

Heisenberg   But in the meanwhile, in this most precious meanwhile, there it is. The trees in Faelled Park. Gammertingen and Biberach and Mindelheim. Our children and our children's children. Preserved, just possibly, by that one short moment in Copenhagen. By some event that will never quite be located or defined. By that final core of uncertainty at the heart of things.

POSTSCRIPT

Where a work of fiction features historical characters and historical events it's reasonable to want to know how much of it is fiction and how much of it is history. So let me make it as clear as I can in regard to this play.

The central event in it is a real one. Heisenberg *did* go to Copenhagen in 1941, and there *was* a meeting with Bohr, in the teeth of all the difficulties encountered by my characters. He probably went to dinner at the Bohrs' house, and the two men probably went for a walk to escape from any possible microphones, though there is some dispute about even these simple matters. The question of what they actually said to each other has been even more disputed, and where there's ambiguity in the play about what happened, it's because there is in the recollection of the participants. Much more sustained speculation still has been devoted to the question of what Heisenberg was hoping to achieve by the meeting. All the alternative and co-existing explications offered in the play, except perhaps the final one, have been aired at various times, in one form or another.

Most anxious of all to establish some agreed version of the meeting was Heisenberg himself. He did indeed go back in 1947 with his British minder, Ronald Fraser, and attempted to find some common ground in the matter with Bohr. But it proved to be too delicate a task, and (according to Heisenberg, at any rate, in his memoirs) 'we both came to feel that it would be better to stop disturbing the spirits of the past.' This is where my play departs from the historical record, by supposing that at some later time, when everyone involved had become spirits of the past themselves, they argued the question out further, until they had achieved a little more understanding of what was going on, just as they had so many times when they were alive with the intractable difficulties presented by the internal workings of the atom.

The account of these earlier discussions in the twenties reflects at any rate one or two of the key topics, and the passion with which the argument was conducted, as it emerges from the biographical and autobiographical record.

I am acutely aware of how over-simplified my version is. Max Born described the real story as not so much 'a straight staircase upwards, but a tangle of interconnected alleys', and I have found it impossible to follow these in any detail (even where I can begin to understand them). In particular I have grossly understated the crucial role played by Born himself and by his pupil Pascual Jordan at Göttingen in formulating quantum mechanics (it was Born who supplied the understanding of matrices that Heisenberg lacked, and the statistical interpretation of Schrödinger's wave function), and of Wolfgang Pauli in Hamburg, whose exclusion principle filled in one of the key pieces in the puzzle.

But the account of the German and American bomb programmes, and of the two physicists' participation in them, is taken from the historical record; so is the fate of Danish Jewry; Heisenberg's experiences in Germany before and during the war, his subsequent internment, and the depression that clouded his later years. I have filled out some of the details, but in general what he says happened to him – at the end of the First World War, on Heligoland, during his nocturnal walk in Faelled Park, during the Berlin air-raid and his internment, and on his ride across Germany, with its near-fatal encounter along the way – is based very closely upon the accounts he gave in life.

The actual words spoken by my characters are of course entirely their own. If this needs any justification then I can only appeal to Heisenberg himself. In his memoirs dialogue plays an important part, he says, because he hopes 'to demonstrate that science is rooted in conversations'. But, as he explains, conversations, even real conversations, cannot be reconstructed literally several decades later. So he freely reinvents them, and appeals in his turn to Thucydides. (Heisenberg's father was a professor of classics, and he was an accomplished classicist himself, on top of all his other distinctions.) Thucydides explains in his preface to the *History of the Peloponnesian War* that, although he had avoided all 'storytelling', when it came to the speeches, 'I have found it impossible to remember their exact wording. Hence I have made each orator speak as, in my opinion, he would have done in the circumstances, but keeping as close as I could to the train of thought that guided his actual speech.' Thucydides was trying to give an account of speeches that had actually been made, many of which he had himself heard. Some of the dialogue in my play represents speeches that must have been made in one form or another; some of it speeches that were certainly never made at all. I hope, though, that in some sense it respects the Thucydidean principle, and that speeches (and indeed actions) follow in so far as possible the original protagonists' train of thought.

But how far is it possible to know what their train of thought was? This is where I have departed from the established historical record – from any possible historical record. The great challenge facing the storyteller and the historian alike is to get inside people's heads, to stand where they stood and see the world as they saw it, to make some informed estimate of their motives and intentions – and this is precisely where recorded and recordable history cannot reach. Even when all the external evidence has been mastered, the only way into the protagonists' heads is through the imagination. This indeed is the substance of the play.

*

I can't claim to be the first person to notice the parallels between Heisenberg's science and his life. They provide David Cassidy with the title (*Uncertainty*) for his excellent biography (the standard work in English). 'Especially difficult and controversial,' says Cassidy in his introduction, 'is a retrospective evaluation of Heisenberg's activities during the Third Reich and particularly during World War II. Since the end of the war, an enormous range of views about this man and his behaviour have been expressed, views that have been fervently, even passionately, held by a variety of individuals. It is as if, for some, the intense emotions unleashed by the unspeakable horrors of that war and regime have combined with the many ambiguities, dualities, and compromises of Heisenberg's life and actions to make

Heisenberg himself subject to a type of uncertainty principle
. . .' Thomas Powers makes a similar point in his
extraordinary and encyclopaedic book *Heisenberg's War*, which
first aroused my interest in the trip to Copenhagen; he says
that Heisenberg's later reticence on his role in the failure of
the German bomb programme 'introduces an element of
irreducible uncertainty'.

Cassidy does not explore the parallel further. Powers even
appends a footnote to his comment: 'Forgive me.' The
apology seems to me unnecessary. It's true that the concept
of uncertainty is one of those scientific notions that has
become common coinage, and generalised to the point of
losing much of its original meaning. The idea as introduced
by Heisenberg into quantum mechanics was precise and
technical. It didn't suggest that everything about the
behaviour of particles was unknowable, or hazy. What it
limited was the simultaneous measurement of 'canonically
conjugate variables', such as position and momentum, or
energy and time. The more precisely you measure one
variable, it said, the less precise your measurement of the
related variable can be; and this ratio, the uncertainty
relationship, is itself precisely formulable.

None of this, plainly, applies directly to our observations
of thought and intention. Thoughts are not locatable by pairs
of conjugate variables, so there can be no question of a ratio
of precision. Powers seems to imply that in Heisenberg's case
the uncertainty arises purely because 'questions of motive
and intention cannot be established more clearly than he was
willing to state them'. It's true that Heisenberg was under
contradictory pressures after the war which made it
particularly difficult for him to explain what he had been
trying to do. He wanted to distance himself from the Nazis,
but he didn't want to suggest that he had been a traitor. He
was reluctant to claim to his fellow-Germans that he had
deliberately lost them the war, but he was no less reluctant
to suggest that he had failed them simply out of
incompetence.

But the uncertainty surely begins long before the point
where Heisenberg might have offered an explanation. He

was under at least as many contradictory pressures at the time to shape the actions he later failed to explain, and the uncertainty would still have existed, for us and for him, even if he had been as open, honest, and helpful as it is humanly possible to be. What people say about their own motives and intentions, even when they are not caught in the traps that entangled Heisenberg, is always subject to question – as subject to question as what anybody else says about them. Thoughts and intentions, even one's own – perhaps one's own most of all – remain shifting and elusive. There is not one single thought or intention of any sort that can ever be precisely established.

What the uncertainty of thoughts does have in common with the uncertainty of particles is that the difficulty is not just a practical one, but a systematic limitation which cannot even in theory be circumvented. It is patently not resolved by the efforts of psychologists and psycho-analysts, and it will not be resolved by neurologists, either, even when everything is known about the structure and workings of the brain, any more than semantic questions can be resolved by looking at the machine code of a computer. And since, according to the so-called 'Copenhagen Interpretation' of quantum mechanics – the interconnected set of theories that was developed by Heisenberg, Bohr, and others in the twenties – the whole possibility of saying or thinking anything about the world, even the most apparently objective, abstract aspects of it studied by the natural sciences, depends upon human observation, and is subject to the limitations which the human mind imposes, this uncertainty in our thinking is also fundamental to the nature of the world.

'Uncertainty' is not a very satisfactory word to come at this. It sits awkwardly even in its original context. You can be uncertain about things which are themselves entirely definite, and about which you could be entirely certain if you were simply better informed. Indeed, the very idea of uncertainty seems to imply the possibility of certainty. Heisenberg and Bohr used several different German words in different contexts. Bohr (who spoke more or less perfect

German) sometimes referred to *Unsicherheit*, which means quite simply unsureness. In Heisenberg's original paper he talks about *Ungenauigkeit* – inexactness – and the most usual term now in German seems to be *Unschärfe* – blurredness or fuzziness. But the word he adopts in his general conclusion, and which he uses when he refers back to the period later in his memoirs, is *Unbestimmtheit*, for which it's harder to find a satisfactory English equivalent. Although it means uncertainty in the sense of vagueness, it's plainly derived from *bestimmen*, to determine or to ascertain. This is reflected better in the other English translation which is sometimes used, but which seems to be less familiar: indeterminacy. 'Undeterminedness' would be closer still, though clumsy. Less close to the German, but even closer to the reality of the situation, would be 'indeterminability'.

Questions of translation apart, Heisenberg's choice of word suggests that, at the time he wrote his paper, he had not fully grasped the metaphysical implications of what he was saying. Indeed, he concludes that the experiments concerned are affected by *Unbestimmtheit* 'purely empirically'. He was not, as Bohr complained, at that time greatly interested in the philosophical fallout from physics and mathematics (though he became much more so later on in life), and he was publishing in a hurry, as Bohr also complained, before he had had a chance to discuss the work with either Bohr or anyone else. His paper seems to imply that electrons have definite orbits, even if these are unknowable; he talks about a quantum of light completely throwing the electron out of its 'orbit', even though he puts the word into inverted commas, and says that it has no rational sense here. The title of the paper itself reinforces this impression: *Über den anschaulichen Inhalt der quantentheoretischen Kinematik und Mechanik*. Again there are translation problems. '*Anschaulich*' means graphic, concrete, 'look-at-able'; the title is usually translated as referring to the 'perceptual' content of the disciplines concerned, which again seems to suggest a contrast with their unperceived aspects – as if Heisenberg were concerned merely about our difficulties in visualising abstractions, not about the physical implications of this.

*

The Copenhagen Interpretation of quantum mechanics was scientific orthodoxy for most of the twentieth century, and is the theoretical basis (for better or worse) on which the century's dramatic physical demonstrations of nuclear forces were constructed. But it has not gone unchallenged. Einstein never accepted it, though he could never find a way round it. The mathematician Roger Penrose regards the present state of quantum theory as 'provisional', and quotes Schrödinger, de Broglie, and Dirac as forerunners in this view.

An alternative to the Copenhagen Interpretation, explaining the apparent superimposition of different states that appears at the quantum level in terms of a multiplicity of parallel worlds, was developed after the Second World War by Hugh Everett III, who had been a graduate student of John Wheeler, Bohr's associate in the famous paper which opened the way to an understanding of uranium fission. David Deutsch, who proposes an extreme version of Everett's ideas in his book *The Fabric of Reality*, claims that 'hardly anyone' still believes in the Copenhagen Interpretation. I have put this view to a number of physicists. They all seemed greatly surprised by it; but maybe I have hit upon precisely the supposed handful who remain in the faith.

Another follower of Everett (though he seems to differ quite sharply from Deutsch) is Murray Gell-Mann, who with Yuval Ne'eman revolutionised elementary particle theory in the sixties with the introduction of the quark, in its three different 'colours' and six different 'flavours', as the fundamental unit of the material world. Gell-Mann believes that quantum mechanics is the fundamental tool for understanding the universe, but he sees the Copenhagen Interpretation, with its dependence upon an observer and the human act of measurement, as anthropocentric, and as characterising merely a special case that he calls 'the approximate quantum mechanics of measured systems'. I hesitate to express any reservations about something I understand so little, particularly when it comes from such an authority, but it seems to me that the view which Gell-Mann favours, and which involves what he calls alternative 'histories' or 'narratives', is precisely as anthropocentric as Bohr's, since histories and narratives are not freestanding elements of the universe, but human constructs as subjective and as restricted in their viewpoint as the act of observation.

The relevance of indeterminacy to quantum mechanics has also been challenged. A version of the famous thought experiment involving two slits has now actually been carried out in the laboratory (at the University of Konstanz). It confirms, as Bohr hypothesised, that while an unobserved particle seems to pass through both slits, so that it forms a characteristic interference pattern on a screen beyond them, any act of observation that attempts to determine which of the two paths the particle actually follows necessarily destroys the phenomenon, so that the interference pattern vanishes. But the experiment appears to suggest that, although the uncertainty principle is true, it accounts for discrepancies far too small to explain the loss of interference. The observation in the laboratory experiment, moreover, was carried out not, as in the old thought experiment, by hitting the particle involved with a photon, which transfers part of its energy to the particle and so alters its path, but by a way of marking with microwaves which has almost no effect on the particle's momentum.

Some physicists now accept that the loss of interference is caused by a much stranger and less quasi-classical aspect of the quantum world – entanglement. The notion was introduced by Schrödinger in 1935, and suggests that where quantum-mechanical entities become involved with each other (as with the particle and the photon), they form states of affairs which continue to have a collective identity and behaviour, even though their components have physically separated again. The difficulties in this are obvious, but there is no interpretation of quantum-mechanical phenomena that does not involve breathtaking challenges to the logic of our everyday experience.

For the references to all these developments see the

bibliography at the end of this Postscript.

*

What about my characters? Are they anything like their originals?

It's impossible to catch the exact tone of voice of people one never knew, with only the written record to go on, especially when most of what their contemporaries recall them as saying was originally said in other languages. There are also more particular problems with all three of my protagonists.

Bohr, for a start, was as notorious for his inarticulacy and inaudibility as he was famous for his goodness and lovability. He was fluent in various languages, but I have heard it said that the problem was to know which language he was being fluent in. Schrödinger, after his epic confrontation with Bohr in 1926, described him as often talking 'for minutes almost in a dreamlike, visionary and really quite unclear manner, partly because he is so full of consideration and constantly hesitates – fearing that the other might take a statement of his [Bohr's] point of view as an insufficient appreciation of the other's . . .' My Bohr is necessarily a little more coherent than this – and I have been told by various correspondents who knew him that in private, if not in public, he could be much more cogent and incisive than Schrödinger evidently found him.

The problem with Margrethe is that there is relatively little biographical material to go on. She and Niels were plainly mutually devoted, and everything suggests that she was as generally loved as he was. She had no scientific training, but Bohr constantly discussed his work with her, presumably avoiding technical language – though she must have become fairly familiar with even that since she typed out each draft of his papers. I suspect she was more gracious and reserved than she appears here, but she plainly had great firmness of character – in later life she was known as *Dronning* (Queen) Margrethe. She was always cooler about Heisenberg than Bohr was, and she was openly angry about his visit in 1941. According to Bohr she objected strongly to his being invited to the house, and relented only when Bohr promised to avoid politics and restrict the conversation to physics. Bohr himself always refused to be drawn about Heisenberg's trip in 1941, but she insisted, even after the war, even after all Heisenberg's attempts to explain, 'No matter what anyone says, that was a hostile visit.'

The problem with Heisenberg is his elusiveness and ambiguity, which is of course what the play is attempting to elucidate. The one thing about him that everyone agreed upon was what Max Born, his mentor in Göttingen, called 'his unbelievable quickness and precision of understanding'. The contrast with Bohr is almost comic. 'Probably [Bohr's] most characteristic property,' according to George Gamow, 'was the slowness of his thinking and comprehension.'

As a young man Heisenberg seems to have had an appealing eagerness and directness. Born described him as looking like a simple farm boy, with clear bright eyes, and a radiant expression on his face. Somebody else thought he looked 'like a bright carpenter's apprentice just returned from technical school'. Victor Weisskopf says that he made friends easily, and that everyone liked him. Bohr, after their first meeting in 1922, was delighted by Heisenberg's 'nice shy nature, his good temper, his eagerness and his enthusiasm'. There was something about him of the prize-winning student, who is good at everything required of him, and Bohr was not the only father-figure to whom he appealed. He had a somewhat similar relationship to Sommerfeld, his first professor in Munich, and in his difficulties with the Nazis he turned to two elders of German physics for counsel, Max Planck and Max von Laue. His closest friend and colleague was probably Carl Friedrich von Weizsäcker, who was younger than him, but it is striking that during his internment the person he chose to confide his explanation of the Hiroshima bomb to was not Weizsäcker, who was interned with him (although he may well have discussed it with him already), but the 66-year-old Otto Hahn.

The American physicist Jeremy Bernstein says that 'he

had the first truly quantum-mechanical mind – the ability to take the leap beyond the classical visualising pictures into the abstract, all-but-impossible-to-visualise world of the subatomic . . .' Cassidy believes that a great part of his genius was his 'ability to adopt a serviceable solution regardless of accepted wisdom'. Rudolf Peierls stresses his intuition. He would 'almost always intuitively know the answer to a problem, then look for a mathematical solution to give it to him'. The obverse of this, according to Peierls, is that 'he was always very casual about numbers' – a weakness that seems to have contributed to his downfall – or his salvation – in the atomic bomb programme.

Margrethe always found him difficult, closed, and oversensitive, and this propensity to be withdrawn and inturned was exacerbated as life went on – first by his political problems in the thirties, and then by his efforts to reconcile the moral irreconcilables of his wartime work. His autobiographical writing is rather stiff and formal, and his letters to Bohr, even during the twenties and thirties, are correct rather than intimate. Throughout the period of their closest friendship they addressed each other with the formal *Sie*, and switched to *Du* only when Heisenberg also had a chair.

The conversations that Heisenberg claimed such freedom to recreate in his memoirs are stately. Much more plausibly colloquial is the transcript of David Irving's long interview with him for *The Virus House*, Irving's history of the German bomb programme, though he is still (naturally) watchful. In the transcripts of the relatively unguarded conversations that the German atomic team had among themselves during their internment, where Heisenberg emerges as the dominant figure, both morally and practically, a certain hard-headed worldliness can be detected. He is much concerned with professional prospects, and with how they might make some money out of their wartime researches. When one of the others says that if they agree to work on atomic matters under Allied control they will be looked down upon as traitors 'in the eyes of the masses', Heisenberg replies: 'No. One must do that cleverly. As far as the masses are

concerned it will look as though we unfortunately have to
continue our scientific work under the wicked Anglo-Saxon
control, and that we can do nothing about it. We will have
to appear to accept this control with fury and gnashing of
teeth.'

There was always something a little sharp and harsh about
him, something that at its best inspired respect rather than
love, and that after the war occasioned really quite
astonishing hostility and contempt. Even Samuel Goudsmit
turned against him. Goudsmit was an old friend
and colleague; when the investigators of the Alsos mission, the
Allied agency for gathering intelligence on German atomic
research, for which he was working, finally broke into
Heisenberg's office in 1945, one of the first things they saw
was a picture of the two of them together that Heisenberg
had kept there as a memento of happier days. But when
Goudsmit subsequently interrogated Heisenberg he found
him arrogant and self-involved. Goudsmit had
understandably bitter feelings at the time – he had just
discovered the record of his parents' death in Auschwitz.
Heisenberg was also caught in a false position. Confident
that his team had been far ahead of the Americans, he
offered Goudsmit his services in initiating them into the
secrets of uranium fission. (Goudsmit did nothing to correct
his misapprehension, which gave Heisenberg, when the truth
finally came out, grounds for returning Goudsmit's
bitterness.) In his superficial and strangely unimpressive book
on Alsos, Goudsmit wrote about Heisenberg and his team
with contemptuous dismissal, and in the year-long
correspondence in the American press that followed its
publication, accused him of self-importance and dishonesty.

Weisskopf gave a reception for Heisenberg during his trip
to America in 1949, but about half the guests – including
many people from the Los Alamos team – failed to appear,
explaining to Weisskopf that they didn't want to shake the
hand of the man who had tried to build a bomb for Hitler.
Even Cassidy, who gives full measure to Heisenberg as a
physicist in his biography, is notably cool and cautious in his
assessment of Heisenberg's role in the German bomb

programme. Ronald Fraser, the British intelligence officer who escorted Heisenberg back to Copenhagen in 1947 (the British seem to have been frightened that he would defect to the Russians, or be kidnapped by them) replied to Irving's inquiry about the trip in tones of patronising contempt that seem slightly unhinged. 'The whole story of "a kind of confrontation",' he wrote to Irving, 'in the matter of his 1941 natter with Bohr in the Tivoli Gardens [sic] is a typical Heisenberg fabrication – maybe a bit brighter than a thousand others, but like them all a product of his *Blut und Boden* guilt complex, which he rationalises that quickly that the stories become *for him* the truth, the whole truth, and nothing but the truth. Pitiful, in a man of his mental stature.'

The historian Paul Lawrence Rose, who has focused upon Heisenberg as an emblem for what he regards as the general failings of German culture, also takes a remarkably high moral tone. In a paper he wrote in 1984, entitled *Heisenberg, German Morality and the Atomic Bomb*, he talked about Heisenberg's 'guff', his 'self-serving, self-deluding claims', and his 'elementary moral stupidity'. After a further fourteen years research Professor Rose returned to the subject in 1998 in a full-length book which was published after the play was produced, and which has attracted considerable attention, *Heisenberg and the Nazi Atomic Bomb Project: a Study in German Culture*. His contempt for Heisenberg remains unmoderated. He believes that Heisenberg failed, in spite of his perfect readiness to serve the Nazi regime, because of his arrogance and wrong-headedness, and because he embodied various vices of German culture in general, and of the Nazi regime in particular, whose values he had absorbed.

It is a difficult book to read – Rose can scarcely quote a word of Heisenberg's without adding his own disparaging qualification. Here is a selection of his interjections on two facing pages taken more or less at random: ' . . . self-incriminating . . . a somewhat inadequate explanation . . . this inconsistency . . . the falseness of these lame excuses . . . a characteristic Heisenberg lie . . . Heisenberg's usual facile rationalising ability . . . Heisenberg then went on glibly to

recollect . . . the delusory nature of Heisenberg's
memory . . .'

You wonder at times whether it wouldn't look better if it
were handwritten in green ink, with no paragraph breaks.
Rose seems to be aware himself of the effect he is producing.
He realises, he says, that some readers may 'find distasteful
the recurrent moral judgments passed on Heisenberg'. They
may also, he thinks, be put off by what seems a 'lack of
sympathy with German culture' – he cannot say, he
confesses, that his 'British background' has made him
entirely sympathetic to it. He is at pains to distance himself
from any unfortunate echoes that this attitude may awaken:
he hopes that readers will not accuse him of 'unthinkingly
preaching a crude view of German "national character",
whatever that term may mean'. What he is concerned with,
he explains, is not that at all, but 'the enduring nature of
what one might call the "deep culture" of Germany . . . In
this book I have tried to penetrate into how Germans think
– or rather, perhaps, used to think – and to show how
radically different are German and what I have termed
"Western" mentalities and sensibilities.' It is this that
underlies what he calls, without apparent irony, 'the
Heisenberg problem'.

Some of his evidence induces a certain dizziness. He
quotes without comment, as the epigraph to a chapter, a
remark by Albert Speer, the Nazi Minister of Armaments: 'I
do hope Heisenberg is not now claiming that they tried, for
reasons of principle, to sabotage the project by asking for
such minimal support!' It's true that any claim to have
sabotaged the project, particularly for reasons of principle,
would represent an astonishing departure from Heisenberg's
habitual caution on the subject. But the question is not what
Speer hoped, but whether Heisenberg *did* make such a claim.

So did he or didn't he? Rose doesn't tell us, and the only
reference he gives is Gitta Sereny's new book, *Albert Speer: His
Battle with Truth*. The allusion is to the crucial meeting at
Harnack House in 1942, mentioned in the play. Speer said
in his memoirs that he was 'rather put out' by the very small
amount of money that Heisenberg requested to run the
nuclear research programme. In an earlier draft of the

manuscript (the 'Spandau draft'), says Sereny, he had added in brackets the remark that Rose quotes – and Heisenberg, she says, 'did in fact try precisely that after the war'.

So he *did* make the claim! But when and where? Sereny doesn't tell us. The only references to the smallness of the sums of money he asked for that I can find in the record are the one quoted, by Speer himself, and another by Field Marshal Milch, Goering's deputy in the Luftwaffe, who was also present at the meeting. There's certainly nothing about it in Heisenberg's memoirs, or in Robert Jungk's book, *Brighter Than a Thousand Suns*, or in Heisenberg's long interview with Irving, or in the other two obvious places, his interview with *Der Spiegel* in 1967, when Irving's book was published, or his review of the book in the *Frankfurter Allgemeine Zeitung*. I hardly like to put myself forward to fill the gap, but so far as I know the only reference he made to the subject was posthumously and fictitiously in my play.

Sereny, like Rose, is markedly unenthusiastic about Heisenberg in general. She goes on to argue that Heisenberg's claims about his intentions in meeting Bohr in 1941 'are now shown by Speer's Spandau account to be false', though quite how this is so she doesn't explain. About what she calls 'the facts' of the Copenhagen meeting she is remarkably brisk. In the conversation '. . . which Bohr subsequently reported to his associates at the Niels Bohr Institute, Heisenberg had made his political stand crystal clear. His team, he told Bohr, had gone some way towards discovering a way to produce an atom bomb. Germany was going to win the war, probably quite soon, and Bohr should join them now in their efforts.'

The idea that Heisenberg was inviting Bohr to work on the German bomb is on the face of it the least plausible out of all the possible interpretations that have been offered. It is completely at odds with what Weisskopf recalls Bohr as saying in 1948, and with what Bohr is on record as telling Chadwick at the time. In any case, the suggestion that Heisenberg thought he might be able to import someone half-Jewish into the most secret research programme in Nazi Germany is frankly preposterous.

So what is Sereny's evidence for her account of the
meeting? At this point the sense of vertigo returns, and one
begins to have the feeling that one is in an Escher drawing,
where the stairs up to the floor above somehow lead back to
the floor one is already on, because the only reference she
gives is . . . Powers, Heisenberg's great champion, in
Heisenberg's War.

And it's true – Powers *does* quote an opinion to this effect
(and it's the only possible source for it anywhere, so far as I
know). He says he was told by Weizsäcker that some person
or persons unnamed in Copenhagen, 44 years after the
event, had told *him* that this is what Bohr had said he had
believed Heisenberg's intention to be. One might think that
this is rather faint evidence. In any case, even if it really is
what Bohr believed, it is of course not what Weizsäcker
believed, or Powers either. They are reporting Bohr's alleged
belief as a possible misapprehension on his part which might
have explained his anger. Indeed, Powers's own reading of
the situation is precisely the one that Sereny claims to be
discredited by Speer's remark.

*

Goudsmit gradually modified his opinion, and his final
judgment on Heisenberg, when he died in 1976, was a
generous one which goes some way to expunging the
dismissive tone of his book: 'Heisenberg was a very great
physicist, a deep thinker, a fine human being, and also a
courageous person. He was one of the greatest physicists of
our time, but he suffered severely under the unwarranted
attacks by fanatical colleagues. In my opinion he must be
considered to have been in some respects a victim of the
Nazi regime.'

Robert Jungk, one of the few authors who have ever
attempted to defend Heisenberg, modified his opinion in the
opposite direction. In *Brighter Than a Thousand Suns*, originally
published in 1956, he suggested that the German physicists
had managed to avoid building nuclear weapons for
conscientious reasons, and quoted Heisenberg as saying that,

'under a dictatorship active resistance can only be practised by those who pretend to collaborate with the regime. Anyone speaking out openly against the system thereby indubitably deprives himself of any chance of active resistance.' But Jungk later changed his mind, and described the notion of passive resistance on the part of the German physicists as a 'myth'. He had contributed to spreading it, he said, out of an 'esteem for those impressive personalities which I have since realized to be out of place'.

For a really spirited and sustained defence Heisenberg had to wait until Powers published his book in 1993. It is a remarkable piece of work, journalistic in tone, but generous in its understanding and huge in its scope. A little too huge, perhaps, because Powers is unable to resist being side-tracked from the main narrative by the amazing byways that he perpetually finds opening off it. I recommend it particularly to other dramatists and screenwriters; there is material here for several more plays and films yet.

His central argument is that the Allied bomb programme succeeded because of the uninhibited eagerness of the scientists to do it, particularly of those exiles who had known Nazism at first hand, and who were desperate to pre-empt Hitler; while the German programme failed because of the underlying reluctance of scientists in Germany to arm Hitler with the bomb, however strong their patriotism, and however much they wanted to profit from the possibilities for research. 'Zeal was needed,' he says; 'its absence was lethal, like a poison that leaves no trace.'

But he goes further, and argues that Heisenberg 'did not simply withhold himself, stand aside, let the project die. He killed it.' He tries to show that at every point Heisenberg was careful to hold out enough hope to the authorities to ensure that he and his team were left in charge of the project, but never enough to attract the total commitment and huge investment that would have offered the only real hope of success. 'Heisenberg's caution saved him. He was free to do what he could to guide the German atomic research effort into a broom closet, where scientists tinkered until the war ended.'

Cassidy, reviewing the book in *Nature*, described it as a good story, but insisted that 'as history it is incredible'. Rose dismisses it as 'entirely bogus' and 'a scholarly disaster'. Powers acknowledged ruefully, in a recent letter to the *Times Literary Supplement*, that he had failed to convince any historian who had pronounced upon the matter.

The play is not an attempt to adjudicate between these differing views of Heisenberg's personality, or these differing accounts of his activities. But it would have been impossible to write it without taking *some* view of Powers' version of events, so here, for what it is worth, is a brief summary of the case, and of my own hesitant view of it. The evidence is confused and contradictory, and making any sense of it involves balancing probabilities and possibilities almost as indeterminable as Heisenberg found events inside the atom.

*

Some of the evidence undoubtedly appears to support Powers's thesis in its stronger form, that Heisenberg deliberately sabotaged the project.

In the first place there are two scraps of direct testimony. One is a message brought to America in 1941 by a departing German Jewish academic called Fritz Reiche. It was from Fritz Houtermans, the German physicist who had just realised that if they could get a reactor going it would produce plutonium, and that plutonium would be a fissile alternative to the U-235 that they could not separate. Reiche testified later that he had passed it on to a group of scientists working at Princeton, including Wolfgang Pauli, John von Neumann, and Hans Bethe. As Rudolf Ladenburg, the physicist who arranged the meeting, recorded it afterwards, Houtermans wanted it to be known that 'a large number of German physicists are working intensively on the problem of the uranium bomb under the direction of Heisenberg', and that 'Heisenberg himself tries to delay the work as much as possible, fearing the catastrophic results of a success'.

Rose dismisses Houtermans as a proven liar, and records that Reiche later appeared to withdraw his belief in

Heisenberg's opposition to the project. But neither of these objections seems immediately relevant to the consistency of Reiche's and Ladenburg's testimony.

The second scrap of evidence is even more direct, but much more dubious. Heisenberg's American editor, Ruth Nanda Anshen, records receiving a letter from him in 1970 in which he claimed that, 'Dr Hahn, Dr von Laue and I falsified the mathematics in order to avoid the development of the atom bomb by German scientists.'

The letter itself has apparently vanished from the record. Rose nonetheless accepts it as beyond doubt genuine, and sees it as a yet more blatant attempt at self-justification. It is not, however, called into evidence by Powers, even though it would appear to support his case, and he mentions it only in his notes, and with the greatest reserve. Jeremy Bernstein, who seems to me the best-informed and most fair-minded of all Heisenberg's critics, and whose book *Hitler's Uranium Club* will be relied upon in understanding the scientific considerations that follow, dismisses it as 'incredible' and 'a chimera'. It is entirely at odds with Heisenberg's careful moderation in all his other references to the matter, and the inclusion of Hahn and von Laue in the plot is nonsensical. Hahn was a chemist, not a physicist, and, as will be plain from what comes later, had no knowledge whatsoever of the relevant mathematics, while von Laue is famous as an outspoken opponent of Nazism who never worked on the German nuclear programme at all.

So much for the direct evidence, true or false. All the rest of the evidence is indirect, and relates to whether Heisenberg did actually have some understanding of the relevant physics and concealed it, or whether he failed out of ignorance. It centres on the question of critical mass, the amount of fissile material (U-235 or plutonium) large enough to support an explosive chain reaction. An estimate of this amount was crucial to the decision about proceeding with a serious nuclear weapons programme because of the enormous difficulty and expense of separating the U-235 from the U-238 that makes up the vast bulk of natural uranium, and the length of time it would take to develop a reactor capable of transmuting the uranium into plutonium. At the beginning of the war it was believed by scientists on both sides that the answer would be in tons, which put the possibility of producing it beyond practical consideration. The idea became imaginable only when two scientists working in Britain, Rudolf Peierls and Otto Frisch, did the calculation and realised quite how fast the reaction would go with fast neutrons in pure U-235, and consequently how little fissile material you would need: not tons but kilograms. (The various ironies associated with this are explored in the play, and I will not repeat them here.)

Powers argues that the idea never became imaginable in Germany because Heisenberg 'cooked up a plausible method of estimating critical mass which gave an answer in tons'. He believes that Heisenberg 'well knew how to make a bomb with far less, but kept the knowledge to himself'.

There is a certain amount of evidence that the German team did at one point arrive at a much lower figure for the critical mass – indeed, for one in kilograms, that bore some relation to the estimate made by Frisch and Peierls, and to the actual mass of the Hiroshima bomb (56 kg). Manfred von Ardenne, who was running an alternative nuclear programme for the German Post Office, later claimed in his memoirs that in the late autumn of 1941 he was informed independently by both Heisenberg and Hahn that they had worked out the critical mass for a U-235 bomb and found it to be about 10 kilograms. This information was subsequently withdrawn by von Weizsäcker, who told him that he and Heisenberg had decided that a U-235 bomb was impossible (because the heat of the reaction would expand the uranium too fast for it to continue). But Heisenberg, so far as I know, never commented on this, and von Weizsäcker, according to Bernstein, 'essentially denied' that any such conversation ever took place.

As Bernstein says, it is difficult to know what to make of all this – it is 'one of several brick walls anyone who studies this subject runs into'. I think it's difficult to take von Ardenne's recollection entirely literally. Hahn, as I noted before, plainly had no understanding of the mathematics, nor of any of the other issues involved, and, as we shall see, had to have them explained to him by Heisenberg later. On the other hand (and this story has more other hands than a Hindu god), in von Weizsäcker's report on the possibility of an American bomb programme, written in September 1941, he talked about the destructive effects of a bomb weighing 5 kg. Then again, in February 1942 a brief progress report for German Army Ordnance, authors unnamed, suggested without further explanation a critical mass of between 10 and 100 kg. And at the crucial meeting with Speer at Harnack House in June 1942, when Field Marshal Milch asked him how large an atomic bomb would have to be to destroy a city, Heisenberg replied, or so he said in his interview with Irving, that it, or at any rate its 'essentially active part', would have to be 'about the size of a pineapple'.

In the end, though, I believe that the crucial piece of evidence lies elsewhere, in a source that was denied to everyone who wrote about Heisenberg until recently – the transcripts of the Farm Hall recordings. Bernstein, Powers, and Rose were the first commentators to have access to them.

Though of course they still don't reach the same conclusions from them.

*

The story of Farm Hall is another complete play in itself. Sir Charles Frank, the British atomic physicist, in his admirably fair and clear introduction to the text of the transcripts that was published in Britain, regrets that they were not released in time for Dürrenmatt to make use of.

At the end of the war troops of the Alsos mission, to which Goudsmit was attached, made their way through what was left of the German front line and located the remains of the German reactor at Haigerloch, with the intention of finally reassuring themselves that Germany would not be able to spring some terrible nuclear surprise at the last moment. They also seized the team of scientists themselves, making a special armed sortie to Urfeld, in Bavaria, to collect Heisenberg from his home. Hechingen, the nearby town where the team was based, and Haigerloch itself were in the French sector. The scientists were abstracted secretly, from under the noses of the French, and brought back to Britain, where they were held, under wartime laws and without anyone's knowledge, in a former Intelligence safe house – Farm Hall, near Cambridge. The intention seems to have been partly to prevent their passing on any atomic secrets to either of our other two allies, the Russians and the French; partly to forestall any discussion of the possibility of nuclear weapons until we had completed and used our own; and partly, perhaps, to save Heisenberg and the others from the alternative solution to these problems proposed by one American general, which was simply to shoot them out of hand.

They were detained at Farm Hall for six months, during which time they were treated not as prisoners but as guests. Hidden microphones, however, had been installed, and everything they said to each other was secretly recorded. The existence of the transcripts from these recordings was kept as secret as that of the prisoners. General Groves, the head of the Allied bomb programme, quoted from them in his memoirs (1962), and Goudsmit plainly had access to them, which he drew upon in his book on Alsos, but the British Government, perhaps to protect the feelings of the former detainees, some of them now prominent in post-war German science, perhaps merely out of its usual pathological addiction to secrecy, continued to block the release of the papers themselves. Even Margaret Gowing was refused access when she wrote her official history of British atomic policy in 1964, and David Irving was refused again, in spite of strenuous efforts, for *The Virus House* in 1967. The ban was maintained until 1992, when the Government finally gave way to a combined appeal from leading scientists and historians.

The German originals are lost, and the translation was plainly done under pressure, with little feeling for colloquial nuance, but the transcripts are direct evidence of what

Heisenberg and the others thought when they were talking,
as they believed, amongst themselves. The ten detainees
represented a wide range of different attitudes. They ranged
from Walther Gerlach, the Nazi Government's administrator
of nuclear research, and Kurt Diebner, who had been a
member of the Nazi party, to Max von Laue, who had been
openly hostile to the regime, who had never worked on the
atomic programme, and whose inclusion in the party seems
on the face of it mysterious. Their conversations over the six-
month period reflect a similarly wide range of attitudes and
feelings. The general tone is pretty much what one might
expect from any group of academics deprived of their liberty
without explanation and cooped up together. There is, as
one might suppose, quite a lot of complaining, scheming,
and mutual friction.

One thing, though, seems to me to emerge quite clearly:
for all practical purposes German thinking had stopped at a
reactor, and there had been no eagerness at all to look
beyond this to the possibility of weapons. Their shocked
comments in the moment of unguarded horror that followed
the announcement of Hiroshima are particularly revealing.
The internees had been given the news by their (almost)
endlessly sympathetic and urbane gaoler-cum-host, Major
Rittner, at dinner-time, but Heisenberg had not believed it
until he had heard it with his own ears on the BBC nine
o'clock news. 'They were completely stunned,' reported
Rittner, 'when they realised that the news was genuine. They
were left alone on the assumption that they would discuss the
position . . .'

'I was absolutely convinced,' says Heisenberg, in the
conversation that followed, 'of the possibility of our making
an uranium engine [reactor] but I never thought that we
would make a bomb and at the bottom of my heart I was
really glad that it was to be an engine and not a bomb. I
must admit that.' Weizsäcker says that he doesn't think that
they should make excuses now for failing, 'but we must
admit that we didn't want to succeed.' Gerlach: 'One cannot
say in front of an Englishman that we didn't try hard
enough. They were our enemies, although we sabotaged the
war. There are some things that one knows and one can

discuss together but that one cannot discuss in the presence of Englishmen.'

In a letter written fourteen years later von Laue complained that, during their conversations at table in the following weeks, 'the version was developed that the German atomic physicists really had not wanted the atomic bomb, either because it was impossible to achieve it during the expected duration of the war or because they simply did not want to have it at all.' Von Laue's account of the elaboration of this sanitised 'version' (*Lesart* in German) has been seized upon by unsympathetic commentators, and contrasted with the encouraging prospects for atomic weapons that some of the physicists had undoubtedly held out to the Nazi authorities at various times during the earlier part of the war.

Well, we all reorganise our recollections, consciously or unconsciously, as time goes by, to fit our changed perceptions of a situation, and no doubt Heisenberg and his fellow-detainees did the same. But Bernstein locates the origins of the *Lesart* in those immediate reactions to the announcement of Hiroshima on the nine o'clock news. If this is so then I can only say that the team began to get their story together with quite remarkable spontaneity, speed, presence of mind, and common purpose. If they all thought as fast as this, and co-operated as closely, it's even more surprising that they didn't get further with the bomb.

To me, I have to say, those immediate and unprepared reactions suggest quite strongly that the first part of Powers's thesis, at any rate, is right, and that there *had* been the 'fatal lack of zeal' that he diagnosed. Perhaps Gerlach's claim, unchallenged by the others, that they had actually 'sabotaged the war' suggests at the very least a consciousness that quite a lot of stones had been left unturned.

*

But do the transcripts support Powers's contention that Heisenberg 'cooked up a plausible method of estimating critical mass which gave an answer in tons, and that he well knew how to make a bomb with far less, but kept the knowledge to himself'?

One preliminary point needs to be cleared out of the way first: the question whether Heisenberg understood an even more fundamental point, the difference between a reactor (which is operated by slow neutrons in natural uranium, or some other mixture of U-238 and U-235) and a bomb (which functions with fast neutrons in pure U-235 or plutonium). Goudsmit, who plainly had access to the transcripts when he wrote his book on Alsos, seems to have thought they supported his view that Heisenberg didn't. Before the transcripts were published Rose shared Goudsmit's dismissive view.

But, according to the transcripts, what Heisenberg tells Hahn that same night, when Gerlach has retired to sob in his room, and they are finally alone together, is that 'I always knew it could be done with 235 with fast neutrons. That's why 235 only [presumably = "only 235"] can be used as an explosive. One can never make an explosive with slow neutrons, not even with the heavy water machine [the German reactor], as then the neutrons only go with thermal speed, with the result that the reaction is so slow that the thing explodes sooner, before the reaction is complete.'

Bernstein (unlike Goudsmit) reads this and what follows as showing that Heisenberg *did* understand the difference between a reactor and a bomb, 'but that he did not understand either one very well – certainly not the bomb'. Rose now seems to accept that Heisenberg's remarks do indicate that he realised the bomb would have to be fissioned with fast neutrons (though he shows that in the past Heisenberg had been toying with the idea of some kind of vast exploding reactor).[1]

[1]Bernstein takes the trouble to explain in his book what few other commentators do – the difference between slow and fast neutrons: 'By definition, slow neutrons move with speeds of the order of a few kilometers a second, about the speeds that molecules at room temperature move in a gas. That is why these neutrons are also referred to as thermal. Fast neutrons, the kind that are emitted in many nuclear processes, move at speeds of tens of thousands of kilometers a second.'

This same conversation between Heisenberg and Hahn, when they were alone together on that terrible night, seems to me also to resolve the question of Heisenberg's understanding of the critical mass beyond any reasonable doubt. He takes Hahn through what he believes to be the relevant calculation and tells him that the answer is 'about a ton'. I can't see any earthly reason why he should be rehearsing a fabricated calculation or a fabricated answer at this stage, in a private conversation with someone he seems to have trusted, after the German team are out of the race and in custody, and after someone else has in any case already built the bomb. If he had had the right calculation and the right answer up his sleeve all the time, now would surely have been the moment to produce them. I find it much more plausible that he was telling the simple truth when he said to Hahn just before this that 'quite honestly I have never worked it out as I never believed one could get pure 235'.

Earlier on in the evening, it's true, when everyone was present during the conversation immediately after the news bulletin, Hahn says to Heisenberg: 'But tell me why you used to tell me that one needed 50 kilograms of 235 in order to do anything.' (To which Heisenberg replies that he wouldn't like to commit himself for the moment.) This does seem to suggest that he *had* made a calculation of some sort earlier, as von Ardenne claimed – though it also surely destroys once and for all the improbable proposition that Hahn had been involved in it, or had made some kind of estimate of his own. Perhaps Heisenberg had made not so much a calculation as some kind of guess or estimate. Even if it *was* a serious calculation, it seems most unlikely that it was the right calculation, or that it was one he had adhered to.

This is made clear to me (at last) by Jeremy Bernstein. I should explain that when I first read the Farm Hall transcripts, before I wrote the play, I was using the bare uncommented text published in Britain, unaware that there was also a completely different edition published in the US, incorporating Bernstein's detailed commentary. After the play was produced and published he was kind enough to send me it, and it illuminated a great many matters that I had not understood before. These are after all scientists talking to scientists, and they are reported verbatim with all the ellipses of spoken conversation, and with a further haze cast over the proceedings by translation. Bernstein is both a distinguished journalist and a professor of physics, and he has a long acquaintance with the history of atomic research. (He recalls being given the bare plutonium core of a bomb to hold on the Nevada test site in 1957; 'it was slightly warm to the touch, since plutonium is marginally radioactive.') He has a thorough understanding of the scientific issues involved, and is the ideal guide to the physics – though a slightly less percipient one, I think, to the psychology of the physicists.

I'm pleased to discover for a start that he takes the same view of Heisenberg's admission to Hahn about never having worked out the critical mass. He believes that it has to be taken at its face value, and he asks how it can be reconciled with the figure of 50 kg recalled by Hahn. He demonstrates that when Heisenberg attempts to do the calculation for Hahn he 'gets it wrong at every level' – he does the arithmetic wrong, and is in any case doing the wrong arithmetic. 'Knowing how scientists work,' says Bernstein, 'I find it implausible that he ever did the calculation correctly before. One can imagine even a Heisenberg forgetting a number – he was, in any case, not very good with numbers – but it is very difficult to imagine his forgetting a general method of calculation, a method that once led him to a more reasonable answer.'

The calculation of the critical mass is not the only thing that Heisenberg got wrong that night. Even when he revealed to Hahn that he understood how the critical mass could be reduced by the use of a reflective shield he suggested a material, carbon, that would have had the opposite effect to the one intended. Carbon is a good moderator for a reactor, and Heisenberg's proposing it for the 'tamper' in a bomb, says Bernstein, 'shows he was thinking like a reactor physicist, which, for the last two years, he was'.

These were of course Heisenberg's first thoughts off the top of his head in the wake of Hiroshima. A week later, with the help of what few details the newspapers had given of the two bombs, Heisenberg offered all his fellow-internees a lecture in which he presented a complete and considered account of how the Allies had done it. The inclusion in the lecture of quite fundamental matters, argues Powers, together with the questions which his hearers asked, make it clear that it was all news to everyone present except his closest associates. 'What the Farm Hall transcripts show unmistakably,' he says, 'is that Heisenberg did not explain basic bomb physics to the man in charge of the German bomb program [Gerlach] until after the war was over.' They 'offer strong evidence that Heisenberg never explained fast fission to Gerlach'. At the end of the lecture, says Powers, 'the German scientists, given a second chance, would have been ready to start building a bomb'.

Bernstein sees the lecture very differently. He demonstrates that Heisenberg's exposition is still marred by quite fundamental misconceptions. Heisenberg now seems to have 'the first inkling' of how to calculate the critical mass (though he still does the arithmetic wrong), but is not much nearer to the practicalities of building a bomb than his audience. What the novelty of a lot of this material suggests to Bernstein is simply that communications between the different sections of the German project were very poor.

As a non-scientist I can't offer any opinion on the physics. To my eyes, I have to say, Heisenberg does seem to have come a remarkably long way in a week – if, that is, he was starting more or less from scratch. And he surely must have been. It's really not plausible that he hadn't recollected more by this time if he actually had done the work. The conclusion seems to me inescapable: he hadn't done the calculation. If he had kept the fatal knowledge of how small the critical mass would be from anyone, as Powers argues, then it was from himself.

*

In the end, it seems to me, your judgment of Heisenberg comes down to what you make of his failure to attempt that fundamental calculation. Does it suggest incompetence or arrogance, as his detractors have claimed? It's possible. Even great scientists – and Bernstein agrees that Heisenberg was one of them – make mistakes, and fail to see possibilities that lesser men pick up; Heisenberg accepted that he had made a mistake in the formulation of uncertainty itself. And I think we have to accept Bernstein's judgment that, although he was the first person to be able to grasp the counter-intuitive abstraction of quantum mechanics, he was not so good at the practicalities of commonsense estimates and working arithmetic.

Or does the failure suggest something rather different? An unconscious reluctance to challenge the comforting and convenient assumption that the thing was not a practical possibility? Comforting and convenient, that is, if what he was trying to do was *not* to build a bomb. Is it all part of a general pattern of reluctance, as the first and more plausible part of Powers's thesis suggests? If so, you might wonder whether this reluctance was a state definite enough to be susceptible of explanation. Heisenberg was trapped in a seamless circle which explains itself: he didn't try the calculation because he didn't think it was worth doing – he didn't think it was worth doing because he didn't try it. The oddity, the phenomenon that requires explaining, is not this non-occurrence but its opposite – the escape of Frisch and Peierls from that same circle. It seems almost like a random quantum event; in which case, of course, it is no more explainable than its not happening.

After the war, certainly, Heisenberg was not just passively reluctant about any military application of nuclear power, but very actively so. In the 1950s, when there was a proposal to arm Federal Germany with nuclear weapons, he joined forces with Weizsäcker and others to fight a vigorous campaign that entirely and permanently defeated it.

There is also one small piece of evidence about his attitude during the war that Powers rather curiously doesn't comment on: the question of the cyclotron.

At the crucial meeting between Heisenberg and Speer in 1942, which seems finally to have scuppered all possibility of a German bomb, Heisenberg is reported to have emphasised the need to build a cyclotron. A cyclotron could have been used, as the cyclotrons in America were, for isotope separation, the great sticking-point in the German programme. In the account of this meeting in his memoirs Speer says: 'Difficulties were compounded, Heisenberg explained, by the fact that Europe possessed only one cyclotron, and that of minimal capacity. Moreover, it was located in Paris and because of the need for secrecy could not be used to full advantage.' Powers mentions this, but does not go on to the obvious corollary: that if Speer's recollection is accurate, then Heisenberg was plainly lying, because he knew perfectly well that there was a second cyclotron to hand – at Bohr's institute in Copenhagen. This would suggest that his apparent anxiety to lay his hands on a machine that might actually separate some U-235 was not quite what it seemed. Or, at the very least, that he placed Germany's war aims below his desire to protect Bohr's institute.

Perhaps Speer is simply wrong. It seems uncharacteristic of Heisenberg to have risked such a blatant falsehood, and he makes no mention of it in his own accounts of the meeting. All the same, when he went back to Copenhagen in 1944, after Bohr had fled, to adjudicate a German proposal to strip the institute of all its equipment, presumably including the cyclotron, he seems to have contrived to leave it even then still in Danish hands.

*

One of the forms of indeterminacy touched upon in the play is the indeterminacy of human memory, or at any rate the indeterminability of the historical record. There are various examples which I left out, for fear of making the play even more tangled than it is. Some, such as the difficulties about the amazingly realistic figure for the critical mass that von

Ardenne recollected being given by Heisenberg and Hahn in 1941, I have already mentioned in this Postscript. There were others. A minor one concerns whether there were two ships sent to load the Jews of Copenhagen for deportation, as some witnesses recall, or a single one (named as the *Wartheland*). A more significant point of dispute is the drawing which Heisenberg did or didn't make for Bohr during their meeting in 1941.

According to Hans Bethe, who was one of the team at Los Alamos, Heisenberg drew a rough sketch to show Bohr the work that was being done in Germany. Bohr evidently took it to Los Alamos with him when he went, because Bethe (and others) recall it being passed around at a meeting there. Bethe told Powers that Bohr believed it represented a bomb; but the consensus of opinion at the meeting was that it was a reactor. However, Aage Bohr, Niels's son, a physicist himself (and another Nobel prizewinner), who was with his father in Copenhagen during Heisenberg's visit, and with him again in Los Alamos, was absolutely insistent that there was no drawing.

If the story is true it might help to explain Goudsmit's insistence, in the teeth of the evidence from Farm Hall, that Heisenberg couldn't tell the difference between a reactor and a bomb. It would certainly cast doubt on Heisenberg's recollection that the entire discussion with Bohr in 1941 took place during the walk, and that Bohr broke off the conversation almost as soon as it was broached. It seems improbable to me that Heisenberg would have risked putting anything down on paper, and if even so he had then I can't see why he didn't seize upon it after the war, to support his claim that he had hinted to Bohr at the German research on a bomb. I suppose it's possible that Bohr made the sketch himself, to illustrate to his colleagues at Los Alamos what he thought Heisenberg was getting at, but the truth of the matter seems to be irretrievable.

*

I have had many helping hands with this play, both before it was produced in London and since. Sir John Maddox kindly read the text for me, and so did Professor Balázs L. Gyorffy, Professor of Physics at Bristol University, who made a number of corrections and suggestions. I am also indebted to Finn Aaserud, the Director of the Niels Bohr Archive in Copenhagen, and to his colleagues there, for much help and encouragement. Many scientists and other specialists have written to me after seeing the play on the stage. They have mostly been extraordinarily generous and supportive, but some of them have put me right on details of the science, for which I am particularly grateful. They also pointed out two mathematical errors so egregious that the lines in question didn't make sense from one end to the other – even to me, when I re-read them. All these points have now been addressed, though I'm sure that other mistakes will emerge. So much new material has come to hand, in one way or another, that I extensively overhauled and extended this Postscript to coincide with the production of the play in New York.

One matter of dispute that I have not been able to resolve completely concerns the part played by Max Born in the introduction of quantum mechanics. The matter was raised (with exemplary temperance) by his son, Gustav Born, who was concerned about the injustice he felt I had done to his father's memory. I was reluctant to make the play any more complex than it is, but I have since made adjustments both to the play itself and to this Postscript which go at any rate some way to meeting Professor Born's case. We are still at odds over one line, though, in which Heisenberg is said to have 'invented quantum mechanics'. I am quoting the judgment of other physicists here (including one not especially sympathetic to Heisenberg), but I realise that it is a huge over-simplification, and that it seems to compound the original injustice committed when Heisenberg was awarded the Nobel Prize in 1932 'for the creation of quantum mechanics', while Born had to wait another 22 years to have his part acknowledged in the same way. The trouble is that I have not yet been able to think of another way of putting it briefly enough to work in spoken dialogue.

The American physicist Spencer Weart, in a letter to Finn Aaserud, very cogently pointed out that the calculation of the critical mass was much harder than I've made it seem for Heisenberg once Bohr has suggested it to him. 'Perrin failed to get it and his publication of a ton-size critical mass subtly misled everyone else, then Bohr and Wheeler failed, Kurchatov failed, Chadwick failed, all the other Germans and Russians and French and British and Americans missed it, even the greatest of them all for such problems, Fermi, tried but missed, everyone except Peierls . . . Physics is hard.'

Some correspondents have also objected to Heisenberg's line about the physicists who built the Allied bomb, 'Did a single one of them stop to think, even for one brief moment, about what they were doing?', on the grounds that it is unjust to Leo Szilard. It's true that in March 1945 Szilard began a campaign to persuade the US Government not to use the bomb. A committee was set up – the Committee on Social and Political Implications – to allow the scientists working on the project to voice their feelings, and Szilard also circulated a petition among the scientists, 67 of whom signed it, which mentioned 'moral considerations', though it did not specify what exactly these were.

But the main stated reasons for Szilard's second thoughts were not to do with the effects that the bomb would have on the Japanese – he was worried about the ones it would have on the Allies. He thought (presciently) that the actual use of the bomb on Japan would precipitate an atomic arms race between the United States and the Soviet Union. The Committee's report (which Szilard himself seems to have written) and the petition stressed the same points. By this time, in any case, the bomb was almost ready. It had been Szilard who urged the nuclear programme in the first place, and at no point, so far as I know, while he worked for it (on plutonium production) did he ever suggest any hesitation about pursuing either the research or the actual manufacture of the bomb.

I think the line stands, in spite of Szilard's afterthoughts. The scientists had already presented their government with the bomb, and it is the question of whether the German scientists were ready or not to do likewise that is at issue in the play. If Heisenberg's team *had* built a bomb, I don't think they would have recovered very much moral credit by asking Hitler to be kind enough not to drop it on anyone – particularly if their objection had been the strain it might place upon post-war relations among the Axis powers.

*

One looming imponderable remains. *If* Heisenberg had made the calculation, and *if* the resulting reduction in the scale of the problem had somehow generated a real eagerness in both the Nazi authorities and the scientists, could the Germans have built a bomb? Frank believes that they could not have done it before the war in Europe was over – 'even the Americans, with substantial industrial and scientific advantage, and the important assistance from Britain and from ex-Germans in Britain did not achieve that (VE-Day, 8 May 1945, Trinity test, Alamogordo, 16 July 1945).' Speer (who as Armaments Minister would presumably have had to carry the programme out) suggests in his memoirs that it might have been possible to do it by 1945, if the Germans had shelved all their other weapons projects, then two paragraphs later more cautiously changes his estimate to 1947; but of course he needs to justify his failure to pursue the possibility. Powers makes the point that, whatever the timetable was, its start date could have been much earlier. Atomic energy in Germany, he argues, attracted the interest of the authorities from the first day of the war. 'The United States, beginning in June 1942, took just over three years to do the job, and the Soviet Union succeeded in four. If a serious effort to develop a bomb had commenced in mid-1940, one might have been tested in 1943, well before the Allied bomber offensive had destroyed German industry.'

If this 'serious effort' had begun only after Heisenberg's visit to Copenhagen, as the play suggests might have happened if the conversation with Bohr had gone differently, then even this timetable wouldn't have produced a bomb until late 1944 – and by that time it was of course much less

likely that German industry could have delivered. In any
case, formidable difficulties remained to be overcome. The
German team were hugely frustrated by their inability to
find a successful technique for isolating U-235 in any
appreciable quantity, even though the experimental method,
using Clusius-Dickel tubes, was of German origin. They
could have tried one of the processes used successfully by the
Allies, gaseous diffusion. This was another German
invention, developed in Berlin by Gustav Hertz, but Hertz
had lost his job because his uncle was Jewish. (It was,
incidentally, the delays in getting the various American
isotope-separation plants to function which meant that the
Allied bomb was not ready in time for use against Germany.)

The failure to separate U-235 also held up the reactor
programme, and therefore the prospect of producing
plutonium, because they could not separate enough of it
even for the purposes of enrichment (increasing the U-235
content of natural uranium), so that it was harder to get the
reactor to go critical. The construction of the reactor was
further delayed because Walther Bothe's team at Heidelberg
estimated the neutron absorption rates of graphite wrongly,
which obliged the designers to use heavy water as a
moderator instead. The only source of heavy water was a
plant in Norway, which was forced to close after a series of
attacks by Norwegian parachutists attached to Special
Operations Executive, American bombers, and the
Norwegian Resistance. Though perhaps, if a crash
programme had been instituted from the first day of the war,
enough heavy water might have been accumulated before
the attacks were mounted.

If, if, if. . . . The line of ifs is a long one. It remains just
possible, though. The effects of real enthusiasm and real
determination are incalculable. In the realm of the just
possible they are sometimes decisive.

*

Anyone interested enough in any of these questions to want
to sidestep the fiction and look at the historical record should
certainly begin with:

Thomas Powers: *Heisenberg's War* (Knopf, 1993; Cape, 1993)

David Cassidy: *Uncertainty: The Life and Science of Werner Heisenberg* (W H Freeman, 1992)

Abraham Pais: *Niels Bohr's Times* (OUP, 1991) – Pais is a fellow nuclear physicist, who knew Bohr personally, and this, in its highly eccentric way, is a classic of biography, even though Pais has not much more sense of narrative than I have of physics, and the book is organised more like a scientific report than the story of someone's life. But then Bohr notoriously had no sense of narrative, either. One of the tasks his assistants had was to take him to the cinema and to explain the plot to him afterwards

Werner Heisenberg: *Physics and Beyond* (Harper & Row, 1971) – in German, *Der Teil und das Ganze*. His memoirs

Jeremy Bernstein: *Hitler's Uranium Club, the Secret Recordings at Farm Hall,* introduced by David Cassidy (American Institute of Physics, Woodbury, New York, 1996)

or the British edition of the transcripts:

Operation Epsilon, the Farm Hall Transcripts, introduced by Sir Charles Frank (Institute of Physics Publishing, 1993)

Also relevant:

Heisenberg: *Physics and Philosophy* (Penguin, 1958)

Niels Bohr: *The Philosophical Writings of Niels Bohr* (Oxbow Press, Connecticut, 1987)

Elisabeth Heisenberg: *Inner Exile* (Birkhauser, 1984) – in German, *Das politische Leben eines Unpolitischen*. Defensive in tone, but revealing about the kind of anguish her husband tended to conceal from the world; and the source for Heisenberg's ride home in 1945

David Irving: *The German Atomic Bomb* (Simon & Schuster, 1968) – in UK as *The Virus House* (Collins, 1967). The story of the German bomb programme

Paul Lawrence Rose: *Heisenberg and the Nazi Atomic Bomb Project* (U of California Press, 1998)

Records and Documents Relating to the Third Reich, II German Atomic Research, Microfilms DJ29-32. (EP Microform Ltd, Wakefield) – Irving's research materials for the book, including long verbatim interviews with Heisenberg and others. The only consultable copy I could track down was in the library of the Ministry of Defence

Archive for the History of Quantum Physics, microfilm. Includes the complete correspondence of Heisenberg and Bohr. A copy is available for reference in the Science Museum Library. Bohr's side of the correspondence is almost entirely in Danish, Heisenberg's in German apart from one letter

Leni Yahil: *The Rescue of Danish Jewry* (Jewish Publication Society of America, Philadelphia, 1969)

There are also many interesting sidelights on life at the Bohr Institute in its golden years in:

French & Kennedy, eds: *Niels Bohr, A Centenary Volume* (Harvard, 1985)

and in the memoirs of Hendrik Casimir, George Gamow, Otto Frisch, Otto Hahn, Rudolf Peierls, and Victor Weisskopf.

For the subsequent challenges to the Copenhagen Interpretation:

David Deutsch: *The Fabric of Reality* (Allen Lane, 1997)

Murray Gell-Mann: *The Quark and the Jaguar* (W H Freeman, 1994; Little, Brown, 1994)

Roger Penrose: *The Emperor's New Mind* (OUP, 1989)

The actual 'two-slits' experiment was carried out by Dürr, Nonn, and Rempe at the University of Konstanz, and is reported in *Nature* (3 September 1998). There is an accessible introduction to the work in the same issue by Peter Knight, and another account of it by Mark Buchanan (boldly entitled 'An end to uncertainty') in *New Scientist* (6 March 1999).

POST-POSTSCRIPT

I made a number of changes to the text of the play, as I have explained above, in response to suggestions and criticisms I received during the run of the play in London, and to new material I came across. The production in New York, however, opened up a much broader and more fundamental debate. A number of commentators expressed misgivings about the whole enterprise. Paul Lawrence Rose, the most outspoken of the play's critics, even managed to detect in it a 'subtle revisionism . . . more destructive than Irving's self-evidently ridiculous assertions – more destructive of the integrity of art, of science, and of history'.

One of the most frequent complaints about the play in America was that I should have laid more stress on the evils of the Nazi regime, and in particular upon the Holocaust; it was pointed out that Heisenberg's visit to Copenhagen in 1941 coincided with the Wannsee Conference. It was argued that I should have put the visit in the context of a number of subsequent trips he made during the course of the war to other occupied countries. It was also felt that I should have laid more stress than I did on Heisenberg's stated view that Germany's conquests, at any rate in Eastern Europe, were justified, and that her victory over Russia was to be welcomed.

With hindsight, I think I accept some of these criticisms. I should perhaps have had Heisenberg justify Germany's war aims on the Eastern front direct, instead of having Bohr refer to his arguments in one angry but passing aside. I should perhaps have found some way to make the parallel with all the other trips that were found offensive, and about whose purpose there was none of the mystery which had seemed to attach to the one to Copenhagen.

About a greater stress on the evil of the Nazi regime I'm not so sure. I thought that this was too well understood to need pointing out. It is after all the *given* of the play; this was precisely why there was (or should have been) a problem facing Heisenberg, and us in understanding him. In any case, the play returns to the persecution of Jews in

Nazi Germany again and again, from the suppression of so-called 'Jewish physics' (relativity) to the enforced flight of all the Jewish physicists, the death of Goudsmit's parents in Auschwitz, and the attempt by the SS to deport the Jewish population of Denmark to the death camps, which Margrethe Bohr describes as 'that great darkness inside the human soul . . . flooding out to engulf us all'.

Some of the criticisms were even more radical. The play turns on the difficulty of determining why Heisenberg made his trip. For a number of commentators there was no problem at all – they knew the correct explanation for certain; though what that explanation was varied from one to another. For some it was Heisenberg's desire to persuade Bohr of the rightness of Germany's war aims and of its inevitable victory; for Rose and others, he was on a spying mission, to find out through Bohr if the Allies were also working on an atomic bomb.

I agree that Heisenberg may have wished to present the German case to Bohr; but he surely didn't go all the way to Copenhagen *just* to do that. I also agree about the spying. But then so does my Heisenberg. He tells Bohr that he wanted 'some hint, some clue' about whether there was an Allied nuclear programme. This seems to me to be common sense; he would have had to be insanely incurious not to seize any chance he could to find out whether the Allies might drop atomic bombs on his country. There is surely no contradiction at all with what he himself claimed his purpose was – to discuss whether the German team were justified in working on a German weapon. Any information he could get about the other side's intentions would have been a prerequisite for deciding what to do.

Some criticisms I reject, and I should like to put the record straight. Professor Rose suggested that I had 'fantasized' Heisenberg's fear that he was in danger of his life from the Gestapo for talking to Bohr. Not so – I was simply expanding upon what the real Heisenberg said. Jonothan Logan, a physicist writing in *American Scientist*, dismissed as misleading the fictitious Bohr's assertion that in June 1942 Heisenberg had been slightly ahead of Fermi in

Chicago. The context makes plain that this was in terms of neutron multiplication, and the claim was based on what David Cassidy says in his biography of Heisenberg. The correctness of Cassidy's assessment was verified for me, after much inquiry on my part, by Al Wattenberg, one of the editors of Fermi's *Collected Papers*.

All these are at any rate debatable points. Other criticisms I found extremely difficult to make sense of – some even to credit. Professor Rose, who detected the subtle revisionism of the play, found a particularly sinister significance in one detail – the fictitious Heisenberg's remarking upon the neatness of the historical irony whereby the crucial calculation (of the critical mass), which persuaded the Allies of the possibility of building a nuclear weapon, was made by a German and an Austrian, driven into exile in Britain because they were Jewish. Professor Rose saw this as an attempt to blame 'the Jews' for the bomb's invention.

A little more extraordinary still was the view of the play taken by Gerald Holton, Professor of Physics and Professor of the History of Science Emeritus at Harvard. He saw it as being 'structured in good part' to reflect the thesis advanced by Powers, that Heisenberg had correctly calculated the critical mass, but concealed it by 'cooking up' a false result. By the time the play was produced in New York, he believed, I had been forced (by Bernstein) to lay this idea aside, so that I now had an 'unsolvable problem' with the motivation of the play.

I can only suppose that Professor Holton was misled because in the Postscript I speak warmly and gratefully about Powers's book. It has been much attacked, but I continue to admire the generosity of its tone, and the range of Powers's research. I also agree with the first part of his thesis (lack of zeal). But then so does Holton himself, and so, he says, does everyone else who has studied the matter. In the Postscript, however, I make abundantly clear that I don't accept Powers's view about the 'cooking up' and never did.

But you don't even need to read the Postscript to

discover this, because it's all over the play itself. The central argument turns on Heisenberg's confession to Otto Hahn that he had *not* attempted the calculation. By my count, there are something like thirty-five speeches devoted to establishing this, to asking why he hadn't attempted it, and to suggesting what might have happened if he had. How anyone could give the play even the most cursory glance and fail to notice this is difficult to understand.

Even harder to credit was the reaction in some quarters to the 'strange new quantum ethics' proposed by the fictitious Heisenberg. I suppose I should have erected a flashing 'IRONY' sign in front of it. The allusion is to his insight, in his original introduction of quantum mechanics, that physics should be limited to the measurement of what we could actually observe – the external effects of events inside the atom. We should need a similar kind of ethics, he suggests in my play, if we judged people purely on the external effects of their actions, without regard to their intentions. According to Professor Holton, Heisenberg 'exults' that under the new dispensation there would be a place in heaven even for him. Professor Holton fails to mention that Heisenberg also 'exults' that, under the new quantum ethical rules, there would also be a place in heaven for the SS man who seemed ready to murder him in 1945, simply because in the end he settled for a pack of American cigarettes instead. Jonothan Logan manages to believe that I am seriously proposing even the SS man's assumption into heaven.

Let me make it absolutely unambiguous: my Heisenberg is saying that we *do* have to make assessments of intention in judging people's actions. (The epistemology of intention is what the play is about!) He is saying that Bohr will continue to inspire respect and love, in spite of his involvement in the building of the Hiroshima and Nagasaki bombs; and that he himself will continue to be regarded with distrust in spite of his failure to kill anyone. The reaction of Holton, Rose, and others to the play is perhaps an oblique testimony to the truth of this judgement.

*

One of the most striking comments on the play was made by Jochen Heisenberg, Werner Heisenberg's son, when I met him, to my considerable alarm, after the première of the play in New York. 'Of course, your Heisenberg is nothing like my father,' he told me. 'I never saw my father express emotion about anything except music. But I understand that the characters in a play have to be rather more forthcoming than that.'

This seems to me a chastening reminder of the difficulties of representing a real person in fiction, but a profoundly sensible indication of the purpose in attempting it, which is surely to make explicit the ideas and feelings that never quite get expressed in the confusing onrush of life, and to bring out the underlying structure of events. I take it that the nineteenth-century German playwright Friedrich Hebbel was making a similar point when he uttered his great dictum (one that every playwright ought to have in pokerwork over his desk): 'In a good play everyone is right.' I assume he means by this not that the audience is invited to approve of everyone's actions, but that everyone should be allowed the freedom and eloquence to make the most convincing case that he can for himself. Whether or not this is a universal rule of playwriting, it must surely apply to this particular play, where a central argument is about our inability, in our observation of both the physical world and the mental, ever to escape from particular viewpoints.

I suppose that this is what sticks in some people's throats – that my Heisenberg is allowed to make a case for himself – even to criticise others. His claims about his intentions are strongly contested by another character in the play, Margrethe Bohr. Neither Heisenberg nor Margrethe Bohr, so far as I can see, is presented as winning the argument. I don't see why my Margrethe shouldn't be allowed to express her suspicions of Heisenberg much more sharply and woundingly than the real Margrethe's habitual courtesy would ever have permitted, and I don't see why my Heisenberg shouldn't be free to express the deeper feelings that the real Heisenberg remained silent about. Why shouldn't he have the same conflicting loyalties and the same mixed motives and emotions that we all have? Why shouldn't he try to juggle principle and expediency, as we all do? Why shouldn't he fear his country's defeat, and its destruction by nuclear weapons? Why shouldn't he lament its ruin and the slaughter of its citizens?

I can imagine it being asked how far I think this principle should be carried. Do I believe that a fictitious Hitler should be accorded the same privileges? I can see all the problems of exhibiting Hitler on the stage, but I can't see any point in attempting it at all if he is to be simply an effigy for ritual humiliation. Why should we be asked to endure a representation of his presence if he doesn't offer us some understanding of what was going on inside his head from his own point of view? The audience can surely be trusted to draw its own moral conclusions.

*

The most surprising result of the debate set off by the production of the play, though, has been the release of the Bohr documents.

I was told privately about the existence of at any rate one of the documents at a symposium on the play organised in Copenhagen by the Niels Bohr Archive in the autumn of 1999. Heisenberg had made public his own version of the 1941 meeting with Bohr, chiefly in two places: a memorandum written in 1957 to Robert Jungk, who was preparing the material for *Brighter Than a Thousand Suns*, and his memoirs, published in 1969. Bohr, however, had never publicly given his side of the story, and historians had been obliged to rely upon what other people (chiefly his son Aage – also a physicist, and later a Nobel prizewinner himself – and his colleague Stefan Rozental) recalled him as saying about it.

In 1957, however, Bohr had apparently been so angered by Heisenberg's version, when he read it in Jungk's book, that he had written to Heisenberg, dissenting and giving his own account. He had never sent the letter, though, and at his death in 1962 it had been placed in the Archive by his family, not to be released for another fifty years. This was all my informant was prepared to tell me.

I said nothing about this because I believed that I had been told in confidence. The existence of the letter was first publicly mentioned, so far as I know, by Professor Holton, at a further symposium on the play organised in New York in March 2000 on the occasion of its production there. He said that he had actually seen the letter – he had been shown it by the Bohr family. He felt bound not to divulge its contents, but I recall him as promising that when it was finally made public, in 2012, it would entirely change our view of the meeting.

Now the cat was out of the bag, and at yet another symposium on the play, at the Niels Bohr Archive in September 2001, it was announced that the Bohr family had decided to release the letter early. It also turned out that there was not just the one letter but various alternative drafts and notes relating to it. When they were finally published on the web in February 2002, the whole question of the visit was accorded even wider attention in the press than ever before.

The documents seem to me to bear out remarkably well the very detailed reconstruction made of Bohr's attitude by Powers from other sources. The most surprising thing to me in Bohr's first attempt at the letter is its remarkably sharp tone – particularly coming from a man so celebrated for his conciliatoriness:

> I think that I owe it to you to tell you that I am greatly amazed to see how much your memory has deceived you . . .
>
> Personally, I remember every word of our conversations, which took place on a background of extreme sorrow and tension for us here in Denmark. In particular, it made a strong impression both on Margrethe and me, and on everyone at the Institute that the two of you spoke to, that you and Weizsäcker expressed your definite conviction that Germany would

win and that it was therefore quite foolish for us to maintain the hope of a different outcome of the war and to be reticent as regards all German offers of cooperation. I also remember quite clearly our conversation in my room at the Institute, where in vague terms you spoke in a manner that could only give me the firm impression that, under your leadership, everything was being done in Germany to develop atomic weapons and that you said that there was no need to talk about details since you were completely familiar with them and had spent the past two years working more or less exclusively on such preparations. I listened to this without speaking since [a] great matter for mankind was at issue in which, despite our personal friendship, we had to be regarded as representatives of two sides engaged in mortal combat.

It is a revelation to have all this in Bohr's own voice, and I wish it had been available when I wrote the play. I recognise that the real Bohr remained much angrier for much longer than my character, that he claimed to have paid much closer attention to what Heisenberg said, and that he claimed to recall it much more clearly.

Does it really modify our view of what Heisenberg said, though, and of what his intentions were?

Slightly, I think, but not fundamentally. There has never been any disagreement, for a start, that Heisenberg publicly told various people at the Institute that Germany was going to win the war, and that her aims, at any rate in the East, were justified. Then again, Aage and Rozental were both already on record as recalling Bohr's saying that Heisenberg had talked about the military applications of atomic energy. According to Aage, 'My father was very reticent and expressed his scepticism because of the great technical difficulties that had to be overcome, but he had the impression that Heisenberg thought that the new possibilities could decide the outcome of the war if the war dragged on.' According to Rozental: 'I can only remember how excited Bohr was after that conversation and that he quoted Heisenberg for having said something like, "You must understand that if 1 am taking part in the project then it is in the firm belief that it can be done." '

The letter, however, is the first direct confirmation that Bohr believed he was being urged to accept German 'offers of cooperation', which is what Weizsäcker suspected he may have understood Heisenberg to be suggesting. It's not clear from the letter what Bohr thought this 'co-operation' would entail, and the recollection may not be entirely at odds with what Weizsäcker recalls Heisenberg as telling Bohr – that he ought to establish contact with the staff of the German Embassy for his own safety.

Some of the differences between Bohr's account of the meeting and Heisenberg's are less clear-cut than Bohr's indignation makes them appear. According to Heisenberg, in his memorandum to Jungk, he told Bohr he knew that the use of uranium fission for making weapons was 'in principle possible, but it would require a terrific technical effort, which one can only hope cannot be realized in this war'. Bohr, he said, was shocked, 'obviously assuming that I had intended to convey to him that Germany had made great progress in the direction of manufacturing atomic weapons'. This is not all that different in substance, it seems to me, from what Bohr recalls.

The same is true when Bohr goes on to dispute Heisenberg's interpretation of his reaction:

> That my silence and gravity, as you write in the letter, could be taken as an expression of shock at your reports that it was possible to make an atomic bomb is a quite peculiar misunderstanding, which must be due to the great tension in your own mind. From the day three years earlier when I realized that slow neutrons could only cause fission in Uranium 235 and not 238, it was of course obvious to me that a bomb with certain effect could be produced by separating the uraniums ... If anything in my behaviour could be interpreted as shock, it did not derive from such reports but rather from the news, as I had to understand it, that Germany was participating vigorously in a race to be the first with atomic weapons.

The difference between the 'shock' that Heisenberg diagnosed and the more dignified 'silence and gravity' that Bohr himself recalled dissolves a little in a later draft of the letter, where Bohr refers to his reaction as 'alarm'. His assertion that he already understood about the possibility of producing a weapon based on fission is moreover a simplification which is not quite supported by his subsequent behaviour. He had in fact up to that moment believed that it was a practical impossibility, because of the difficulty of separating the fissile U-235, and Heisenberg could not tell him why the balance of probability had now changed – because of the German team's realisation that a reactor, if they could get one going, would produce plutonium as an alternative. After Heisenberg's visit, according to Rozental, he was sufficiently shaken by Heisenberg's confidence to go back to the blackboard and rework all his calculations. Even so, he seems to have remained unconvinced when he got his guarded report on the meeting through to Chadwick, his contact with British intelligence, and said: 'Above all I have to the best of my judgment convinced myself that in spite of all future prospects any immediate use of the latest marvelous discoveries of atomic physics is impracticable.'

The real kernel of the apparent disagreement about the meeting emerges only in later drafts of the letter, where Bohr says that 'there was no hint on your part that efforts were being made by German physicists to prevent such an application of atomic science'. This appears to be a rebuttal of some claim made by Heisenberg. The belief that Heisenberg made some such claim seems to be widespread. Professor Holton suggests that my play is 'based in large part on Heisenberg's published claim that for him an impeding moral compunction may have existed about working on atomic energy'.

But nowhere, so far as I know, did Heisenberg ever make the claim that Bohr seems to have attributed to him. There is no mention of it in the memorandum to Jungk. Even in the expanded account of the meeting that he gave in his memoirs he remained extremely cautious:

I hinted that . . . physicists ought perhaps to ask
themselves whether they should work in this field at all
. . . An enormous technical effort was needed. Now this,
to me, was so important precisely because it gave
physicists the possibility of deciding whether or not the
construction of atom bombs should be attempted. They
could either advise their governments that atom bombs
would come too late for use in the present war, and that
work on them therefore detracted from the war effort, or
else contend that, with the utmost exertions, it might just
be possible to bring them into the conflict. Both views
could be put forward with equal conviction . . .

One might think this sounds a quite implausibly judicious
rendering of anything he might have said. The fact
remains, however, that he is not claiming to have made
any efforts to prevent work on weapons. He is not even
claiming that up to this point the German team had
exercised the option of offering discouraging advice, only
that they might at some point if they so chose. In any case,
Heisenberg says that Bohr 'was so horrified by the very
possibility of producing atomic weapons that he did not
follow the rest of my remarks'.

Some reports on the release of the documents have
suggested that they refute a claim made by Heisenberg to
have offered Bohr a 'deal', whereby the German physicists
would discourage their government from proceeding with
nuclear weapons if Allied physicists would do likewise. I
suppose the implication of Heisenberg's indeterminate
phrase 'the physicists' is that this applied to the physicists
on both sides, but the only evidence I can find for
Heisenberg having made any more definite suggestion than
this is in a part of the memorandum to Jungk which is
quoted by Powers: 'I then asked Bohr once again if,
because of the obvious moral concerns, it would be possible
for all physicists to agree among themselves that one should
not even attempt work on atomic bombs. . .' This might
perhaps be interpreted as a tentative hint at some possible
arrangement, though in the interview he gave to David
Irving for *The Virus House* in 1965 he seems to be retreating

even from this, and says merely that Bohr 'perhaps sensed that I should prefer it if physicists in the whole world would say: We will not make atom bombs'. The remark to Jungk was not quoted by him in his book, and so presumably not seen by Bohr in 1957. In his letter, in any case, Bohr makes no reference to any such claim, or to having understood any such offer at the time.

There are discrepancies in every other aspect of the evidence relating to this meeting, and it is scarcely surprising that there are some to be found between the two participants' own accounts. In both cases they are attempting to recollect something that happened sixteen years earlier, and their perceptions are inevitably coloured by strong feelings and conflicting loyalties. On the whole, I think, what's surprising is how slight the differences of substance are, and how readily most of them can be understood in the circumstances.

The most remarkable point of agreement, it seems to me now that I have had time to reflect upon it, was missed by everyone who wrote about the letters at the time of their release, myself included: Bohr's confirmation of Heisenberg's claim to have overriden all normal obligations of secrecy. Heisenberg did indicate to him, he agrees, that there was a German atomic programme; that he himself was involved in it; and that he now believed it in principle possible to build atomic weapons.

Whatever Heisenberg was officially licensed or ordered to do in Copenhagen, I cannot believe that it included revealing the existence of one of the most secret research programmes in Germany – least of all to an enemy alien who was known to be in contact with Allied scientists (Bohr was at this point still contributing to the US journal *The Physical Review*), and also to be under observation because of his hostile attitude to Nazism and his extensive help for its victims. Heisenberg must have done this of his own initiative, and he must have been aware that Bohr would pass the information on, if he possibly could, to his contacts in Britain or the US. This, it seems to me, goes a considerable way to supporting the account that Heisenberg subsequently gave of his intentions.

*

The only really clear-cut disagreement between the two accounts is about a circumstantial detail – where the meeting took place. Bohr talks about 'our conversation in my room at the Institute'. Heisenberg, on the other hand, recalls in his memoirs visiting the Bohrs' home in Carlsberg, and finally broaching 'the dangerous subject' on their evening walk. This version is reinforced by what he recalls of his attempt to reconstruct with Bohr the 1941 meeting when he returned to Copenhagen in 1947. He was convinced, he said, that the conversation had taken place during 'a nocturnal walk on Pile Allé', which is very close to Carlsberg, and four kilometres from the Institute. (Bohr at the time, according to Heisenberg, thought it had been in his study – but in his study at home in Carlsberg.)

Bohr himself lends some colour to the Carlsberg version by his remark in the letter that 'every word of our conversation . . . made a strong impression both on Margrethe and me'. It seems highly unlikely that Margrethe would have been present at any of the various meetings in the Institute; I don't think that any of the other participants mention her. Jochen Heisenberg recalls his father showing him the street where he said he had walked with Niels Bohr in 1941, though he can't now remember the name of it, only that it was tree-lined (which Pile Allé is).

There is a secondhand account of the meeting given to Thomas Powers by Ruth Nanda Anshen, Heisenberg's American editor, who said that she was told it by Bohr, and that his assistant Aage Petersen confirmed it. According to Powers, in *Heisenberg's War*, Bohr told Anshen that 'the invitation had cost him much agony – he wanted to sit down to dinner with Heisenberg, but his wife, Margrethe, objected, and Bohr couldn't make up his mind what to do. Finally his assistant Aage Petersen suggested that Bohr should write down his objections to Heisenberg's visit, then read them carefully a day or two later, and decide. This Bohr did; the old friendship seemed to him stronger than the objections, and he told his New York friend that he finally obtained Margrethe's agreement with a solemn promise to discuss only physics with Heisenberg – not politics.'

On the other hand Abraham Pais, Bohr's biographer, after making inquiries among Bohr's surviving colleagues just before his own death in 2000, concluded that Heisenberg had never been to the Bohrs' home.

Even Heisenberg's own testimony is not entirely consistent. According to his biographer, David Cassidy, he made an earlier statement in which he 'remembered that his most important talk with Bohr occurred one evening as they strolled along a tree-lined path in the large and secluded Faelledpark, just behind Bohr's institute'. Weizsäcker, who recalled that he met Heisenberg only ten minutes after the meeting with Bohr was over (the two men had parted company, he said, 'in a friendly way', but Heisenberg had immediately told him: 'I'm afraid it's gone completely wrong') agreed that it had taken place in the open air, but introduced another location altogether – Langelinie, the raised walk beside the harbour, miles from either Carlsberg or the Institute.

*

Some further light on this question was cast, nine months after the release of the Bohr documents, by the emergence of yet another letter. This one was written by Heisenberg, and revealed by Dr Helmut Rechenberg, the director of the Werner Heisenberg Archive in Göttingen.[1] The Heisenberg family, who released it, seem not to have taken in its implications earlier.

It makes no direct reference to the disputed conversation itself, but is a much more reliable guide to the

[1] In a Heisenberg Centenary Festschrift issued by the Sächsische Akademie der Wissenschaften. The letter was published in 2003 in a collection of his correspondence edited by his daughter Maria Hirsch.

circumstances surrounding it than the accounts we have had so far, because it was written not sixteen years after the event but during the week that Heisenberg was actually there. In fact it's in three sections, dated respectively to three different evenings – Tuesday (September 16, the day after he arrived), Thursday, and Saturday – and it was posted to his family in Leipzig as soon as he got back to Berlin.

The letter clears up one small point of dispute completely. Heisenberg *did* go to the house – and more than once. He also records various visits to the Institute, and the sheer number and variety of meetings that the two men had during the week supports the claim that Heisenberg's chief reason for making the trip was to see Bohr. The conflation of the different occasions in the participants' memories also probably explains some of the later discrepancies.

The first visit to the Bohrs was late on the Monday evening, as soon as Heisenberg had got off the train from Berlin. The sky, he recorded, was clear and starry, but in the Bohrs' house he found rather darker weather. 'The conversation swiftly turned to the human questions and misfortunes of our time; about the human ones there was spontaneous agreement; on the political questions I found it difficult to cope with the fact that even in a man like Bohr, thoughts, feelings, and hatred cannot be completely separated.'

It is just possible that the fateful conversation occurred at this first meeting, either in the house – where, said Heisenberg, 'later I sat for a long time alone with Bohr' – or later still, after midnight, when Bohr saw him to the tram. But they were accompanied to the tram-stop by Hans, one of Bohr's sons, who would surely have remembered and remarked upon it if it had happened then. And if Weizsäcker's recollection is even remotely accurate then the conversation can't have occurred at any point during this first meeting, because he himself arrived in Copenhagen only on the Wednesday.

The most likely occasion was two days later, during Heisenberg's second visit, on the Wednesday evening. (This

time there was a young Englishwoman present, who
'decently withdrew' during 'the unavoidable political
conversations, in which the role of defending our system of
course automatically fell upon me'.) Dr Rechenberg suggests
plausibly that Bohr accompanied Heisenberg alone part of
the way back to his hotel, where Weizsäcker was waiting
for him.

The real surprise of the letters, though, is that
Heisenberg was invited back to the Bohrs' home for a *third*
time, on the Saturday evening, three days after this (and
the conversation can't have occurred during this visit,
because this time Weizsäcker was accompanying him). 'It
was in many ways particularly nice,' wrote Heisenberg later
that same night. 'The conversation turned for a great part
of the evening around purely human problems. Bohr read
something aloud, I played a Mozart sonata (A major).'

The immediate rupture of the two men's friendship is
almost the only aspect of the story which has up to now
seemed reasonably unambiguous (I certainly take it for
granted in the play). Now even this turns out to be as
clouded as everything else.

Rechenberg suggests that it may have been at this
farewell meeting that Heisenberg and Weizsäcker urged
Bohr to maintain contact with the German Embassy. If so
it could have been Bohr's anger at this that coloured his
recollection of the earlier conversation. It is in any case
clear that the quarrel took the form it did only later, in the
recollection of the participants, as they reflected upon it –
probably also as the circumstances of the war got worse, as
the deepest horrors of the Nazi period were uncovered, and
as the actual development of nuclear weapons called into
question the two men's participation.

History, in other words, is not what happens when it
happens, but what seems to people to have happened when
they look back upon it.

*

I can't help being moved, though, by the picture that the new documents give of Bohr drafting and redrafting the text of the letter over the last five years of his life – and still never sending it. He was famous for his endless redrafting of everything he wrote, and here he was trying not only to satisfy his characteristic concern for the precise nuance, but also to reconcile that with his equally characteristic consideration for Heisenberg's feelings. There is a sad parallel with the account which Professor Hans-Peter Dürr gave, at the Heisenberg Centenary symposium in Bamberg last year, of Heisenberg's rather similar efforts to understand what had happened.

Professor Dürr, who worked for many years with Heisenberg in Göttingen after the war, said that Heisenberg had continued to love Bohr to the end of his life, and he recalled his going over the fatal meeting again and again, trying to work out what had happened. Professor Dürr offered what seems to me the most plausible common-sense estimate of Heisenberg's intentions that has yet been advanced. He thought that Heisenberg had simply wanted to have a talk. Heisenberg and Bohr had been so close that they could finish each other's sentences, and he assumed that he would have only to hint at what was on his mind for Bohr to grasp the significance of it. What he had entirely failed to grasp was that the situation had changed, and that Bohr's anger about the German occupation would make the old easy communication entirely impossible.

Whatever was said at the meeting, and whatever Heisenberg's intentions were, there is something profoundly characteristic of the difficulties in human relationships, and profoundly painful, in that picture of the two ageing men, one in Copenhagen and one in Göttingen, puzzling for all those long years over the few brief moments that had clouded if not ended their friendship. It's what their shades do in my play, of course. At least in the play they get together to work it out.

Overleaf: a diagram outlining *Copenhagen*'s scientific and historical background.

From the beginnings of modern atomic theory to Hiroshima: an outline sketch of the scientific and historical background to the play.

Electrons
1895 Thomson discovers the electron, the extremely light, negatively charged particles orbiting inside the atom which give it its chemical properties.

Quantum Theory
1900 Planck discovers that heat energy is not continuously variable, as classical physics assumes. There is a smallest common coin in the currency, the quantum, and all transactions are in multiples of it.

The Nucleus
1910 Rutherford shows that the electrons orbit around a tiny nucleus, in which almost the entire mass of the atom is concentrated.

Photons
1905 Einstein realises that light, too, has to be understood not only as waves but as quantum particles, later known as photons.

The Quantum Atom.
1913 Bohr realises that quantum theory applies to matter itself. The orbits of the electrons about the nucleus are limited to a number of separate whole number possibilities, so that the atom can exist only in a number of distinct and definite states. (The incomplete so-called 'old quantum theory'.)

Quantum mechanics
1925 Heisenberg abandons electron orbits as unobservable. Max Born finds instead a mathematical formulation in terms of matrices for what can be observed - the effects they produce upon the absorption and emission of light.

Uncertainty
1927 Heisenberg demonstrates that all statements about the movement of a particle are governed by the uncertainty relationship: the more accurately you know its position, the less accurately you know its velocity, and vice versa.

Matter as Waves
1924 De Broglie in Paris suggests that, just as radiation can be treated as particles, so the particles of matter can be treated as a wave formation.

The Wave Equation
1926 Schrödinger finds the mathematical equation for the wave interpretation, and proves that wave and matrix mechanics are mathematically equivalent.

The Copenhagen Interpretation
1928 Bohr relates Heisenberg's particle theory and Schrödinger's wave theory by the complementarity principle, according to which the behaviour of an electron can be understood completely only by descriptions in both wave and particle form. Uncertainty plus complementarity become established as the pillars of the Copenhagen (or 'orthodox') interpretation of quantum mechanics.

Neutrons
1932 Chadwick discovers the neutron - a particle which can be used to explore the nucleus because it carries no electrical charge, and can penetrate it undeflected.

Into the Nucleus
1932 Heisenberg opens the new era of nuclear physics by using neutron theory to apply quantum mechanics to the structure of the nucleus.

Transmutation

1934 Fermi in Rome bombards uranium with neutrons and produces a radio-active substance which he cannot identify.

Identification

1939 Hahn and Strassmann in Berlin identify the substance produced by Fermi's bombardment as barium, which has only about half the atomic weight of uranium.

The Liquid Drop

1937 Bohr explains the properties of the nucleus by analogy with a drop of liquid.

Fission

1939 Lise Meitner and Frisch in Sweden apply Bohr's liquid drop model to the uranium nucleus, and realise that it has turned into barium under bombardment by splitting into two, with the release of huge quantities of energy.

The Neutrons Multiply

1939 Bohr and Wheeler at Princeton realise that fission also produces free neutrons. These neutrons are moving too fast to fission other nuclei in U-238, the isotope which makes up 99% of natural uranium, and will fission only the nuclei of the U-235 isotope, which constitutes less than 1% of it.

The Chain Reaction

1939 Joliot in Paris and Fermi in New York demonstrate the release of two or more free neutrons with each fission, which proves the possibility of a chain reaction in pure U-235.

The Critical Mass

1940 Frisch and Peierls in Birmingham calculate, wrongly but encouragingly, the minimum amount of U-235 needed to sustain an effective chain reaction.

The War

1939 The Second World War begins, and Germany at once commences research into the military possibilities of fission.

The Manhattan Project

1942 The Allied atomic bomb programme begins.

Germany Defeated

1945 The Allied advance into Germany halts the atomic programme there.

The Reactor

1942 Fermi in Chicago achieves the first self-sustaining chain reaction, in a prototype reactor.

The Bomb

1945 The bomb is successfully tested in July, and in the following month used on Hiroshima.

Notes

3 *But why?*: a detective story on one level, the play opens with four questions.

Lingering like ghosts: the characters exist in an 'afterlife', from which they can revisit events in the past.

We were under German occupation: Germany invaded Denmark in April 1940. Only two German divisions were required and on 9 April Copenhagen was taken within twelve hours.

4 *One is the uncertainty principle*: Heisenberg is therefore famous for two types of uncertainty.

Too quick. Too eager: rival interpretations will dominate the exchanges.

5 *quantum theory applied to matter as well as to energy*: atomic theory began with the ancient Greeks. But in 1913 Bohr established a link between classical and quantum physics with his explanation of atomic structure and atomic dynamics. Atoms are not things, atoms are energy. For this, he is known as the father of the atom.

and in just over a year: characters share the narration. This technique, common in adaptations of novels, here becomes part of the play's structure and theme.

Max Born: one of Heisenberg's teachers, Born (1882–1970) was a theoretical physicist who reformulated the first law of thermodynamics. He worked with Heisenberg on the mathematical formulation of quantum mechanics (see p.126). A Jew, Born fled Germany for Britain in 1933.

Pascual Jordan: another student of Born's, Jordan (1902–80) was an expert in matrix mechanics.

complementarity: in 1927 Bohr proposed the idea that two different but complementary concepts were needed to describe quantum behaviour – one was in terms of waves, the other was in terms of particles.

6 *Then the Nazis came to power*: Hitler became Chancellor of Germany on 30 January 1933.

For years I had it down in my memory as October: the fallibility of memory is a recurrent theme.

A curious sort of diary memory is: the characters move in and out of time-zones in a way that reflects this observation.

September, 1941, Copenhagen: the deft transitions in time depend on a non-naturalistic setting. 'This is not a naturalistic play,' the director Michael Blakemore has said. 'We're not trying to pretend that what we're seeing is real. The audience must listen to the arguments, empathise with the characters' emotions, and create the reality for themselves' (www.nucnews.net [9 April 2000]).

Weizsäcker: Carl Friedrich von Weizsäcker (1912–). Theoretical physicist and influential younger colleague and friend of Heisenberg's. His father, Ernst, was the second highest official in Hitler's Foreign Office, who was sentenced to jail at Nuremberg. His brother Richard later became President of the Federal Republic of Germany (1984–94).

7 *Occupation of Poland*: Germany invaded Poland on 1 September 1939. Two days later Britain and France declared war on Germany.

Christian Møller: professor of mathematical physics in Copenhagen. Møller (1904–81) contributed to atomic and nuclear theory and wrote *The Theory of Relativity*.

8 *Our tanks are almost at Moscow*: Germany invaded Russia on 22 June 1941. On 19 September the Germans launched the Moscow offensive.

the basement at Prinz-Albrecht-Strasse: this was the headquarters of the SS in Berlin.

White Jew: in 1937, in the SS weekly *Das Schwarze Korps*, the Nobel prizewinner Johannes Stark attacked Heisenberg for being too indebted to 'Jewish' quantum physics. A 'white Jew' was a toxic term of abuse for a German who helped spread the Jewish 'spirit'.

9   *Still a professor*: Margrethe's testiness is essential in drawing out information for the audience.

Goudsmit: Dutch-American physicist and scientific head of the Alsos mission, Samuel A. Goudsmit (1902–78) was responsible for arresting Heisenberg, and the other scientists detained at Farm Hall, at the end of the war.

10   *We'll stick to physics*: the subtle shifts in time and perspective are evident here, when Bohr talks about what he *thinks* will happen at the 1941 meeting.

So now here I am: the encounter moves into the present tense. For the first few pages the Bohrs have shared the stage with Heisenberg without meeting him. Now the three of them are together.

11   *nuclear fission*: the splitting of a heavy atomic nucleus, which releases nuclear energy.

Wolfgang Pauli: (1900–58), won the 1945 Nobel Prize for the 'exclusion principle' which explained the electronic make-up of atoms.

Otto Frisch: (1904–79), nephew of Lise Meitner. The Nazi racial laws forced him to emigrate. He worked with Bohr in Copenhagen. With Meitner he wrote the paper that gave the first correct description of fission.

Lise Meitner: during the thirties Meitner (1878–1968) and Otto Hahn investigated what happened to uranium when it was bombarded with neutrons. In 1939 Meitner and her nephew Otto Frisch realised that a new process – fission – had occurred.

Sommerfeld: German physicist (1868–1951) Arnold Sommerfeld worked on quantum theory, making a significant contribution to Bohr's atomic theory by extending the theory to include elliptical paths for electrons.

Von Laue: won the Nobel Prize for Physics in 1914 for his research on X-rays. Max von Laue (1879–1960) was bewildered by his detainment at Farm Hall after the Second World War. He had engaged in no war-related research during the war.

Wirtz: German physicist, detained at Farm Hall. Karl Wirtz (1910–94) was an expert in heavy water and isotope separation.

Harteck: professor of physical chemistry. Paul Harteck (1902–85) was detained at Farm Hall. During the war he worked on heavy-water production and reactor construction.

12 *Otto Hahn*: a radiochemist, he worked with Lise Meitner for thirty years. Like the other detainees at Farm Hall, Hahn (1879–1968) learnt about the Hiroshima bomb during his internment. He also learnt that he had been awarded the Nobel Prize for Chemistry.

Enrico Fermi: made major contributions in experimental and theoretical physics. In 1934 Fermi (1901–54) showed that bombarding uranium with slow neutrons resulted in a radioactive substance (fission had taken place), but he did not realise quite what he had achieved. He later worked on the Manhattan Project at Los Alamos.

13 *And of course*: Margrethe steps out of the scene just as Heisenberg steps into it.

15 *A few months ago they started deporting*: two vast events lie, like shadows, behind the play – the Holocaust and the atomic bomb. In 1941 neither of these horrors had been realised.

16 *Silence again*: Margrethe comments on the scene in 1941 even as it is taking place, and then her memory flashes back to 1924.

17 *nuclei*: the nucleus is the central core of the atom, composed of protons and neutrons.

deuterons: the nucleus of a deuterium atom (deuterium is also known as heavy hydrogen).

cyclotron: invented in 1931 to smash atoms. It accelerates charged particles by means of a magnetic field. It is used to break down atoms or combine them. (See p. 124.)

We mustn't jump to conclusions: the next four lines, like a number of others, achieve a choric effect as if the three characters had joined together to become a single narrator.

18 *Schrödinger*: the Austrian physicist Erwin Schrödinger (1887–1961) formulated his wave equation in 1926 which used wave function as the mathematical expression for measuring the co-ordinates of a particle in space. (See also note to p.25.)

I'm not teaching: Heisenberg is not entirely candid about the work he is doing.

19 *Chadwick*: confirmed the existence of the neutron in 1932 and received the Nobel Prize for its discovery in 1935. During the war James Chadwick (1891–1974) headed the British atomic bomb project.

Oppenheimer: in 1942 J. Robert Oppenheimer (1904–67) was put in charge of the scientific side of the Manhattan Project.

mesons: a sub-particle of the atom.

25 *particle . . . goes through two different slits at the same time*: one of the mind-bending aspects of quantum mechanics is that when a particle is faced with the choice of going through one of two slits it appears to go through both of them. (Don't ask.) See also p.102.

Schrödinger's wretched cat: Bohr maintained that the position of a particle remains indeterminate until it has been observed. In response to this, Schrödinger posed a famous question that was of more interest to physicists than to cat lovers: if a cat were placed in a sealed box with some radioactive material, how could we know if or when the cat had died?

26 *Hendrik Casimir*: (1909–) made important contributions to applied mathematics, theoretical physics and low-temperature physics.

George Gamow: one of the originators of the big bang theory, a professor of physics, Gamow (1904–68) wrote popular science books.

29 *Christian and Harold*: see p.xlviii.

30 *Elsinore*: Hamlet's home. Heisenberg is a Hamlet figure, unable to decide what it is he should do. Elsinore becomes a term for the destructive impulses, the dark side of humanity, which recurs throughout the play.

32 *Goodbye*: the end of the first visit. What follows is the rival interpretations of that first meeting.
John Wheeler: American physicist (1911–). Working with Bohr in 1939 at Princeton, he realised that fission also produces free neutrons.

33 *neutron*: one of the two components of an atomic nucleus. Separated on its own, a neutron undergoes radioactive decay.
isotope: one of two or more atoms of the same chemical element, which have the same number of protons, but differ in the number of neutrons in the nucleus. From the Greek 'isos' (the same) and 'topos' (place).

37 *plutonium*: a man-made heavy metal, discovered at the University of California in 1940, formed by the radioactive decay of neptunium, that was ideal for use in nuclear weapons.

38 *Weisskopf*: leading theoretical physicist, Victor Weisskopf (1908–) was a Viennese Jew who emigrated to the US in 1937 and worked at Los Alamos from 1943.

40 *Geiger counters*: developed in 1928, the counters detect and measure radioactivity.

42 *It's just getting under way even as you and I are talking*: his mind moves forwards in time as well as backwards.

43 *Teller*: a Hungarian Jew, Edward Teller (1908–) went to the United States in 1935 and to Los Alamos in 1943 to work on a fusion weapon. He is known as the 'father of the H-bomb'. He has been caricatured in the movie *Dr Strangelove*.
Szilard: in 1934, four years before fission was identified, the Hungarian Leo Szilard (1898–1964) conceived the idea of a 'chain reaction', involving neutrons. In 1939 he warned Einstein of the possibility of a chain reaction. Einstein wrote to President Roosevelt (with Szilard's support) warning the President of the possibility

of an atomic arms race (see p.127).

48   *our meeting with Albert Speer*: Hitler's favourite architect,
Speer, became Minister for Armaments and War
Production. Heisenberg briefed him on nuclear research
on 4 June 1942.
the RAF have begun terror-bombing: the RAF began its
strategic bombing offensive on 15 May 1940. After the
German bombing of London the RAF attacked Berlin
on 25 August 1940.

50   *Hambro*: Sir Charles Hambro, a prominent banker
and commander of SOE (Special Operations Executive).
On 21 April 1945, after supper in a local hotel,
Hambro and Perrin went into the cave at Haigerloch to
inspect the nuclear pile that Heisenberg had been
building.
Perrin: Michael Perrin, physicist and official of the
British atomic programme. He discussed the German
bomb programme with Bohr when Bohr reached
England in 1943. He inspected Heisenberg's reactors at
Haigerloch. He was one of those who received the
weekly transcripts from Farm Hall.

53   *Another draft of the paper*: although the second attempt to
explain the visit was heralded fifteen pages ago ('let's
start all over again'), it starts here.

54   *And from those two heads*: in the final moment of the first
act, Margrethe restates what is at stake.

Act Two

59   *Dirac*: Paul Dirac (1902–84), British physicist, best
known for the Dirac Equation (1928). This gave a
relativistic wave equation for electrons that replaced
Schrödinger's non-relativistic equation in situations when
relativity is a factor (for instance, high speed).
de Broglie: French physicist Louis de Broglie (1892–1987)
was best known for his theory of wave-particle duality.
In 1924 he hypothesised that particles should exhibit
certain wave-like properties. He received the Nobel

Prize in 1929.

Landau: Lev Landau (1908–68), Russian physicist, who early on saw the possibility of a bomb.

Uhlenbeck: in the 1920s, George Uhlenbeck (1900–88), working with Goudsmit, introduced the idea of 'electron spin'.

Stern: an experimental physicist, Otto Stern (1888–1969) worked with Walther Gerlach, one of the Farm Hall detainees, on the influential 1922 atomic-beam experiment.

60 *Ehrenfest*: with Max Planck, Einstein and Bohr, Paul Ehrenfest (1880–1933) was a pioneer of the quantum revolution.

62 *Any more than*: Margrethe states a central theme in the play: how we can never understand one another's thoughts.

63 *Schrödinger's wave formulation*: see note to p.18.

matrix mechanics: the first formulation of quantum mechanics, made by Heisenberg in 1925, was presented in terms of mathematical matrices.

68 *photon*: in 1905 Einstein realised that light had to be understood not only as waves but as quantum particles, later known as photons.

70 *Klein*: Oskar Klein (1894–1977) joined Bohr in 1918 and later remarked on the great progress that Bohr had made in the early 1920s 'in spite of the abyss, whose depth he never ceased to emphasize, between the quantum theoretical mode of description and that of classical physics'.

75 *the plot against Hitler*: on 20 July 1944, at a conference at Hitler's headquarters at Rastenberg in East Prussia, Count von Stauffenberg left a suitcase bomb in a room where Hitler was holding a meeting. Hitler was not seriously injured. Many of the plotters and their relations were executed.

76 *Better to stay on the boat*: the question of what action people should take in desperate situations, and whether it is right to make a sacrifice that is heroic and

probably useless, parallels Heisenberg's dilemma in Nazi
Germany.

82 *diffusion equation*: diffusion is the atomic process by which
substances mix or spread. In a solid or liquid, diffusion
can only take place when an atom or molecule acquires
enough energy to jump to another place.

83 *Peierls*: working in Birmingham in the late-thirties, the
German physicist Rudolf Peierls (1907–95) calculated
that pure uranium 235 could make an atom bomb. A
memo was sent to the British government. It was
immediately classified as top secret and Peierls, an
enemy alien, was not allowed to read the document he
had written. Peierls later wrote about Heisenberg that
'though a brilliant theoretician he was always very
casual about numbers'.

86 *One more draft*: in the play's three-act structure this is the
beginning of the third act. From now on the play
moves inside the characters' thoughts. Michael
Blakemore said in an interview: 'The play moves away
from science towards what Michael [Frayn] tells me is
late-Wittgenstein – into a sort of philosophical position
– where, having examined this meeting twice, in terms
of history and in terms of science, the exhausted
participants have to actually examine very specifically
what happens when three people encounter one
another' (www.nucnews.net [9 April 2000]).

89 *To leave him misunderstood*: this is as close as we get to
the reason for the visit.

Questions for Further Study

1. What is the dramatic purpose and function of the role of Margrethe in *Copenhagen*?
2. What are the advantages/disadvantages of staging the play as a discussion in an afterlife rather than as an imagined historical reconstruction?
3. 'I sometimes feel very envious of your cyclotron' (p.17). Do you need to be able to make sense of the science to make sense of *Copenhagen*?
4. 'The emotional currents between the three characters in *Copenhagen* give the play its questing energy.' Discuss.
5. The language of indeterminacy, alternative narratives, alternative histories belongs to the realm of literary theory as well as science. To what extent does *Copenhagen* suggest that the separation of the spheres of science and literature (the 'Two Cultures' idea) is a myth?
6. 'The play deals with politics on the largest scale imaginable, and personal relationships at their most private and unspoken.' How successfully does Frayn succeed in dramatising the relationship between the political and the personal in *Copenhagen*?
7. Some critics felt that *Copenhagen* would fare better as a play for radio. Give your reasons for agreeing or disagreeing with this view.
8. 'No one is going to develop a weapon based on nuclear fission' (p.11). How does Frayn deploy historical and scientific knowledge which is available to us but not to the protagonists?
9. To what extent does the play seem to be preoccupied with moral relativity or moral indeterminacy, given that Heisenberg describes Bohr towards the end of the play as a 'good' man?

10. In the commentary, Michael Frayn is quoted as saying that the play is 'about audiences' (p. xxxviii). What do you think he means and how might this affect the staging of *Copenhagen*?

11. 'I wanted to get into the question of how we know why we do what we do. We can't come to any moral judgements of people or ourselves until we can make some estimation of motivations. The difficulties of doing this point to a fundamental difficulty in making moral judgements' (Michael Frayn). How essential are the particular people and situations in the play to the philosophical problems posed and how successfully does *Copenhagen* deal with them?

12. What kind of moral or other issues does *Copenhagen* raise in portraying a half-Jewish Dane who triggers an atomic bomb used against the Japanese on behalf of the Americans, and a loyal German scientist under the Nazis who contributes to the development of atomic weaponry which might have been deployed against the Allies?

13. What do you make of the fact that, unlike most plays, *Copenhagen* makes a virtue of eliminating conventional dramatic indicators including stage directions?

14. According to the author, 'The epistemology of intention is what the play is about' (p. 136). Given the indeterminate nature of its subject matter can he be so sure?

15. How has Frayn designed the play so that a vehicle for ideas becomes an absorbing theatrical experience? You might like to consult reviews of previous productions in considering this question.

16. In what ways does *Copenhagen* bear comparison with either Brecht's *Galileo* or Dürrenmatt's *The Physicist*?

17. 'Everyone remembers the paper – no one remembers the postscript' (p. 69). Do the author's postscripts have anything important to say affecting our understanding and appreciation of the actual play?

18. In the commentary (pp. xvii-xviii) the search for

motivation in *Copenhagen* is compared with Stanislavsky's notion of the super-objective. In what ways might a Stanislavskyan approach to the play help or hinder a performance?

19. In what ways is *Copenhagen*'s contribution to the indeterminacy debate significantly different from the formulation offered by the ancient philosopher Cratylus (a follower of Heraclitus, *c.*540–480 BC) who declared that 'you cannot step twice into the same river'?

20. Why should it be important, for all our sakes, that Heisenberg's unconscious motive for visiting Bohr was, as is suggested at one point in *Copenhagen*, to be 'misunderstood'?

Methuen Drama Student Editions

Jean Anouilh *Antigone* • John Arden *Serjeant Musgrave's Dance*
Alan Ayckbourn *Confusions* • Aphra Behn *The Rover* • Edward Bond
Lear • *Saved* • Bertolt Brecht *The Caucasian Chalk Circle* • *Fear and
Misery in the Third Reich* • *The Good Person of Szechwan* • *Life of Galileo* •
Mother Courage and her Children • *The Resistible Rise of Arturo Ui* • *The
Threepenny Opera* • Anton Chekhov *The Cherry Orchard* • *The Seagull* •
Three Sisters • *Uncle Vanya* • Caryl Churchill *Serious Money* • *Top Girls*
• Shelagh Delaney *A Taste of Honey* • Euripides *Elektra* • *Medea* •
Dario Fo *Accidental Death of an Anarchist* • Michael Frayn *Copenhagen*
• John Galsworthy *Strife* • Nikolai Gogol *The Government Inspector* •
Robert Holman *Across Oka* • Henrik Ibsen *A Doll's House* • *Ghosts* •
Hedda Gabler • Charlotte Keatley *My Mother Said I Never Should* •
Bernard Kops *Dreams of Anne Frank* • Federico García Lorca *Blood
Wedding* • *Doña Rosita the Spinster* (bilingual edition) • *The House of
Bernarda Alba* • (bilingual edition) • *Yerma* (bilingual edition) • David
Mamet *Glengarry Glen Ross* • *Oleanna* • Patrick Marber *Closer* • John
Marston *Malcontent* • Martin McDonagh *The Lieutenant of Inishmore* •
Joe Orton *Loot* • Luigi Pirandello *Six Characters in Search of an Author*
• Mark Ravenhill *Shopping and F***ing* • Willy Russell *Blood Brothers*
• *Educating Rita* • Sophocles *Antigone* • *Oedipus the King* • Wole
Soyinka *Death and the King's Horseman* • Shelagh Stephenson *The
Memory of Water* • August Strindberg *Miss Julie* • J. M. Synge *The
Playboy of the Western World* • Theatre Workshop *Oh What a Lovely
War* Timberlake Wertenbaker *Our Country's Good* • Arnold Wesker
The Merchant • Oscar Wilde *The Importance of Being Earnest* •
Tennessee Williams *A Streetcar Named Desire* • *The Glass Menagerie*

Methuen Drama Modern Classics

Jean Anouilh *Antigone* • Brendan Behan *The Hostage* • Robert Bolt *A Man for All Seasons* • Edward Bond *Saved* • Bertolt Brecht *The Caucasian Chalk Circle* • *Fear and Misery in the Third Reich* • *The Good Person of Szechwan* • *Life of Galileo* • *The Messingkauf Dialogues* • *Mother Courage and Her Children* • *Mr Puntila and His Man Matti* • *The Resistible Rise of Arturo Ui* • *Rise and Fall of the City of Mahagonny* • *The Threepenny Opera* • Jim Cartwright *Road* • *Two & Bed* • Caryl Churchill *Serious Money* • *Top Girls* • Noël Coward *Blithe Spirit* • *Hay Fever* • *Present Laughter* • *Private Lives* • *The Vortex* • Shelagh Delaney *A Taste of Honey* • Dario Fo *Accidental Death of an Anarchist* • Michael Frayn *Copenhagen* • Lorraine Hansberry *A Raisin in the Sun* • Jonathan Harvey *Beautiful Thing* • David Mamet *Glengarry Glen Ross* • *Oleanna* • *Speed-the-Plow* • Patrick Marber *Closer* • *Dealer's Choice* • Arthur Miller *Broken Glass* • Percy Mtwa, Mbongeni Ngema, Barney Simon *Woza Albert!* • Joe Orton *Entertaining Mr Sloane* • *Loot* • *What the Butler Saw* • Mark Ravenhill *Shopping and F***ing* • Willy Russell *Blood Brothers* • *Educating Rita* • *Stags and Hens* • *Our Day Out* • Jean-Paul Sartre *Crime Passionnel* • Wole Soyinka • *Death and the King's Horseman* • Theatre Workshop *Oh, What a Lovely War* • Frank Wedekind • *Spring Awakening* • Timberlake Wertenbaker *Our Country's Good*